CHURCHILL'S THIRD
WORLD WAR

CHURCHILL'S THIRD WORLD WAR

BRITISH PLANS TO ATTACK THE SOVIET EMPIRE, 1945

JONATHAN WALKER

The
History
Press

For Professor Peter Simkins
An inspirational historian and leading member of the
Cabinet War Rooms Restoration Team

First published as *Operation Unthinkable* in 2013
This paperback edition first published 2017

The History Press
The Mill, Brimscombe Port
Stroud, Gloucestershire, GL5 2QG
www.thehistorypress.co.uk

British Library Cataloguing in Publication Data.
A catalogue record for this book is available from the British Library.

ISBN 978 0 7509 5838 7

Typesetting and origination by The History Press
Printed and bound by CPI Group (UK) Ltd

CONTENTS

LIST OF MAPS

ACKNOWLEDGEMENTS

The story of Operation Unthinkable is particularly significant for Poland, since the venture might have provided the Poles with their last chance of freedom before total Soviet domination. My thanks, therefore, to Katarzyna Kienhuis, Head of International Relations at the Institute of National Remembrance (INR) in Warsaw. Dr Tomasz Łabuszewski and Dr Jacek Sawicki of the INR offered helpful advice on the state of the Polish resistance in 1945 and I am most grateful for the benefit of their wide knowledge. My thanks to Mikołaj Książek and Marta Hiscox for their help with translations. Similarly, my thanks to Piotr Śliwowski, Head of History at the Museum of the Warsaw Rising and also the staff of the Archiwum Akt Nowych in Warsaw. Professor Anita Prażmowska gave me valuable insights into the state of post-war Polish society. Dr Andrzej Suchcitz, Keeper of Archives at the Polish Institute and Sikorski Museum in London was most helpful with sources and advice; likewise Dr Halik Kochanski, whose recent book, *The Eagle Unbowed*, is a most valuable source for historians and researchers. Dr Ross Bastiaan gave me the benefit of his deep knowledge of Australian and Empire history, while Sofie Miłkowska, a former member of the Polish resistance, kindly kept me supplied with details of the underground in 1945.

My special thanks to the following friends and colleagues who have helped me with checking drafts, or providing sources and contacts: Keith Northover, Peter Hall, Paul and Sarah Arnott, Minnie Churchill, Jasper Humphreys and Simon Tidswell. Scandinavia played a part in the 'Unthinkable' story and I am grateful to Lieutenant-Colonel David Summerfield RM for conveying his expert knowledge of the region. Archive and library specialists have also been very helpful in locating material and I am grateful to Meriel Santer, Kate O'Brien and staff from both the Churchill Archive Centre and the Liddell Hart Centre for Military Archives.

ACKNOWLEDGEMENTS

I have made every effort to obtain the necessary permission to reproduce copyright material in this work, though in some cases it has been impossible to trace the current copyright holders. Any omissions are entirely unintentional and if any are brought to my notice, I will be most happy to include the appropriate acknowledgements in any future re-printing. I acknowledge permission to quote passages from the following: Pen & Sword Books for *Bomber Pilot on the Eastern Front*, by Vasiliy Reshetnikov, and *Finale at Flensburg*, by Charles Whiting; Constable & Robinson for *Winston Churchill: The Struggle for Survival 1940–1956*, by Lord Moran; Macmillan Publishers for *Truman*, by Roy Jenkins; Orion Books for *Harold Nicolson Diaries 1907–1964*, edited by Nigel Nicolson; WW Norton for *Witness to History* by Charles Bohlen; extracts from Professor George Kennan's interview are reproduced from www.nsarchive.org with the kind permission of the National Security Archives.

My thanks to the following archives and individuals for permission to reproduce images: Narodowe Archiwum Cyfrowe, The Harry S Truman Library, The UK National Archives, The Trustees of the Imperial War Museum, The US Library of Congress, The US National Archives and Records Administration.

Permission was kindly given by The Trustees of the Liddell Hart Centre for Military Archives (LHCMA) to quote from the papers of Field Marshal Lord Alanbrooke and Major-General FHN Davidson; similarly, The Trustees of the Imperial War Museum gave their permission to quote from the Field Marshal Montgomery Papers; UK Crown copyright material is reproduced under the conditions of the Open Government Licence; the US National Security Archives have allowed permission under limited licence to quote from material in their collections.

As always, Shaun Barrington and Chrissy McMorris of Spellmount and The History Press have offered useful help and advice. And finally, my greatest thanks to my wife, Gill, who has given me so much support during the writing of *Operation Unthinkable* (now *Churchill's Third World War*) and who has cheerfully accompanied me on my research adventures into Eastern Europe.

Jonathan Walker, 2017

GLOSSARY

AK	*Armia Krajowa* (Polish Home Army)
COS	Joint Chiefs of Staff Committee (British)
DSZ	*Delegatura Sił Zbrojnych* (Armed Forces Delegation for Poland). Successor to Nie. Set up May 1945 and disbanded August 1945. Aimed to bring together all partisan bands opposing Soviet domination inside Poland.
JPS	Joint Planning Staff
JWPC	US Joint War Plans Committee
LWP	*Ludowe Wojsko Polskie* (Polish People's Army). Soviet-sponsored Polish army. Established 1943.
Nie	*Niepodleglo* ('No'). Set up in spring 1944 and disbanded May 1945.
NKGB	*Narodnyi Kommissariat Gosudarstvennoi Bezopastnosti* (Soviet Security and Intelligence Service)
NKVD	*Narodnyi Kommissariat Vnutrennikh Del* (People's Commissariat for Internal Affairs)
NSZ	*Narodowe Siły Zbrojne* (National Armed Forces). Nationalist resistance group established in September 1942. Partly merged with AK in 1944 but elements maintained a separate NSZ. This group survived the war to continue the fight against the communists until the 1950s.
PKWN	*Polski Komitet Wyzwolenia Narodowego.* (Polish Committee of National Liberation). Also known as the Lublin Committee. Soviet-sponsored administration, which later became the Provisional Government of Poland.
PPR	*Polska Partia Robotnicza.* (Polish Workers Party). Polish Communist Party.
SBZ	Soviet Occupation Zone of Germany

SMERSH *Smert Shpionam* (Death to Spies)
SSR   Soviet Socialist Republics
TRJN   *Tymczasowy Rząd Jedności Narodowej* (Polish Provisional
        Government of National Unity).
UB   *Urząd Bezpieczeństwa* (Polish Secret Police)
USAAF   United States Army Air Force
WiN   *Wolność i Niezawisłość* (Freedom and Independence). Successor
        to Nie. Set up in the summer of 1945. Became the largest post-
        war underground organisation in Poland. Infiltrated by the
        communist Polish Secret Police, WiN was largely destroyed by
        late 1947.

INTRODUCTION

At 3 p.m. on VE Day, 8 May 1945, Prime Minister Winston Churchill broadcast to the British nation from the Cabinet room in 10 Downing Street. He still used the familiar hand gestures as if he were addressing a public meeting and his voice betrayed little of the massive strain he had endured since 1940. The speech echoed from loudspeakers to vast crowds in Parliament Square, Trafalgar Square and across Britain. It was picked up by wirelesses across Europe and beyond. Churchill announced that the war against Germany was finally over and reminded his listeners of the magnitude of the struggle that they had endured. 'We may allow ourselves a brief period of rejoicing', he warned, 'but let us not forget for a moment the toil and efforts that lie ahead'. While he reminded his audience that Japan was the devil still to be vanquished, he was well aware of another, more unpredictable peril that lay in wait to the east. He would later recall:

> When in these tumultuous days of rejoicing I was asked to speak to the nation,
> I had borne the chief responsibility in our island for almost exactly five years.
> Yet it may well be there were few hearts more heavily burdened with anxiety
> than mine.[1]

The cause of Churchill's private agony during the days of celebration was Josef Stalin, and his determination to totally control Poland and Eastern Europe. Not without good reason did Churchill name his account of the end of the war *Triumph and Tragedy*. By May 1945 he was deeply worried about not only Stalin's tightening grip on continental Europe, but also his designs on Britain and her Empire. The omens during the last months of the war had not been good.

In the spring of 1945 the Red Army continued its advance towards Western Europe, reaching the Adriatic in the south and approaching to within 100 miles of the River Rhine in the west. Meanwhile Germany was shattered and the great powers of Britain and France were financially exhausted. The United States was already turning its attention to the Pacific region and looked set to evacuate Europe. With such bleak prospects Churchill saw one last chance to save Poland from total Soviet domination. Even Britain herself looked vulnerable, and there seemed only one solution – to push back the Soviet Empire by force. Without delay he ordered Operation 'Unthinkable' to be prepared, to examine the possibility of an Allied force attacking the Red Army and regaining the lost ground in Europe.[2]

Churchill felt isolated. The late President Roosevelt, with his 'progressive' advisors, Army chief of staff General George Marshall, Ambassador Joseph Davies, Harry Hopkins and even his own son Elliott Roosevelt, had all sought to accommodate Stalin. Indeed, the president considered himself the best man to deal with Stalin, telling Churchill, 'I can personally handle Stalin better than either your Foreign Office or my State Department.' Given the capacity of the Soviet leader for devious and brutal behaviour, it was a bold boast and one the US Joint Chiefs of Staff did not, at least privately, endorse. 'No one in the West', they admitted, 'really knows which direction Soviet policy will take.'[3]

As far as Stalin was concerned, after the enormous sacrifices of his people, the Soviet Union deserved the spoils of war. During 'The Great Patriotic War', as the Soviets called the Second World War, in excess of 8.5 million Red Army soldiers had perished, as well as more than 17 million civilians. This total estimate of more than 25 million deaths dwarfed the losses suffered by any other participating power and the war also cost the Soviet Union about 30 per cent of its natural wealth.[4] Although the country's contribution to the Allies' success was irrefutable, its motives and future agenda in Europe were not quite so clear. Churchill was profoundly concerned about Soviet intentions, and although his angst was not widely shared, even a cursory look at Soviet and Russian history should have alarmed his colleagues. Stalin was, after all, the standard bearer of Marxism, and an avowed enemy of small nations. He clung to the old Russian belief that she was a 'mother country' entrusted with the protection of the Slav nations in Eastern Europe. Furthermore, the ultimate victory of the Soviet Union in the Second World War imbued the people with a confidence that they could achieve anything through sacrifice – a confidence that was boosted by Stalin's ruthless denials of Allied help through Lend-Lease or the Arctic Convoys. The vast outpouring of pro-Soviet articles by the British press during the war must surely have strengthened Stalin's self-confidence even more. So, as his assurance grew, Stalin believed that there was no future in a post-war partnership with the West, and although he did not relish the prospect, he saw no alternative but conflict with his erstwhile allies.[5]

If Stalin's ambitions were to be checked, and diplomacy failed to deliver, the West might have to resort to military means. Anglo-American military strength was at its peak in May 1945, but that would rapidly diminish due to general demobilisation and the re-deployment of forces to the Far East. Churchill felt he would have to act quickly and decisively to combat the Soviet threat. On 12 May 1945 he cabled Roosevelt's successor, President Truman:

I am profoundly concerned about the European situation, as outlined in my No. 41. I learn that half the American Air Force in Europe has already begun to move to the Pacific theatre. The newspapers are full of the great movements of the American Armies out of Europe. Our Armies also are under previous arrangements likely to undergo a marked reduction. The Canadian Army will certainly leave. The French are weak and difficult to deal with. Anyone can see that in a very short space of time our armed power on the Continent will have vanished except for moderate forces to hold down Germany.

Meanwhile what is to happen about Russia? I have always worked for friendship with Russia but, like you, I feel deep anxiety because of their misinterpretation of the Yalta decisions, their attitude towards Poland, their overwhelming influence in the Balkans excepting Greece, the difficulties they make about Vienna, the combination of Russian power and the territories under their control or occupied, coupled with the Communist technique in so many other countries, and above all their power to maintain very large Armies in the field for a long time. What will be the position in a year or two, when the British and American Armies have melted and the French has not yet been formed on any major scale, when we may have a handful of divisions, mostly French, and when Russia may choose to keep two or three hundred on active service?

An iron curtain is drawn down upon their front. We do not know what is going on behind. There seems little doubt that the whole of the regions east of the line Lübeck-Trieste-Corfu will soon be completely in their hands. To this must be added the further enormous area conquered by the American Armies between Eisenach and the Elbe, which will I suppose, in a few weeks, be occupied when the Americans retreat, by the Russian power. All kinds of arrangements will have to be made by General Eisenhower to prevent another immense flight of the German population westward, as this enormous Muscovite advance into the centre of Europe takes place. And then the curtain will descend again to a very large extent, if not entirely. Thus a broad band of many hundreds of miles of Russian-occupied territory will isolate us from Poland.

Meanwhile, the attention of our peoples will be occupied in inflicting severities upon Germany, which is ruined and prostrate, and it would be open to the Russians in a very short space of time to advance, if they chose, to the waters of the North Sea and the Atlantic.[6]

Churchill was always at his most articulate and inventive when faced with a grave situation. As his doctor, Lord Moran, observed, 'In adversity Winston becomes gentle, patient and brave.' Even if events did not favour him, 'he will not spend the rest of his days brooding on the past. Whatever happens, nothing can hold up for long the stream of ideas that rush bubbling through his head.'[7] One such idea was Operation Unthinkable.

The remarkable thing about this plan was that it was unique. Churchill, alone among Western leaders, was prepared to consider a pre-emptive strike against Soviet forces in the summer of 1945. President Roosevelt and his successor, President Truman, would not, at first, countenance the Soviet threat, and even when it became impossible to ignore, they would not endorse the first use of arms against the Soviet Union.

The alarming aspect of the attitudes of national leaders in the West during the fast-moving events of the spring and summer of 1945 was their capacity for dramatic mood swings. Churchill, Roosevelt and Truman took it in turns to be either bullish or conciliatory towards Stalin, while he remained resolutely unyielding in his demands.[8] Consequently, what seemed an inevitable and logical course of action for the Western Allies one week could well be discarded the next. It is in the light of this frighteningly volatile atmosphere that Operation Unthinkable was born. In his VE Day speech Churchill exhorted 'Advance Britannia', but if she did indeed advance, would Poland really stand a chance of recovering her freedom in 1945? And just how close did the world come to a Third World War?

NOTE ON WORD USAGE

The term 'the Soviet Union' is always used in the text, rather than 'Russia', which is the usual word found in contemporary documents and may appear in quotations. Russia was only one of the fifteen socialist republics that made up the USSR (Union of Soviet Socialist Republics), which existed between 1922 and 1991. Since the break-up of the Soviet Union the individual republics have become independent states, of which Russia remains the strongest.

I

'AN UNSPOKEN FEAR'

Winston Churchill, 23 February 1945

Winston Churchill was no stranger to the Soviet Union, or to its previous form as Tsarist Russia. Indeed, it was the threat of a Russian invasion of India, via Afghanistan at the end of the nineteenth century that had seen the 'young Winston' engaged in his first war. As a subaltern, he had fought with the Malakand Field Force on the North-West Frontier, which was dispatched to keep control of the vital mountain passes between Afghanistan and India. Writing of the campaign, Churchill was unimpressed by British military tactics, but he did support the strategy of warding off Russian expansion in the region.

During the Great War, the Russian Army was eventually overwhelmed on the Eastern Front. Although Churchill declared at the time that 'Russia is unconquerable', he was surprised at the speed of the collapse in 1917 of both the Tsarist regime and the subsequent Provisional Government. The success of the Bolsheviks troubled Churchill. Not only was he passionately opposed to their ideology, but as Minister of Munitions he was also appalled that Bolshevik Russia could sign a peace treaty with Germany and pull out of the war.

Several months after the armistice he became Secretary of State for War and his fear of Bolshevism became all-consuming. Though he did not instigate the Allied intervention in Russia during her post-revolution civil war, he was enthusiastic about the mission. He endorsed the expansion of military operations in 1919, sending further troops and supplies to support the White Russians who were attempting to topple the Bolshevik government. But the sheer scale of the territory, the divisions amongst the White Russians, and a war-weariness amongst the Allies all conspired to extinguish the venture.

In the 1930s Stalin's appalling crimes reinforced Churchill's belief that the Soviet dictator and the communist system were tantamount to 'a plague'. Nevertheless, the advent of Nazism made them a convenient bulwark in the East. Even the 1939 Nazi–Soviet pact failed to dent Churchill's conviction that it was Hitler who was the greater evil. Compromise with Stalin was, he held, the only way to defeat Germany. And when Hitler invaded the Soviet Union in 1941, Churchill was quick to counter those who predicted Stalin's demise. 'I will bet you a Monkey to a Mousetrap,' he growled, 'that the Russians are still fighting, and fighting victoriously, two years from now.'

So Churchill took up the mantle of chief sceptic about Stalin only later in the war. Before that it had been up to the Poles to warn the West in vain of Stalin's ambitions, which they had learned about from bitter experience. The annexation of eastern Poland by Stalin in 1939 was a blatant act of double-dealing as well as naked aggression. Subsequently, the need for an alliance against Hitler had compelled the Poles to accept the Soviets as allies, but this abrasive relationship was finally shattered in April 1943, when the Soviet Union broke off relations with the London-based Polish government-in-exile. This crisis erupted after the Poles had demanded a Red Cross inquiry into the Katyn massacres, when more than 21,000 members of Poland's elite, including officers, professors and writers, were found to have been murdered on Stalin's orders.[1] Despite pressure from the Western Allies, Stalin had refused to re-establish relations with the London Poles in 1944, claiming that they had rejected his demands for the ceding of eastern Polish territory. He even alleged that Polish intransigence had forced him to establish a Lublin-based 'National Committee of Liberation' in July 1944, which comprised communist and left-wing Poles. This committee, also known as the PKWN (*Polski Komitet Wyzwolenia Narodowego*), would shortly emerge as Stalin's sponsored Polish government, and it would dash Western hopes of a democratic government.

As 1944 drew to a close, Stalin's strategy for the domination of Poland was all coming together. The Polish resistance, in the shape of the Home Army, had been effectively destroyed by the Warsaw Rising and although their spirit was undiminished, their command structure and operations were seriously depleted by the end of the year.[2] By then, Soviet forces had overrun Romania, Bulgaria, the Baltic States and large parts of Hungary. They had advanced into East Prussia and occupied a large swathe of Poland up to the River Vistula. Stalin envisaged that he would soon have almost total possession of Eastern Europe, and with it the power to dictate his terms to the Allies. Meanwhile Churchill and particularly Roosevelt were becoming desperate to avoid a total fall-out with Stalin over Poland.

Churchill pressured the Polish government-in-exile to accept the loss of their eastern territory, especially as it was softened by the offer, once the war was over, of a similar-sized chunk of German territory to the west.

But Britain, or more precisely her military commanders, did not entirely roll over before Stalin. Barely a month after the June D-Day landings, post-war planning was being discussed in the British War Office, and on 27 July, the Chief of the Imperial General Staff, Field Marshal Sir Alan Brooke, met with the Secretary of State for War, Sir James Grigg, to discuss the future dismemberment of Germany. Should it be carved up between the Great Powers or, as Brooke favoured, 'gradually converted to an ally to meet the Russian threat of 20 years hence'? That night, he noted in his diary, 'Germany is no longer the dominating power in Europe. Russia is … she has vast resources and cannot fail to become the main threat 15 years from now.'[3] This was certainly at odds with the entrenched view within the British Foreign Office (FO) that any future Soviet threat could easily be contained by the West.[4]

This split between the soldiers and the diplomats was widening, and Brooke baulked at the attitude of the Foreign Office. His diary entry for 2 October 1944 showed his frustration at the diplomats' attitude towards the Soviets:

A longish COS [Chiefs of Staff Committee] where we discussed the Foreign Office attitude to our paper on dismemberment of Germany. We had considered the possible future and more distant threat to our security in the shape of an aggressive Russia. Apparently the FO could not admit that Russia might one day become unfriendly.[5]

Indeed, senior Foreign Office figures such as Christopher Warner, who was head of the FO's Northern Department 'wobbled' constantly over the idea that plans should be prepared for a conflict with the Soviet Union. He feared that France might succumb to a communist take-over after the war, and if such war plans existed, the military would be tempted to try them out in France. To this end he sanctioned that 'special security treatment' should be applied to any FO papers that mentioned the Soviets as a possible enemy. So, as 1944 drew to a close, the predominant view in Whitehall was that Stalin would seek to accommodate the West for another ten years, if only to repair the war damage to the Soviet economy. They perceived that Stalin wished to see that those countries that bordered the Soviet Union followed the same foreign policy, but he would not necessarily insist on them having communist governments. Consequently, such a benign Soviet attitude was not expected to challenge Britain's imperial interests.[6] However, this FO view only looked at the situation through the eyes of a responsible Western democracy, which would realise that huge post-war restoration costs would mean a corresponding reduction in arms spending and a curtailing of foreign policy. No such constraints, of course, bound Stalin, whose spending on military hardware knew no limits.

The British Foreign Office was optimistic, if not naive, about finding a solution with Stalin as to the future of Poland. British analysts did not dismiss the problems of negotiating with the Soviets, but seemed pathetically grateful for any crumbs Stalin discarded:

> We consider that Poland must have the closest and genuinely friendly relations with Russia but that she should herself be genuinely independent and in no sense a puppet of the Soviet Union. A settlement on the above lines would in our view constitute a complete fulfilment of our obligations to Poland. So far as public statements and private assurances go there is no difference between us and the Soviet Government on the above policy. Indeed, Marshal Stalin in his last Moscow conversation with M. Mikołajczyk went further than we should have expected in positively encouraging the Poles to maintain their present relationship with Great Britain and America in addition to entering upon a new relationship of alliance with Russia.[7]

There were even those within the FO who feared the day when the British public might realise that 'Uncle Joe' Stalin was not all that he seemed. Should public pressure then start upsetting the *status quo*, it would ruin the carefully nurtured relationship between London and Moscow.[8]

In October 1944 the Polish prime minister, Stanisław Mikołajczyk, previously rebuffed by Stalin, joined Churchill in Moscow to attempt a last-ditch reconciliation over the issue of the Polish border. But it was all in vain. Mikołajczyk realised that the Soviet Union ultimately wanted to engulf Poland and stood his ground against Churchill. There was a furious row between the pair and Churchill erupted at the Polish leader's intransigence. 'We will tell the world,' Churchill bellowed, 'how unreasonable you are. You will start another war in which 25 million lives will be lost. But you don't care.' So Mikołajczyk was bullied into agreeing to the Curzon Line proposal (the old suggested Polish–Soviet border, mooted by the British in the 1920s), but he metaphorically drew the line at handing over Lwów and the Carpathian oil fields. Even this stance was too much for his rigid government-in-exile colleagues back in London and they refused to allow him to cede any territory. Left with no alternative, Mikołajczyk resigned as prime minister on 24 November 1944, and was replaced by the elderly socialist Tomasz Arciszewski, an implacable opponent of Stalin. Weeks later the Lublin Poles declared themselves the provisional government of the Republic of Poland. As 1945 dawned, the Soviet Union formally recognised the new Polish government, leaving Churchill and Roosevelt with few political options. Even on the military front, events were not going smoothly for the Western Allies, with their forces meeting stiff German resistance in the Ardennes. A further conference with Stalin was a necessity.

However, before the Marshal of the Soviet Union would agree to a conference, he made sure that the Red Army was as far forward as possible and that the three great capitals of Berlin, Budapest and Prague all lay within his grasp. On 17 January 1945 the Red Army also occupied what was left of Warsaw and weeks later they captured Kraków, farther south. So, having placed himself in a commanding position, Stalin now acceded to the Western Allies' request for another meeting of the 'Big Three'.

A suitable meeting-place for the Big Three was determined by Stalin's refusal to move very far from home. President Roosevelt was happy to suggest Yalta, a resort on the 'Crimean Riviera'. To begin with there was some confusion as to whether he meant Malta rather than Yalta, but once that was clarified the only problem for Stalin was the physical state of the place. The Germans had left the Crimea as a wasteland, with its countryside ravaged and its roads pitted with landmines. Nothing if not resourceful, the Red Army was ordered to completely overhaul Yalta and the surrounding area. Thirty thousand Soviet troops were brought in to guard the approaching roads and the resort, while 1,500 train coaches arrived from Moscow bearing vast quantities of linen, food, drink and furniture, as well as glass to repair the shattered windows of the villas.[9]

While Soviet troops were patching up Yalta for the conference, the US and British delegations broke their journeys, stopping off at Malta. But if Churchill and his foreign secretary, Anthony Eden, were hoping for preconference discussions with Roosevelt, they would be disappointed. According to Eden, although the president arrived with a great flourish, he was soon tired by his illness and distracted by his daughter, so that there were no talks with the British. Eden recalled that although Roosevelt was sick, there was an abiding feeling that the president and his aides did not want to be 'ganging up' with their British allies, or be seen to be doing so, before meeting the Soviet delegation. This meant that there was no preparation before going into the ring with Stalin at Yalta. As far as the Polish issue was concerned, it was a fatal mistake.[10]

2

YALTA

Going into the Yalta Conference, the Western Allies were far from unified. Roosevelt, rather than standing shoulder to shoulder with Churchill, increasingly saw himself as 'an honest broker' between Britain and the Soviet Union. Not surprisingly, Roosevelt's son Elliott also saw him in this role. 'The Russians had a Polish government in Moscow,' he observed, 'and the British backed the old Polish government operating outside of Poland. Father's role was mediator and arbitrator – as it was so important for unity that it continue to be.'[1] Yet unity was not Roosevelt's sole objective. He shared the belief, with many of his advisors, that the American mission in the war should not just end with the defeat of Hitler, but should also help to free colonial people from their masters. American foreign policy was at this time avowedly anti-imperial and Roosevelt made his opinions about the British Empire very clear to Churchill. 'I've tried to make it clear to Winston,' he complained, 'that while we're their allies and in it to victory by their side, they must never get the idea that we're in it just to help them hang on to the archaic, medieval Empire ideas.'[2] It seemed that Roosevelt and his advisors were becoming as suspicious of Britain's post-war ambitions as those of the Soviet Union.

Perhaps Churchill had misjudged the Americans more than the Soviets. As John Lukacs has observed, 'the idea of an Anglo-American union evoked no response in American minds and hearts; it all seemed somehow limiting and backward compared to such things as world government or the United Nations.'[3] For his part, Roosevelt believed Churchill to be cleverer and more calculating – a conviction reinforced by Roosevelt's discovery, some months earlier, of Churchill's deal concerning the partition of the Balkans.[4] The 'naughty document', as Churchill himself christened it, had been conceived when he met Stalin in Moscow in October 1944. During their talks, Churchill suddenly proposed that the countries of the Balkans should be split by percentage into areas of Western and Soviet control. Churchill passed a piece of paper to Stalin on which he had scribbled that 'Russia' could dominate 90 per cent of Romania, while Britain and the US would have a 90 per cent stake in Greece. Yugoslavia and Hungary would be split 50/50 and Bulgaria 75/25, but there was no attempt to arbitrarily split influence in the real problem areas of Poland, Austria or Italy.

What seems a cynical document was, in fact, Churchill's reaction to sudden news. He had heard, via ULTRA, that the Germans were about to evacuate Athens and there was an immediate risk that the vacuum would be filled by communist partisans. He was prepared to sacrifice an already Soviet-dominated Romania for a free hand in Greece, so that the British could advance into Athens within days, and stop a communist takeover. This idea of a 'deal' over post-war Europe also cemented Churchill's belief that Stalin would always respond to a spot of bargaining. The prime minister reasoned that as a man devoid of all moral constraints, Stalin might well come to heel if presented with a straightforward percentage split of control over Europe. However, this assumption relied on the unlikely premise that Stalin would keep his word and that the West could rely on some element of anti-Soviet sentiment in the caretaker governments of Eastern Europe. Both these hopes were soon to be dashed and it was this sense of betrayal that increasingly haunted Churchill and persuaded him that force against the Soviet Union might be justified. Unsurprisingly, when Roosevelt heard about this impromptu deal, he was furious. He had not been consulted beforehand and it merely reinforced his belief that Churchill was pushing Britain's imperial ambitions, or at the very least trying to exclude the US from the European negotiations.[5]

When the British and American delegates arrived at the Black Sea resort of Yalta, they found a surreal world that contained superficially grand palaces. But behind the gloss, the place was a wreck. The British were initially impressed by the 'green cypresses, terra-cotta earth and magnificent country villas', including their own base, which resembled a castle from 'a Grimm's fairy-tale'. The building had to accommodate Churchill, the foreign secretary, Anthony Eden, two field marshals, three chiefs of staff and a host of their attendants. Domestic arrangements were bizarre, as Churchill's secretary recalled:

The Vorontsov Villa boasted several banqueting halls, various reception rooms, a conservatory containing lemon trees and so on; but washing facilities seemed to be neglected. It appeared that Prince and Princess Vorontsov had concentrated more on eating than on bathing. One bath and three small washbasins served this enormous Palace, and in the morning one queued with impatient Generals and embarrassed Admirals, all carrying their shaving kit and wishing that their dressing-gowns had been long enough to cover their bare ankles.[6]

As many as twenty generals could be sharing a bathroom, and the sight of Field Marshal Sir Henry 'Jumbo' Maitland Wilson emerging from the bathtub was not for the faint-hearted. Nonetheless, there was much embarrassment and spluttering when local Crimean girls arrived with bath brushes to administer the Russian ritual of back-scrubbing.[7] So, with spotlessly clean delegates, Yalta (also known as the Crimea Conference) convened on 4 February 1945. Stalin ensured that all the accommodation used by the Allies was fitted with bugging devices, and although the delegates swept their rooms for such devices, they missed many of them, including the exterior microphones fitted to pick up outdoor conversations. So throughout the conference, the daily conversations of Churchill, Roosevelt, their chiefs of staff, and numerous advisors and diplomats were analysed by Stalin and the general staff of the Red Army. Stalin, through the offices of his Soviet Security and Intelligence Service (NKGB), had also acquired a mass of British documents concerning the proposed strategy of the British delegation, so he was well aware of the divergent policies of the Western Allies, especially regarding Poland.[8]

For many attendees it was their first sight of the legendary Soviet dictator. George Kennan, a deputy head of the US Mission in Moscow, summed up what it was like to be in Stalin's presence:

> Stalin, when he looked at you, he didn't look at you because he always looked to the side; he held his head on one side, and never looked you straight in the eyes, which to me – I mean I'd read about him obviously – rather betrayed his sort of suspicious, locked-in nature. He had a withered left arm, and he held this in his right hand, with his palms upright, cupped. This was a typical stand of his. But then he'd shake you by the hand very formally; very soft hand, he had … when I first met him, I got rather a shock because of his very marked Georgian accent. He spoke in short sentences.[9]

Both Roosevelt and Churchill were, by now, familiar with Stalin and his operating techniques, yet as Kennan observed, the US president still seemed puzzled by him:

I don't think FDR was capable of conceiving of a man of such profound iniquity, coupled with enormous strategic cleverness as Stalin. He had never met such a creature and Stalin was an excellent actor and when he did meet with leading people at these various conferences, he was magnificent, quiet, affable, reasonable. He sent them all away thinking this really is a great leader. And yes, but behind that there lay something entirely different. And Charles Bohlen, my colleague who succeeded me as ambassador there, was present at the Yalta and the Potsdam Conferences and he told me that he saw, only on one or two occasions, when the assistants to Stalin had said or done something of which he didn't approve, when he turned on them and then the yellow eyes lit up and you suddenly realised what sort of an animal you had by the tail there.[10]

The gaunt and fast-fading Roosevelt felt that he and Stalin stood together on certain issues, not least that they both saw Britain as a spent force, thoroughly exhausted by the war. At one of the first plenary sessions, Roosevelt made a statement that was designed to allay Stalin's concerns about US influence in Europe, but it struck fear into Churchill's heart. The president stated that he did not wish to keep a vast army in Europe after the war and therefore US troops would be pulled out of Germany within two years of the end of the war. This would leave Britain and France responsible for occupying all of western Germany, and it would also leave Britain perilously undefended, should Stalin advance beyond Berlin.[11] There were other indications that the US was lukewarm about any military operations in Europe that might conflict with Stalin. For the US chiefs of staff had persistently turned down requests from Churchill to support Allied operations in the Balkans. Roosevelt believed that the British wanted to establish a presence in Eastern Europe in order to prevent communist takeovers there. This US attempt to curb British aspirations won favour in Moscow and reinforced Roosevelt's conviction that he, and he alone, could hold all the wartime Allies together in the post-war world.[12] Frank Roberts, a British Foreign Office minister, was apprehensive about the US president's apparent lack of interest in Europe, and particularly the fate of Poland. 'A cynic might also add,' he ventured, 'that he [Roosevelt] had already won his re-election, and did not need the Pittsburg Polish vote for the time being.'[13]

Yalta certainly had a packed agenda. Among the main items discussed by Britain, the US and the Soviet Union were the creation of the United Nations, the 'Dismemberment of Germany', reparations and the most contentious of all – Poland. With the first two issues Britain was at odds with the Soviet Union; Stalin's 'dream team' for the UN comprised all fifteen separate Soviet states, which after pressure from the West were whittled down to the Ukraine, Belorussia and Russia itself. As for the dismemberment of Germany, Churchill demanded the inclusion of France as an occupying power. He had no love for General de Gaulle, and the French leader characteristically failed to appreciate Churchill's gesture, but still, France added weight to the West's increasingly fragile position. [14]

There were daily arguments, mainly between Churchill and Stalin, over the composition of Poland's future government; with the Soviet Army occupying Poland, Stalin believed he held all the cards. He was never going to negotiate with an émigré Polish government in London, and as for the Polish borders, Stalin was keen to cite history as his reason for redesigning them in the Soviet interest. He said he feared Poland being used again as a corridor for invading armies to attack his country. 'In future,' he growled, 'we do not want to be shot in the back.' Stalin did indeed receive most of his border demands, and although final confirmation was to be left to the 'future Polish government', it was clear that his client state of Poland would receive part of the old East Prussia on her northern boundary, together with a slab of eastern Germany, including the mineral-rich area of Silesia, and the town of Breslau and port of Stettin. [15] This was supposed to be compensation for the loss of her eastern territory to the Soviet Union, but this effectively placed a productive slice of Germany within Stalin's control. According to Anthony Eden this also meant the expulsion of over 8 million ethnic Germans from the newly acquired territory. Despite all the posturing, a final agreement was hammered out by the time the conference ended on 11 February. The wording was a compromise, but Stalin's threat was clear from the first line:

> A new situation has been created in Poland as a result of her complete liberation by the Red Army. This calls for the establishment of a Polish Provisional Government which can be more broadly based than was possible before the recent liberation of western Poland. The Provisional Government which is now functioning in Poland should therefore be reorganised on a broader democratic basis with the inclusion of democratic leaders from Poland itself and from Poles abroad. This new Government should then be called the Polish Provisional Government of National Unity ... This Polish Provisional Government of National Unity shall be pledged to the holding of free and unfettered elections as soon as possible on the basis of universal suffrage and secret ballot. In these elections all democratic and anti-Nazi parties shall have the right to take part and to put forward candidates. [16]

When Roosevelt's chief of staff, Admiral Leahy, saw the document, he told the president that it could be interpreted any way the Soviets wished. The president shrugged. 'I know it,' he replied, 'but it's the best I can do for Poland at this time.' Roosevelt knew he had a sizable Polish-American vote at home to placate and he did not have time on his side. His health was rapidly declining, though it is debatable whether he knew he had just weeks to live. Yet, despite the publicly announced 'shared intent' over Poland, the two sides were as far apart as ever on who should govern Poland. The more realistic Leahy knew there was trouble ahead. 'Russia will be the dominant power in Europe,' he warned, 'with the prospects of another war.'[17]

As the Red Army continued its relentless westwards advance, Stalin was prepared to concede a few token democrats on his communist-based Lublin Committee. But he was only prepared to consider one final outcome – the installation of a communist and pro-Soviet government in Poland. Meanwhile the Western Allies wanted any new provisional government to include democratic Polish leaders from outside Stalin's orbit, and preferably from the London Polish government-in-exile. They wanted future elections to be 'free and fair', but Stalin could easily circumvent this by refusing to allow the West to participate in observing such elections. Stalin physically held the territory, and the Yalta agreement on Poland was a face-saving agreement for the West, an attempt to paper over widening cracks between the Big Three. Platitudes flowed during the after-dinner speeches at Yalta and Churchill was as enthusiastic as the other leaders to flatter Stalin.[18] But at least Churchill did not extend such largesse to Stalin's chief of police, Lavrenti Beria. When the British ambassador to the Soviet Union, Archibald Clerk-Kerr, toasted Beria at the end of one of the Yalta dinners, Churchill was horrified. 'Be careful,' Churchill admonished, shaking his finger at the ambassador, 'be very careful.' To the prime minister, Beria obviously symbolised the worst excesses of the Soviet system and was indeed Stalin's 'bloody hangman'.[19]

But the West indulged Stalin excessively. It is true that at Yalta the US believed it was imperative to secure the agreement of the Soviet Union to enter the war against Japan. The Americans were still vulnerable in north-west Europe, and that was evident by their recent reversal at the Battle of the Bulge. A long, hard fight towards Berlin still lay ahead and a usable atomic bomb was still some way off. Yet, that hardly excused the wholesale capitulation over Poland. After all, the Poles had stood beside Britain at a time when the Soviet Union and Nazi Germany had made pacts of friendship. At Yalta, even as Polish troops were dying alongside British and American soldiers, her eastern territory was sacrificed to the Soviet Union.

The Allies gave away 69,000 square miles of eastern Poland in return for Stalin's agreement to declare war on Japan. It is true that Poland was compensated with a little more than 39,000 square miles of territory in the west and to the north, taken from the old German Reich; this was rich industrial territory with mineral deposits, good infrastructure and contained a number of important cities and ports.[20] But Stalin was now emboldened and he also demanded that the Allies abandon the Polish government-in-exile and recognise his puppet 'Lublin' government. In February 1945 Soviet support seemed vital if Japan was to be defeated and Roosevelt made a further deal with Stalin, offering him even more concessions in Asia.[21]

Roosevelt's belief that he was better off negotiating direct with Stalin may explain why Britain was only asked to agree to these concessions at a very late stage, for the president did not want any British obstructions.[22] Stalin also demanded the return of any Soviet citizens who found themselves in the west at the end of the war, either because they were POWs or because they had escaped westwards from the communists. Britain caved in easily on this point, perhaps because they couldn't face having to resettle the estimated 2 million Soviet citizens who might refuse to go back to their homeland. In the event their fate was either execution or a life in one of the Soviet slave labour camps or 'gulags'.[23]

By obtaining Soviet help in the war against Japan, Roosevelt was obviously aiming to reduce US casualties. But Stalin extracted a further raft of concessions from the Western Allies in exchange for his agreement to enter the war against Japan 'two or three months after the surrender of Germany'. He demanded, and obtained, control over areas of Mongolia and Manchuria (without China's consent), as well as the restoration of Soviet territorial rights that were lost after its earlier disastrous war against Japan in 1905.[24] The US delegates were delighted. 'We've just saved two million Americans,' Admiral King, Chief of US Naval Staff told colleagues.[25] But there were other, more insidious reasons for the president's reliance on the Soviets. In the Pacific theatre certain elements of the American administration believed that Churchill was as keen on recovering former occupied colonies of the British Empire as he was on defeating Japan. To this end, Admiral King, who exerted great influence on Roosevelt, was anxious that the British should not play a major part in the Pacific war. The US was also determined to prevent France claiming back Indo-China and the Dutch from re-possessing the Dutch East Indies. Consequently, a swift defeat of Japan with Soviet help could certainly stop the old empires from recovering their former colonies.[26] In a sense,

Roosevelt felt he was building up a bank of goodwill with Stalin, from which he could draw in the future. But this belief was fundamentally flawed. The chief of the American Military Mission in Moscow, General Deane, was one of the few Americans who understood how the Soviet negotiators really worked:

> We never make a request or proposal to the Soviets that is not viewed with suspicion. They simply cannot understand giving without taking, and as a result even our giving is viewed with suspicion. Gratitude cannot be banked in the Soviet Union. Each transaction is complete in itself without regard to past favours.[27]

Conversely, Roosevelt's immediate entourage were encouraged to believe that it was the president, rather than Stalin, who dictated the agenda at Yalta. It may have been Roosevelt's vanity that propelled this belief, for his son Elliott was adamant that 'he [Roosevelt] dominated Winston Churchill more completely than before; Joseph Stalin was likewise prepared to heed father's counsel, to accept father's solutions.'[28] But such Soviet largesse did not impress all the members of the American administration. James Byrnes, who was shortly to be appointed secretary of state, lamented that 'the illusion of good feeling and co-operative relationships among the Soviet Union and the Western powers faded quickly in the aftermath of Yalta ... Incident followed incident, recrimination grew, and misunderstanding became the order of the day rather than the exception.'[29]

This growing distrust between the old Allies was exacerbated by Stalin's designs on Poland. He had always nursed a personal dislike for the Poles, fostered no doubt when he witnessed their routing of the Red Army at Warsaw in 1920. He distrusted the Poles but respected their toughness. 'You can scare the Latvians,' he wrote; 'you can't do that with the Poles. The Poles have to be isolated, with them you have to fight.'[30] And when the Polish government-in-exile learned the full details of the Yalta agreement they were ready for a fight. They were appalled at being brushed off by American and British officials, and when they pressed these officials to disclose how this new Polish 'democratic' government would be formed, they were told that 'possibly five, six, perhaps ten governments might be rejected before the United States would agree to one it considered really representative of the Polish people.'[31]

At Yalta Stalin persistently hedged the 'fine detail' of the make-up of the future Polish government and deftly courted Roosevelt with his favourite topic – the creation of the United Nations. By making concessions over Soviet representation at the UN, Stalin made the US president 'very happy' and the controversy over Polish democracy was conveniently side-stepped. The clearly ailing Roosevelt could see his legacy of a new world order coming to fruition. Churchill, too, succumbed to the Soviet ruse, though he was more ambivalent about the outcome of Soviet domination. Harold Nicolson, the political diarist, observed a less than coherent Churchill in the House of Commons, after his return from Yalta:

> He makes an extremely good case for arguing that Poland, in her new frontiers, will enjoy an independent and prosperous existence. But in his closing words before luncheon he rather destroys all this by saying that we will offer British citizenship to those Polish soldiers who are too frightened to return.[32]

Field Marshal Sir Alan Brooke had a visit from his opposite number, the Polish chief of staff, Stanisław Kopański, who offered him a 'sober' view of the Polish concerns. But several days later Brooke recorded an emotional appeal from the charismatic commander of the 2nd Polish Corps, General Władysław Anders, who had just returned from Italy:

> He [General Anders] had been to see the PM yesterday, but was still terribly distressed. According to him the root of the trouble lay in the fact that he could never trust the Russians after his experiences with them whilst Winston and Roosevelt were prepared to trust the Russians. After having been a prisoner, and seeing how the Russians could treat Poles, he considered that he was in a better position to judge what Russians were like than the President or the PM … I felt most terribly sorry for him, he is a grand fellow and takes the whole matter terribly hard. He is to see Winston again next Wednesday and then he is to see me afterwards. I shudder at the thought of this next interview.[33]

The meeting between the Polish commander and Churchill had, indeed, been a bitter one. According to Anders, despite the recent sacrifices of Polish troops in the crucial Battle of Monte Cassino, Churchill lost his temper and remonstrated with him. 'We do not need your help,' Churchill insisted, 'you can take away your divisions. We shall do without them.'[34] In this extraordinary encounter Churchill discounted not only Anders's unique knowledge of the Soviet high command but also the fact that a large number of his forces, who had been with him in the Soviet Union, knew just how the Red Army operated.[35] Yet, even after this showdown, Anders still hoped that Britain and the US would come to their senses about Stalin's designs. Other senior Polish officers voiced similar expectations and they were in no doubt that sooner or later a conflict between East and West would erupt. In this event Poland, they felt, should be ready for another world war when it came. They had their doubts about Britain's loyalty and her willingness to engage in a new war, though they clung to Churchill's Yalta declaration that a non-democratic Polish government would betray the 150,000-strong Polish army in the West.[36] While Anders was still not prepared to give up hope that in the near future the Polish army in the West could be called upon to liberate their homeland, Polish troops were not to be used in the forthcoming assault on mainland Japan. Neither were they to be stationed in a liberated Germany, for fear of antagonising Stalin, so the question arose about their continuing purpose. There was the option of future demobilisation in line with British and American forces, but Anders and other Polish commanders were not prepared to countenance this. Neither would they accept coming under the command of a future Lublin government. They were in limbo.[37]

Whether Anders suspected a war plan or not, there is no evidence that either he or his general staff were aware of the plan for Unthinkable, but there is no doubt that they would have relished the prospect of wresting back their territory from Stalin. With his manifest military power and straightforward patriotism, General Anders, as acting commander-in-chief, was a rallying point for Poles at a time when their government-in-exile was squabbling and splitting into factions.[38] Privately Churchill was gravely concerned that public opinion in the West would not tolerate a capitulation to Stalin over Poland. But the prime minister was almost certainly overestimating the will of the US, let alone British citizens, to go to war again over Poland. Nonetheless, he cabled Roosevelt:

Once it is seen that we have been deceived and that the well-known communist technique is being applied behind closed doors in Poland, either directly by the Russians or through their Lublin puppets, a very grave situation in British public opinion will be reached. How would the matter go in the United States? I cannot think that you personally or they would be indifferent. Thus just at the time when everything is going so well in Europe and when the Japanese policy is also satisfactorily arranged, there would come an open rift between us and Russia, not at all confined, in this country at any rate, to Government opinion, but running deep down through the masses of the people.[39]

The following day, Churchill voiced his concerns about Soviet designs to Sir Arthur Harris, commander-in-chief, Bomber Command. 'The PM was rather depressed, thinking of the possibilities of Russia one day turning against us, saying that Chamberlain had trusted Hitler as he was now trusting Stalin.' The conversation turned to the saturation bombing of German cities, but this only served to remind Churchill of the dangers that lay ahead, once Harris had done his work. 'What will lie between the white snows of Russia and the white cliffs of Dover?' Harris questioned whether the Soviets would advance and conquer the West in a way that the Mongols of old had never achieved. 'Who can say?' Churchill replied. 'They may not want to. But there is an unspoken fear in many people's hearts.'[40]

While Churchill pondered the post-war world and a conflict with his current ally, the very real fight in north-west Europe was reaching a climax. Nearly 4 million soldiers from the US, Britain and Canada were preparing to assault the Rhine. Under their Supreme Commander, General Eisenhower, these forces were moving forward to secure bridgeheads across the river and in early March Churchill, Montgomery and Brooke visited the headquarters of the US general William Simpson to witness the operations. Churchill was eager to visit nearby Aachen, and Brooke recalled that the prime minister was keen to 'pay his respects' to Hitler:

> Simpson asked Winston whether he wished to make use of the lavatory before starting. Without a moment's hesitation he asked, 'How far is the Siegfried Line?' On being told about half an hour's run he replied that he would not visit the lavatory now, but that we should halt on reaching the Siegfried Line! On arrival there the column of 20 or 30 cars halted, we processed solemnly out and lined up along the Line. As the photographers had all rushed up to secure good vantage points, he turned to them and said 'This is one of the operations connected with this great war which must not be produced graphically' ... I shall never forget the childish grin of intense satisfaction that spread all over his face as he looked down at the critical moment.[41]

Relieving himself on the enemy bastions gave Churchill some pleasure, though this was not a part of Germany that he felt the Allies needed to secure. That decision had been taken by Eisenhower, who had insisted that rather than racing to Berlin, the Western Allies should consider the industrial

Ruhr region as a higher priority. He believed that this powerhouse region needed to be occupied by the Allies to prevent its use by a revived nationalist Germany in the future.[42] It would also be a useful asset for the West in a future war with the Soviet Union.

In the aftermath of the Yalta Conference the Polish government-in-exile warned that the Soviet Union would not abide by any agreements, and that Britain and America should prepare for a showdown with Stalin. Indeed, there were very early signs that Soviet domination of Eastern Europe would be complete and merciless. On 7 March 1945 Churchill was interrupted at a dinner to be told that Nicolae Rădescu, the pro-West premier of Romania, had been hounded from office by a communist-dominated clique that now threatened to drag him out of his temporary sanctuary in the British Embassy. This should have been no surprise to Churchill, who had acceded to Stalin's majority control of Romania ever since the 'naughty document'. Nonetheless, the news inflamed the PM. His private secretary voiced his master's alarm:

> It seems that we may be heading for a show-down with the Russians who are showing every sign of going back on the Yalta agreement over Poland and of enforcing aggressive Communism on an unwilling Romania. The PM and Eden both fear that our willingness to trust our Russian ally may have been in vain and they look with despondency to the future.[43]

Churchill was powerless to stop Stalin's domination of Romania, though the reality that Romania was an ex-enemy state meant that he was never going to clash with Stalin over the future of the country. Furthermore, Churchill's frustration and anger quickly abated as he recalled his complicity in the communist domination of the country. He cabled Roosevelt the following day to remind him of how 'reasonably' Stalin had behaved over Greece:

> We have been hampered in our protests against these developments by the fact that, in order to have the freedom to save Greece, Eden and I, at Moscow in October, recognised that Russia should have a largely preponderant voice in Roumania and Bulgaria, while we took the lead in Greece. Stalin adhered very strictly to this understanding during the thirty days fighting against the communists in the city of Athens, in spite of the fact that all this was most disagreeable to him and those around him.[44]

But, while there was little Churchill could do about Romania, Poland was never brought into the 'naughty' deal with Stalin over the post-war spheres of influence. Churchill was determined to take a tough stance over Poland, and even revised his thoughts about Anders's troops. 'We shall need them,' he wrote in the margin of a report from Eden. 'A British Foreign Legion will be a help after the war.'[45] But while Churchill was building up a case for a free Poland, the US State Department took a dim view of his strident attitude. According to the British ambassador to the US, Lord Halifax, they did not wish to join in a combined statement with the British Foreign Office warning off Stalin. The US believed the British approach was 'too unconditional and shows too great a distrust of Soviet intentions in Poland'.[46]

But Churchill was on the right track, for appalling events were unfolding in Poland, many of them under Stalin's direction. While the British Foreign Office could not corroborate the reports (since their intelligence assets in Poland were virtually nonexistent), they received a deluge of information via the Polish government-in-exile. Everyone and everything was being registered – from males between the ages of 16 and 65 to typewriters, printing presses, duplicators and livestock. Ex-Home Army officers were rounded up and arrested, shot or deported in cattle trucks to the Soviet Union. The same fate befell numerous professors, landowners, priests or anyone who might challenge the new order in Poland. In this work the Soviet secret police, or NKVD (People's Commissariat for Internal Affairs) were quick, meticulous and ruthless in rooting out individuals for removal.[47]

The Americans were certainly disturbed by these developments, but only in so far as the reports disrupted their relationship with Stalin. The US secretary of war, Henry Stimson, noted in his diary in April that there was 'increasing strain in the relations between us and Russia', largely over the formation of the 'democratic' government in Poland.[48] Stimson was concerned that the issue of Poland could prove the breaking point:

> The Russians had apparently flatly refused to permit the agreement at Yalta to be carried out to select a mixed delegation from Poland and they are insisting that the Lublin people shall be recognised as the government of Poland.[49]

Roosevelt warned Churchill not to antagonise Stalin over the reports of a police state in Poland. 'You will recall at Yalta,' the president cautioned, 'that Stalin made quite a point of the "terrorist end" activities of the underground forces of the London Government against the Red Army and the Lublin Poles.' Roosevelt deemed it unfair that the Allies should only seek to restrain the Soviet-sponsored Lublin Poles and not the anti-Soviet resistance. 'I very much hope,' the president cautioned, 'that you will not send a message to Uncle Joe.'[50]

Churchill despaired at Western impotence, declaring to Roosevelt that 'at present all entry into Poland is barred to our representatives. An impenetrable veil has been drawn across the scene.'[51] As lists of Western-sponsored representatives for the provisional Polish government were submitted to Stalin, he rejected them and new names had to be submitted. The weeks dragged on. At last it became clear to Churchill what Stalin was up to. 'It is as plain as a pikestaff that his tactics are to drag the business out while the Lublin Committee consolidate their power.'[52] The 'Lublins', sponsored by Stalin and headed by Bolesław Bierut, were far from popular and were desperate to exclude a national figure such as Mikołajczyk, around whom widespread support might rally.[53]

There were other Poles whom Stalin wished to take out of circulation. To this end Colonel Pimenov of Marshal Zhukov's 1st Byelorussian Front had already approached the Polish underground to discuss 'security problems in the rear of the Red Army'. When the underground was slow to respond, the Soviet colonel insisted on a meeting to sort out the question of renegade units from the recently disbanded Home Army still operating inside Soviet lines. Pimenov also wanted to know why the local Polish underground remained active, and therefore in conflict with the Soviet administration. He claimed that he wanted both civilian 'cabinet members' of the underground, as well as its leading military figures, such as the former acting commander-in-chief of the Home Army, General Leopold Okulicki, to meet his superior, General Ivanov. Known as 'Bear Cub' or 'Little Bear', Okulicki's presence was apparently required because any agreements would have to be made at the highest level. He was reluctant to attend, since he had already tasted Soviet 'hospitality' during a stay in the NKVD Lubyanka interrogation centre in Moscow. However, many felt that this might be the last chance for free Poles to have their say in Moscow, and when the Soviets suggested that the sixteen-man Polish underground delegation first fly to London to confer with the Polish government-in-exile, the free Poles were seduced. But first there was the small matter of a preliminary get together to discuss agendas on 27–28 March in Pruszków, inside the Soviet lines.[54]

With a glimmer of hope for some democracy in Poland, Churchill turned his attention to the very late entry into the war of Turkey and Egypt. The former had offered a division for the Allied cause, but rather than dismissing Turkey as a useless adjunct, Churchill was keen to have their support:

The attitude of Russia alone suggests that we should not detach ourselves from Turkey or put her in a more humiliating position than she has been forced to accept as the result of the lack of her military modernization. Turkey may be of service to us in the future ... The changes in the Russian attitude and atmosphere since Yalta are grave.[55]

During the final month of the European war, there was also a growing distrust between Stalin and the Western powers over collusion with Germany. For his part Stalin believed that the British and Americans were agreeing a covert deal with the Germans, which became known as the 'Berg Incident'. Leading Nazi figures, such as Ribbentrop, had indeed sounded out the Western Allies to see if they might ease off the military pressure and form a last-minute alliance with Germany against the Soviet Union. But the British were aware from their ULTRA intelligence intercepts that certain top German leaders were also attempting to talk with Stalin.[56]

In this climate of distrust Churchill was more than ever determined to create 'a fair deal' for Poland. Yet he and his foreign secretary, Anthony Eden, had been fickle in fighting Poland's corner and in squaring up to Stalin. From a position of going to war over Poland in 1939 and initially taking a tough line on her borders, Eden had changed tack in early 1942. No doubt the parlous state of Britain's military resources had persuaded the foreign secretary that closer ties with the Soviet Union were needed and that Stalin's claim to the Baltic States and parts of Poland were worthy of consideration. Churchill was not so minded, and Eden's view did come under attack from Conservative MPs who felt their party leaders were not bullish enough. A common sentiment running through the party ranks by 1945 determined that the British government should stand firm against Soviet hegemony in Europe and if the Soviets took umbrage and boycotted the United Nations talks at the San Francisco Conference, 'then let them'.[57] As Stalin steered the Lublin Committee steadily towards government, he kept up the pretence that this committee was an independent body. Cabling Churchill on 11 April, Stalin portrayed himself as an arbitrator:

Mikołajczyk has come out openly against the decisions of the Crimea [Yalta] Conference on Poland. However, if you think it necessary, I should be ready to use my influence with the Provisional [Lublin] Polish Government to make them withdraw their objections to inviting Mikołajczyk, if the latter would make a public statement accepting the decisions of the Crimea Conference on the Polish question and declaring that he stands for the establishment of friendly relations between Poland and the Soviet Union.[58]

Stalin's ruse appeared to have worked, for several days later Churchill addressed his War Cabinet, telling them that he was encouraged by Stalin's attempts to mediate with the Lublin government and there was genuine cause for optimism.[59] In a new mood of conciliation towards Stalin, Churchill even pushed Mikołajczyk to make a public statement accepting Stalin's demand for a large chunk of eastern Poland including, more controversially, the old Polish city of Lwów.[60] This gesture towards Stalin was not matched by any positive signals from the Kremlin; in fact, there was a deathly silence. The Soviets did not even reply to constant questions from the Poles as to the whereabouts of the Polish underground leaders, who had disappeared since their meeting with the Red Army at Pruszków. At a critical moment, the leaders of the Polish democratic parties had just disappeared, which suited Stalin very well. But another event was about to upset the Soviet leader's carefully managed plan.

3

THREE FISHERMEN

In the early afternoon of 12 April 1945 President Franklin Roosevelt was having his portrait painted. 'We have only 15 minutes left,' he warned the artist. He then clutched his head suddenly and collapsed with a massive cerebral haemorrhage. He died shortly afterwards. The timing of the death of the thirty-second president of the United States could not have been worse. Following Roosevelt's death, Stalin had lost an 'honest broker', as the late president liked to be regarded, and Churchill was faced with establishing a new relationship with an unknown successor. Churchill pointedly did not attend Roosevelt's funeral, perhaps piqued at the late president's failure to support him against Stalin.[1]

But the power machine rolled on relentlessly. Harry Truman was sworn in as the new president only hours later, as startled as anyone else that he should find himself in the White House. The poker-playing farmer from Missouri was a compromise candidate, and he knew it, but he was determined to make his mark. That evening he wrote in his diary:

> I am not easily shocked but was certainly shocked when I was told of the President's death and the weight of the Government had fallen on my shoulders … I knew the President had a great many meetings with Churchill and Stalin. I was not familiar with any of these things and it was really something to think about but I decided the best thing to do was to go home and get as much rest as possible and face the music.[2]

He may have been on the fringes of power for many years, but Truman seemed set to take a firmer line with Stalin than his predecessor. Bracketing Stalin and Hitler together, he had already declared 'neither of them think anything of their pledged word.'[3] For his part, Stalin was alarmed that Roosevelt had departed the stage, for he always believed that the late president would never have the stomach for a fight with the Soviet Union and that while he lived the US would act as a sort of guarantor against an Allied double-cross. If Roosevelt was still alive, Stalin might have agreed to the Allies participating in the fight for Berlin. But as it was, Stalin set the date for his assault on Berlin to start on 16 April 1945.[4]

The fall of Berlin was eagerly awaited by all of the Allies, but even at the end of April there was still plenty of German resistance in the West to be cleared up by British or US forces. North-west Holland, the north German coastal belt, the Frisian Islands and Heligoland all had to be captured. Resistance remained in Denmark and Norway, while southern Germany, parts of Austria and the flanks of Czechoslovakia were still hostile. There were even pockets of German fighters around the French coast, and the Channel Islands still awaited liberation.[5]

There was little doubt that these countries would soon be free of Nazi occupation, but Churchill knew that in certain cases Stalin was ready to fill the power vacuum. This was certainly true of Austria. And if Stalin were successful, would that open the way for a further Soviet advance on the West? Much of Austria had already been swamped from the east by the Red Army. They had reached the suburbs of Vienna on 7 April and a week later, after violent street fighting, they were in complete control of the city, as well as the eastern half of the country. Any ideas that the Soviets came as liberators were quickly dispelled as the invading troops, many of them Ukrainians, or primitive Mongolian farm boys, set about raping and looting. Special treatment was meted out to those Austrian troops who had willingly fought in German divisions on the Eastern Front and scores were settled with the utmost brutality. Rape was systematic and it has been estimated that up to 100,000 Austrian women and girls suffered at the hands of 'liberating' Soviet troops from Konev's 1st Ukrainian Front.[6]

US and British forces had entered the western part of the country and it was agreed that there would be a similar four-power occupation as in Germany. Vienna, within the Soviet domain, was to have Soviet, US, British and French zones, but as usual Stalin had prepared the ground well in advance and swiftly set up a provisional government in Austria. Here, he had a completely free hand, for unlike France or Italy, Austria had no mature resistance movement who could form the nucleus of a government. Although this 'blank canvas' suited Stalin, he nevertheless had to draft in inexperienced communist party members to form the provisional government.[7] On 29 April a cabinet was sworn in, under the chancellorship of the socialist Karl Renner. It was meant to look like a provisional democratic government and indeed, there were moderates in the line-up, but the phalanx of Soviet officers surrounding the ceremony was an ominous sign. Churchill was outraged by this precipitate action but, as in Poland, Stalin had military possession of large parts of the country, including the capital.

There was also friction over the number of airfields in Austria that were allocated to the Western powers, for Stalin had refused to allow any US or British forces to enter Soviet-occupied Austria. Again, Stalin stalled when confronted with outrage from the western Allies, and he seemed unthreatened by their control of large parts of western Austria, even if their formidable military presence included three British and three US divisions. Stalin took his strategy to the brink, even refusing to allow Allied representatives access to Vienna to help determine the zones of occupation.[8] It was the same story across all Soviet-occupied Europe and Allied commanders became increasingly frustrated. The British commander, Field Marshal 'Jumbo' Wilson, was thwarted in his attempts to gain access to the captured German submarine base in Gdansk:

> He [General Deane] suggested that to get our people into Gdynia [Gdansk] we might argue that we should withhold the next Russian convoy unless they agreed. Our convoys had to fight their way through the submarine menace and if we were not given the opportunity to explore that menace at its source then there was no reason why we should accept the risks involved in the convoys.[9]

In effect Stalin's tactic for installing a puppet government in Austria was the same as in Poland – prevaricate with the Western Allies on the issue of the members of the government and then, under pressure, concede a number of ineffectual moderates to mollify the west and give the government some democratic credentials. Any mutterings from the West could be dealt with by referring the matter to a future conference at Potsdam. By this time Stalin would have laid the foundations of Soviet military dominance.[10]

It was no surprise that Churchill was both mentally and physically exhausted. Having spent five years directing the British war effort, there was now the danger that this huge achievement would be overshadowed right at the end by a replacement dictatorship in Europe. Since Yalta he had been considering all possibilities for clawing back lost ground from Stalin, but by mid-April his despair and guilt over Poland had reached new heights. He now approached the Chiefs of Staff Committee and ordered them to prepare a plan for the use of military force to bring Stalin to heel.

The chiefs of staff were the perfect channel for Churchill's top-secret order, since their committee was directly responsible to the prime minister in his dual role as minister of defence. Churchill could be sure of an expert and confidential report from a committee which had proved itself one of the more successful developments in the British war machine, but it had not always functioned so smoothly.[11] Formed in 1923, its initial role was to act as a sub-committee of the Imperial Defence Committee, but from the outset many politicians felt that it gave the armed services too much power. While the earlier chiefs were reluctant to accept collective responsibility, the wartime triumvirate, with Field Marshal Sir Alan Brooke as its chairman, was a formidable and effective team.[12]

The committee also comprised the First Sea Lord (Admiral Sir Andrew Cunningham) and the Chief of Air Staff (Air Marshal Sir Charles Portal), with General Sir Hastings Ismay acting as secretary. Ismay, who was also Churchill's chief of staff, was known universally as 'Pug', and was a big, powerful man who possessed a fund of anecdotes, which according to his deputy he could not deliver without bursting into laughter before the punch line.[13] Humour aside, the chiefs had worked together as a team for some time and, out of hours, even shared a passion for fishing, which they all famously indulged in during the Quebec Conference in 1944. But it was not all harmony at the top. Brooke, as Chief of the Imperial General Staff (CIGS), was responsible for not only the British conduct of the war, but also for liaison with the US chiefs, through the Combined Chiefs of Staff Committee.[14] According to Ismay, it was a role that was not initially satisfactory:

> The Americans at first did not take to Brooke, due to his direct and positive approach to common problems, and his ill-concealed contempt for 'theoretical' soldiers – he spoke fast and abruptly, like a machine-gun, and they could not understand him. Later they came to trust him completely and recognised in him the 'complete master' of his profession ... He was frank to the point of brutality. He held back nothing – there was no finesse, no bluff. At times he could be extremely obstinate. Impatient peppery, quick-tempered, celtic, he was, deep down very kind hearted – consequently he suffered such remorse afterwards for his hasty words.[15]

Portal, too, felt that Brooke 'jarred' on the US chiefs of staff and it was not until the end of the war that senior US commanders, such as General Marshall, established a friendly relationship with him. This was fortunate since Brooke was compelled to spend long periods with the American chiefs – it has been estimated that during his tenure as CIGS he was away from London for some 2½ years.[16] Brook could also be counted on to give a no-nonsense opinion of Churchill's suggestions, and a plan for military force against a resurgent Soviet Union would certainly receive his close scrutiny.

Churchill wanted a contingency plan from the chiefs. He repeated his deep concern that the Soviet Union had reneged on the Yalta agreement and Stalin had tightened his vice-like grip on Poland, a country that Britain had a responsibility to entrust with some democracy. The tension had been heightened when the British government received news on 11 April that Andrzej Witos, a 'moderate' and ex-member of the Lublin Committee, had reportedly been arrested by secret police at his home near Kraków. The stakes were raised again by news that the party of Polish underground leaders, who had met members of the Red Army, had since disappeared.[17] Furthermore, Stalin showed every likelihood of attempting to extend his territory and influence into Western Europe. The chiefs' initial brief from Churchill was to assess Britain's 'potential ability to exert pressure on Russia by the threat or use of force'. They were to calculate the likelihood of success of a pre-emptive strike led by US and British forces against the Soviet Union within two months of the surrender of Germany. The object of such an attack was to force upon Stalin 'the will' of these two former allies by recovering, in the first instance, Polish territory and then penetrating into the Soviet Union. If the Red Army was defeated, it would be the Western powers who dictated the map of post-war Europe.[18]

The subject was highly sensitive and top secret. Only the chiefs of staff and their immediate subordinates would know about the plan. They would put together a number of assumptions and parameters, while the detail and research for the plan would be carried out by the Joint Planning Staff (JPS), a tight group of senior officers who were already Directors of Plans for the three separate services. The normal brief of the JPS was to put together plans and contingencies to cover all eventualities – however improbable. It would be a dereliction of duty for the chiefs not to have a response for all sorts of scenarios, regardless of how remote they might seem, but the time given for submission of these plans could be frighteningly short. Major-General Francis Davidson, Director of Intelligence, recalled that on one occasion he was required to react to the German drive towards the Mediterranean:

> I was rung up by the Director of Plans at 1245 hours and informed that I was to meet the Chief of Staff at 1730 that day and give him an appreciation of the

routes, timings etc of the German plans as far as Athens and Salonica!! ... the C of S had 'passed the buck' to me to produce the answer in about 5 hours.[19]

Fortunately, most planners had the luxury of more time than Davidson, but the sheer demand was staggering; in the spring of 1945 the JPS were inundated with requests for reports on possible military operations in Burma and Borneo, as well as plans for post-war Europe. Reports on the entry into the war of Turkey and Egypt, reviews of personnel, of cargo shipping, of aircraft production and endless reports on plans for the assault on mainland Japan spewed out of the JPS offices. One such report on 12 April attempted to determine the date for the end of the war and there was much talk then of a Nazi redoubt holding out in Bavaria, while German resistance in Norway was expected to be stubborn. Interestingly, the planners believed it would take until the end of June to achieve a viable German surrender, so that any plans for an offensive against the Soviets could only be implemented after that date. This plethora of plans, of course, did not mean that these military adventures would necessarily ever become government policy.[20]

Although the JPS was required to prepare plans for events of worldwide significance, they were surprisingly junior officers, albeit men with good planning pedigrees. Lieutenant-Colonel George Mallaby was secretary to the JPS, which comprised Captain Guy Grantham DSO (Director of Plans at the Admiralty), Brigadier Geoffrey Thompson DSO (Director of Plans, War Office) and Air Commodore Walter Lloyd Dawson (Director of Plans, Air Staff). They were to prepare a plan with certain assumptions, backed up with detailed appendices, maps of deployments and lines of attack.[21] For most plans the JPS would normally call on advisors from the government's service departments, such as the Foreign Office, Home Office and Supply and Transport departments, but for this highly secret plan these advisors would not be consulted.[22]

According to Sir Ian Jacob, Military Assistant Secretary to the War Cabinet, Churchill had little time for the JPS and never really appreciated their work. He recalled on one occasion that Churchill described the planners as 'the whole machinery of negation', though this was probably because their brief was to consider all problems, and to the prime minister this meant 'obstacles'.[23] The individual planners were highly competent, though it was true that the concept of post-war strategic planning was not one of Britain's strongest suits, with inter-departmental rivalry playing a disruptive part.

Particular war plans ordered by the chiefs of staff were always carried out by their designated Joint Planning Staff but there were other departments and committees charged with contingency plans. For example, a Military Sub-Committee (MSC) was first established in 1942 to devise military contingency plans. This evolved in 1944 into the Post-Hostilities Planning Staff (PHPS), tying military plans into Foreign Office 'Basic Assumptions'.[24] However, there was always friction between the FO and the military over their conflicting views of the future role of the Soviet Union. The FO strongly advocated a Soviet-friendly line, with the Deputy Under-Secretary of State, Sir Orme Sargent warning that 'knowledge in the Kremlin that Britain was thinking of a war against the USSR was the surest way of bringing one about'.[25] Some elements within the Armed Forces took a stronger line against the Soviet Union, but the Joint Planners could be relied upon to be objective about their brief. Over the weeks of late April and early May they set to work on one of the most critical projects of their careers. In a plan that would have culminated in a Third World War there were plenty of surprises.

4

THE PLAN – 'QUICK SUCCESS'

During April and May 1945, the Joint Planners worked long into the night in their offices inside the War Office, wrestling with the numerous assumptions, statistics and forecasts of 'Operation Unthinkable'. They began their work by outlining the basic assumptions and object of their study:

WAR CABINET
JOINT PLANNING STAFF

OPERATION 'UNTHINKABLE'
Report by the Joint Planning Staff
We have examined Operation Unthinkable. As instructed, we have taken the following assumptions on which to base our examination:

(a) The undertaking has the full support of public opinion in both the British Empire and the United States and consequently, the morale of British and American troops continues high.

(b) Great Britain and the United States have full assistance from the Polish armed forces and can count upon the use of German manpower and what remains of German industrial capacity.

(c) No credit is taken for assistance from the forces of other Western Powers, although any bases in their territory, or other facilities which may be required, are made available.

(d) Russia allies herself with Japan.

(e) The date for the opening of hostilities is 1st July, 1945.

(f) Redeployment and release schemes continue till 1st July and then stop.

Owing to the special need for secrecy, the normal staffs in Service Ministries have not been consulted.

OBJECT

2. The overall or political object is to impose upon Russia the will of the United States and British Empire.

Even though 'the will' of those two countries may be defined as no more than a square deal for Poland, that does not necessarily limit the military commitment. A quick success might induce the Russians to submit to our will at least for the time being; but it might not. That is for the Russians to decide. If they want total war, they are in a position to have it.[1]

So the planners considered this a 'hazardous undertaking' on two 'hypotheses'. The first premise envisaged a swift military success, which would be enough to gain the political objective of bringing Stalin to heel and imposing the 'will' of the Western Allies, who included forces from the British Empire, the US, Poland and Germany. If this was achieved, no further planning would be required or military commitment considered, beyond holding the frontline. The second hypothesis was, indeed, a nightmare scenario in which a quick success eluded the Allies and the conflict escalated to 'total war', or a Third World War between East and West. However, the planners added a chilling rider to their deliberations that 'if our political object is to be achieved with certainty and with lasting results, the defeat of Russia in a total war will be necessary.'[2]

Both hypotheses involved the same initial planning for an attack on Soviet-occupied territory and the initial offensive would take place in northern Europe. The date chosen was 1 July 1945, early enough to allow the campaign to achieve its targets before the winter set in. It would take the JPS team the best part of a month to draw in all the necessary data, collate the assumptions and draw some conclusions. It is known that the chiefs of staff examined the JPS Unthinkable report towards the end of May, so it is realistic to assume that allowing for a month's planning, the work started in mid-April. However, a report by the same JPS team in early April estimated that the war would end on 30 June. With this date, it allowed no slack in the timetable, for the very same JPS team also determined a start date for Unthinkable of 1 July. The prospect of finishing a war one day and starting another the following day seems incredible.[3]

Preparations for the attack would have been immediately apparent to Soviet agents in Germany. There would be hectic levels of activity in repairing approach roads and communications networks going west to east, while river defences along the Elbe would be reinforced. New airfields and airstrips would be developed to enable short-distance reconnaissance and fighter aircraft to operate, and existing fuel dumps would be topped up. Movements of large troop formations up to the front line would be observed, as would cancellations of leave for servicemen. The rate of demobilisation would slow to a trickle, and Soviet agents would detect the dispersal of aircraft and that that all civilian air movement had come under military control. They would also monitor the activity in allied ports and note that merchant ships had been recalled. Railway stations would become very busy and on the roads armoured columns and artillery brigades would clog the approach routes. Ambulance trains would be heading west to east. Because of the activity in the rearward Allied positions in northern Europe, it would be apparent to Stalin where the main offensive thrust would be launched.

The lack of surprise was not an element that seemed to concern the planners, at least not in the initial stage. They were more concerned with the broad strategy and laying out the assumptions on which they based their plan. Indeed, they were well qualified to do so since the JPS comprised the Directors of Plans from each of the Armed Services. The land operations were devised by Brigadier Geoffrey Thompson, who was based at the War Office. He had previously been attached to French forces in the Middle East and had more recently commanded 1st Field Regiment, Royal Artillery, before becoming Director of Plans.[4] He knew the European terrain well and determined that southern Europe was just too mountainous for a continuous thrust towards the east, with the exception of the Danube Valley. So he calculated that the two-pronged attack would have to take place initially through Soviet-occupied territory in eastern Germany and then into Poland. The northern thrust would advance along the axis, Stettin (later renamed in Polish, Szczecin)-Schneidemuhl (Pila)-Bydgoszcz. The southern thrust would advance along the axis Leipzig-Cottbus-Poznan-Breslau (soon to be renamed Wrocław).

It was likely that Soviet forces would be alerted to heightened Allied activity some weeks before 1 July and would be prepared for the Allied advance. It was also possible that the huge numbers of Soviet defenders could hold any Allied attack on the point of contact. But if a breakthrough was achieved, the Soviets might allow a 'cushion' resistance back to the line of the Oder and Neisse rivers. The mass of their armour would be concentrated to the east of these rivers and it was in this area that a climactic armoured clash might take place.

So the main armoured battle would be joined east of the Oder-Neisse line and in the area between Stettin, Schneidemuhl and Bydgoszcz, which formed the new border with Germany.[5] If the results of this massive engagement were favourable, the objective would be for the Allies to then stabilise the line from Danzig (later Gdańsk) on the north coast to Breslau, 240 miles to the south; any further advance before the winter would mean an extended southern flank, which would be vulnerable to attack from Soviet forces in Bohemia and Moravia (Czechoslovakia). Here, on this southern flank, it was expected that the Czech army (unlike the Polish army) would stand firm behind their Soviet occupiers and support any Red Army operations in this salient. The Czechs were, after all, 'looking west for their cultural inspiration, but east for their security'.[6]

The planners believed that if they could secure this line from Danzig to Breslau by autumn 1945, it might be enough to bring Stalin to heel. This land campaign, rather than the naval or air force operations, would be the deciding factor; but if the Allies reached that line by the autumn (discounting the huge advantage the Soviets held in manpower) and Stalin had not changed his mind about control of Eastern Europe – what then? With the forces available to them, Western commanders could not hold their line through the winter of 1945–46 and they would be forced either to retreat or push on into eastern Poland and the Soviet Union. Pushing on would undoubtedly result in 'total war'.[7]

Breslau, as the limit of the initial objective, could hardly be described as a prize target. The former German city was the capital of Silesia, and had the misfortune to be designated by Hitler as a fortress, to be held at all costs against the advancing Soviet hordes in early 1945. Most of the civilian inhabitants were expelled in January 1945, as the Wehrmacht, supplemented by patchy units of the Home Guard (*Volkssturm*) and Hitler Youth, prepared to withstand a siege. Makeshift defences were bolstered by the efforts of imported slave labour, many of whom had been earlier expelled from Warsaw. From 16 February to 6 May, the day before the surrender of all

German forces in Europe, the 50,000 military defenders and 80,000 civilians were besieged by the encircling Red Army. The city, or what little remained of it, was a desperate and desolated ruin, picked over by the wretched and dehumanised survivors, and the Red Army victors, in scenes that were all too familiar in Berlin, then engaged in an orgy of raping and pillaging what little was left.[8]

A necessary adjunct to the land operations were naval operations, to be carried out in the Baltic. Forty-five-year-old Vice-Admiral Guy Grantham was the JPS member charged with assessing naval strengths and strategies. He had recently been appointed Director of Plans at the Admiralty after a distinguished career commanding various vessels in the Mediterranean and had experience of amphibious operations, having commanded the aircraft carrier HMS *Indomitable* during the landings in Sicily. He was well briefed in all aspects of naval operations and had only recently completed a report for Cunningham on 'Requirements of the Post-War Navy'.[9] He estimated that to carry out supporting flanking operations along the Baltic coast, a naval fleet would have to be assembled in the German port of Brunsbüttel, with advance bases along the north German coast. Brunsbüttel was an ideal naval base, being situated on the mouth of the Elbe near the North Sea and at the western entrance to the Kiel Canal. There would also be facilities at Karlskrona, the main Swedish naval base on the southern tip of the country, though there was no mention by the planners of the poor state of port facilities along the Baltic coast, resulting from the Second World War Allied bombing raids. Similarly, there was no mention of the heavy mining of the sea, especially surrounding the Danish coast, which would prove an obstacle to any shipping.[10]

The Allied Naval force would include two or three Cruisers, two Destroyer Flotillas, four Motor Torpedo Boat (MTB) Flotillas, and one Assault Force. These ships could be taken from the Home Fleet, since the threat from the Soviet fleet in the North Sea was deemed to be 'slight'. But, again, future British naval commitments in the Far East would have to be considered, though there was plenty of confidence that any Soviet ships venturing out of northern Baltic ports, or through the Dardanelles into the Mediterranean, could be easily sunk by superior Allied naval firepower.[11]

All land operations in northern Europe would be supported by naval operations off the Polish coast. The Royal Navy's superiority in the Baltic meant that the Allies' left flank would be protected. An early objective would be the capture of the port of Stettin and thereafter a number of amphibious 'hooks', or assaults along the coast, would ensure the capture of coastal batteries. This expected success at sea would bring rewards, but naval forces would not be a decisive factor in bringing Stalin back to the conference table. However, despite the numerical and technical superiority of the Allied fleet in the Baltic, there were considerable problems in navigating the sea. The average width of the Baltic is only about 100 miles, but the coasts of Finland and Sweden are littered with inlets and islands, while the southern coast of the Baltic, which stretches alongside Germany and Poland, contains sandy beaches and almost no tidal estuaries. Such a shoreline would assist amphibious landings, but large ships could easily run aground on shallows or reefs. The average depth was only about 500ft. Strong north-easterly winds could also whip up the sea and make life difficult for small assault craft.[12]

The Allies could easily control the Baltic and by using carrier air strikes could inflict damage on Soviet installations. Such carriers were vulnerable to Red Air Force strikes, but overall the Soviets had no comparable naval presence and their submarines were far inferior to the German U-boats. The report concluded that 'we should have virtually complete naval superiority in the Baltic and should be able to prevent any Russian move to Sweden or Denmark.'[13]

With such an advantage at sea, the Allied land operations would be well supported, but what about the war in the air? This was an altogether more complicated part of the Unthinkable plan, and was the responsibility of Group Captain Walter Lloyd Dawson. After flying experience with 24 Squadron and 84 Squadron before the war, Dawson had joined the Air Staff in 1939 and then moved to RAF Middle East. Several years later he was involved with Air/Naval co-operation in his role as Director of Operations and his knowledge of tri-service collaboration was therefore a useful skill in calculating how a European conflict or even world war might evolve. He was also involved at the same time in preparing an important paper for his chief, Portal, on 'Requirements of the Post-War RAF'.[14]

Initially it seemed to Dawson that the advantage of any Allied air superiority would be offset by the British strategic bombing force having to operate out of bases in East Anglia. The report stressed that 'the elaborate ground organisation of the bomber force would make it impracticable to move it from the United Kingdom to North West Europe for some months.'[15] Therefore staging and refuelling posts would have to be set up in Europe, but still, the vast distances would present real difficulties, and fighter support would be reduced as the adventure progressed farther eastwards. The Allied air forces could not be expected to perform to the same level as they did against Germany; for one thing, industrial targets in the Soviet Union were far more spread out than in Germany.[16] However, the Red Army's lines of communication would be extended in wartime and its numerous river crossings would be vulnerable to Allied air attacks.[17]

The report estimated that the US, British and Polish air forces could muster 6,714 first line tactical or fighter aircraft which could be utilised from north-west Europe and the Mediterranean, subject to any re-deployments to the Far East in June.[18] Included among these were a number of new jet fighters, which first saw service at the end of the Second World War. The RAF had a number of Gloster Meteor F.3 jets, which had been operational since 1944, while the Luftwaffe had used the Messerschmitt Me262 successfully for bomber interception and ground attack. The Red Air Force did not possess any full jet fighters, though a mixed-power Mikoyan-Gurevich was used to some effect. In short, jet fighters added some weight to an air force's capability in 1945, but there were still too many experimental problems, such as the closing accuracy of cannons at such high speeds.[19] So the Allies would probably rely on the piston-engined US P-51 Mustangs and P-47 Thunderbolts to provide fighter cover, and even then they would have to operate from forward airbases, duly repaired after the end of the Second World War.

The planners also remained confident about the Allied superiority of its strategic bomber force available for an attack on the Soviet Union. This combined force would consist of 2,464 heavy bombers, 1,840 based in Britain and 624 in the Mediterranean, though this was only a proportion of the worldwide compliment.[20] Such aircraft would be used in mass formations, which were well armed, flew at high altitudes and were escorted by modern fighters – a combination which the Red Air Force rarely had to deal with in the Second World War. The Allies would use the Boeing B-29 Superfortress as the main strategic bomber, supplemented by the earlier B-17 Flying Fortresses and Consolidated B-24 Liberator heavy bombers, as well as Lancaster Mk Is and IIIs and Halifax Mk IIIs from RAF Bomber Command.[21] At the time when Unthinkable was mooted, the latest Avro Lincoln bomber had not been tested on operations, but by the summer of 1945 it was one of a number of strategic bombers assigned to *Tiger Force*, the Commonwealth unit earmarked for the assault on the Japanese mainland in October 1945.[22] The Lincoln, which was developed out of the Lancaster stable, was the last of the RAF's piston-engine heavy bombers, and had increased fuel and bomb loads. With its longer range and higher operational ceiling, it would be a thankful addition to later bombing operations against Soviet targets, deep into Poland or Belorussia.

Soviet forward tactical targets might be attacked by the Mosquito and would include fuel and ammunition depots, barracks, repair workshops, headquarters and staff offices, as well as the lines of communication leading to the battlefront.[23] These lines could be easily disrupted since most of the bridges west of Poland's River Vistula were made of wood and were therefore vulnerable to air attack. Strategic targets would be ports, railway junctions and stations, factories, oil refineries and water supplies; it was against such targets that the heavy bombers would be launched. If air bases in Iran could also be utilised by the Allies, so much the better, for this would bring more Soviet oil fields and refineries within range; a typical Lancaster bombing operation against such installations would involve each aircraft carrying fourteen 1,000lb HE bombs. Even then, some of the 32ft-long bomb bay space might have to be utilised for extra fuel tanks.[24]

Providing fighter escorts for the bomber formations would prove a problem, since the long distances involved would require a fighter to have large fuel tanks. These aircraft could be adapted to carry such tanks, but their manoeuvrability in dogfights over enemy territory would be severely hampered, though the USAAF had recently come up with an ingenious solution: the American P-51 Mustang long-range fighter carried cardboard under-wing fuel tanks that could be jettisoned once the fuel was expended. While the Allied air forces were undoubtedly superior, there were no estimates within the plan for their air losses, but based on the Second World War RAF operations, such as the Battle of Berlin, heavy bomber losses could be in the order of 5 per cent of sorties dispatched. Cumulative losses on this scale would certainly strain the resources of the West, especially with engine replacements.[25]

Having outlined the USAAF and RAF strengths, the planners then looked at what competition they would face. The Red Air Force was believed to have a total first-line strength of 16,500 aircraft, which were divided among four separate arms. The Army Air Force was by far the largest arm and was equipped with some 13,600 aircraft, including 9,380 fighters and ground attack aircraft, and 2,380 light bombers. The Long Range Bomber arm comprised 1,000 strategic bombers, but these were deemed to be ineffective. There was also a Naval Air Force, which had more than 1,100 aircraft, mainly engaged in mine laying and anti-submarine operations, and which worked in close co-operation with the Soviet fleets. Finally, there was the Fighter Defence Force, more than 300 aircraft, which were tasked with the role of defending Soviet installations in the rear, but it was a role that had not been tested during the Second World War.[26] Overall, the Red

Air Force was not equipped to oppose a modern-day bomber force, or even a modern-day fighter force; it was not helped by an inferior radar system, and there were more underlying problems.[27]

The main weakness of the Red Air Force was that it depended on the West for nearly half its supplies of high-grade aviation spirit. On commencement of hostilities, the Soviets would be deprived of these supplies and it is unlikely that they could have made up this shortage from occupied territories within six months. The Soviets also relied on Western imports of rubber, aluminium, copper and ferro-alloys – all vital for aircraft construction. In the last months of the Second World War, Soviet aircraft production was running at an unprecedented rate of 3,000 units per month, but if the Allies were to deny the Soviets the vital raw materials, and once the expected heavy losses were inflicted on the Soviet squadrons, it was expected that production rates would be 'totally inadequate to meet the demand'. However, the planners seemed to ignore the fact that two-thirds of the entire German aircraft production plant was inside Austria and Czechoslovakia – territory now occupied by the Red Army. Although it would take some time to tie this into Soviet production, these plants could replenish aircraft shortages by the winter of 1945–46 and also use the latest German technology in rockets and gas-turbine engines to lethal effect.[28]

Due to stale intelligence, the planners also failed to appreciate the rate at which the Soviets were stripping out aircraft plant, resources and technical expertise from occupied territories. Within weeks of the Red Army capturing the Junkers factory at Dessau, the Heinkel plant at Rostock and the Messerschmitt works at Wiener Neustadt, their special engineer squads were dismantling presses, gantries and machine-tools and transporting them swiftly to Soviet works in the east. Furthermore, there were plenty of German technicians, designers and even test pilots who were now prepared to work for the Soviets in exchange for the security of employment and exemption from the work camps.[29]

However, the Red Air Force faced further problems, which were not flagged up by the planners. No sooner had the May Day Parade taken place in Moscow, than Stalin embarked on another, more ruthless purge of his senior commanders. With the object of perpetuating fear and tension among his subordinates, Stalin ripped through the command staff of the Red Air Force, and virtually all the Military Council of the Air Force were jailed, demoted or shipped off to some desolate outpost of the Soviet Empire. Even more bizarre (and heinous) was Stalin's retribution against his airmen or soldiers who had been captured by the Germans during the Second

World War. There were numerous Soviet decorated bomber crews who had been shot down in enemy territory during the war, yet their immediate joy at being liberated and returned to their homeland was shattered when they were interrogated by Soviet intelligence and deemed, because of their spell with the enemy, to be corrupted. They were therefore a danger to the purity of the revolution and were dismissed or expelled to a gulag. In this way, large numbers of experienced and no doubt loyal officers were removed from the Red Air Force to the detriment of the country's defences.[30]

But where the Red Air Force really showed experience and expertise was in their tactical role. Their fighters had given a good account of themselves when faced with old-style German fighters like the JU-87 or Me-109. The main fighter available to Red Air Force squadrons was the Yak 9; its variant the Yak-9D could dog-fight well and had been used to provide fighter cover for US bombers raiding the Romanian oil fields in the Second World War. Although it had large-capacity fuel tanks and could therefore fly long missions, with a range of 845 miles, it was otherwise unexceptional. But the later Yak-9U, which had come into production towards the end of the Second World War, was a fast, nimble fighter that was very effective at low to mid altitude. For tactical and frontline bombing operations the Tupolev Tu-2 twin-engine daylight aircraft was an extremely fast and effective dive-bomber, but fuel restrictions would probably limit its capacity to dive-bomb advancing allied forces.

The planners were also pleased to detect another major weakness of the Red Air Force – its lack of strategic bombers. The Soviets had no experience of aircraft carrier warfare, or indeed attacking high-altitude bombers such as the B-29 Superfortress. In fact, nothing could compete with the American bomber, and Stalin could not believe his luck when, in the autumn of 1944, three USAAF B-29s, returning from bombing Japan, had to make emergency landings in the far east of the Soviet Union. Stalin immediately ordered the construction of copies of the Superfortresses, though it would take some years for the Soviet aviation company Tupolev to turn out operational replicas.[31] So, even by the summer of 1945, the Soviets had still failed to manufacture an effective strategic bomber to compete with either British or US aircraft. The Tupolev Tu-4, which promised to out-perform the B-29, was still at design stage, while the Ilyushin medium bomber, the Il-4 (quick to manufacture, but unreliable and difficult to maintain) and the four-engined Petlyakov Pe-8 could only just about reach European targets. But, while these latter aircraft were already obsolete and were being withdrawn from service, the Il-4 bomber remained the mainstay of the long-range air force. It carried a payload of up to 5,500lb of bombs with a flight range of 2,300 miles but, as one pilot testified, it was no joy to fly:

> The Il-4's directional stability left much to be desired. The controls could not be left for a second: with the most ideal neutral setting of the elevator, a machine with no-one at the controls would unhesitatingly and arbitrarily climb, or, if it felt like it, would drop down at high speed. It cheekily dragged at the pilot's hands and would wear him out during extended flights.[32]

If handling difficulties in the air created problems for Soviet pilots, there was even worse in store when it came to take-off and landing. The condition of many airbase landing strips was appalling, with many heavy bombers unable to take off when the hard frosts of winter thawed in the spring. Colonel General Vasiliy Reshetnikov, an officer in a Soviet long-range bomber regiment, lamented the state of Soviet air bases:

> Our aerodrome came to a standstill during bad weather. Our *chernozem* [topsoil] got waterlogged, the roads became slushy, the town was completely cut off from the outside world … our houses and barracks were lit by candles and kerosene lamps. A pathetic diesel engine gave light in the offices only occasionally in the evenings. I couldn't find a reasonable generator or enough fuel. And I couldn't get hold of building materials to improve the life of the garrison in any way.[33]

Such poor facilities would not be so evident during a summer campaign, as envisaged in Unthinkable, but might be one positive aspect for the Allies in an otherwise gruelling winter campaign. Indeed, because the Soviet long-range bomber force had proved so ineffective during the Second World War, the planners believed it was unlikely to be deployed during Unthinkable for missions deep into Allied-held territory, and would be used only to support Soviet land forces. Consequently, the planners were confident about Allied air superiority:

> Air action would take the form primarily of direct support of the land operations. We should be able to inflict a severe defeat upon the Russian Air Force and seriously interfere with Russian rail communications in rear of their front.[34]

So, while the strength of the Soviet Navy and Air Force could be overcome, the planners believed the overwhelming problem would be the clash against the Red Army. The planners calculated the size of Allied forces in 'North Europe' that could be earmarked specifically 'for offensive operations in the north'. So it is important to remember that these figures did not include the total Allied strength in Europe as a whole. One limiting factor on the size of Allied forces available for operations was the promise to police occupied territories, such as Germany, Italy and Austria, at the end of the war. The planners believed that these internal security obligations would occupy eleven divisions, while a further twenty-five divisions would be required to defend the frontline running from the Baltic down to the Adriatic. After these commitments, this would leave the Allies a total of forty-seven divisions for the offensive in northern Europe, comprising fourteen armoured divisions, twenty-five infantry divisions, five airborne and three 'equivalent' divisions. [35]

These figures would include a proportion of Polish forces, but it is not known whether the bulk of the four Polish divisions in Europe on VE Day would be utilised in recovering their homeland. At the end of the war, units of the Polish army in the west were spread across Europe, but they were nominally assigned to two separate corps. The 1st Polish Corps included the 1st Armoured Division, 1st Independent Parachute Brigade and 16th Independent Armoured Brigade, and although they never fought together as a single formation they each notched up their own bloody battle honours in north-west Europe. Meanwhile, the 2nd Polish Corps (including the 3rd Carpathian Infantry Division, 5th Kresowa Infantry Division, and 2nd Warsaw Armoured Division) finished the war in Italy where they had fought a valiant campaign, including their eventual conquest of Monte Cassino. However, deploying these troops in West Germany for Unthinkable would not be straightforward.

Refugees and ex-POWs from the liberated areas continued to flock to General Anders's colours, so that as each month went by, the Polish army was swelled by thousands of Poles. At the end of the war II Corps had an estimated 75,000 men out of a total Polish army of over 200,000. By 1 July II Corps had probably grown to 90,000, while the whole Polish army in the West would have risen to about 228,000 soldiers (of whom nearly 90,000 were Poles from the west of the country, who had been drafted into the Wehrmacht when western Poland was incorporated into the Reich). [36] However, since this powerful Polish army had become a political football between the Soviet Union and British governments, even Churchill felt it expedient to publicly announce a limit on Polish army recruitment. He also consented to Stalin's demands that this force should not be stationed in the Allied-occupied sector of Germany, since Stalin claimed their presence was a provocation. But it is quite conceivable that if there was a real will to put Unthinkable into effect, the Polish contribution would have exceeded the planners' forecast of available divisions on 1 July. Moving these large concentrations to the north in preparation, however, would destroy any element of surprise in the attack on the Red Army.

It has been estimated that on VE Day, the US army (including the Army Air Force) deployed some 3 million officers and men in the European theatre, with a further 750,000 deployed in the Mediterranean. Fortunately, as far as Unthinkable was concerned, few of these forces would be demobilised in the immediate months after VE Day, since the war against Japan was expected to last for another year. However, during the summer months it was anticipated that US troops would leave Europe in increasing numbers, either to return to the US or to be shipped out to the Far East. It was a sobering thought that by May 1946, only 400,000 US ground and air troops would be left in Europe.[37]

But such numbers would be dwarfed by the Red Army that faced them. The planners estimated that even having lost over 10 million dead in the war, the Red Army still numbered in excess of 7 million men, of whom 6 million were based in the European theatre of operations. In addition there were thought to be 600,000 NKVD troops deployed. Of the Red Army forces mustered in northern Europe (and therefore facing the Allied offensive), it was estimated that they numbered the 'equivalent' in Allied divisions of 140 infantry and 30 armoured divisions, together with 24 tank brigades. 'We should be faced,' the planners concluded, 'with odds in the order of two to one in armour and four to one in infantry.'[38] Fresh from the conquest of Poland and Eastern Germany, Soviet formations had largely remained where they finished at the end of the war. From the Baltic coast down to the south of Poland, some massive Soviet 'Front' formations were lined up, including the 2nd Baltic Front, 1st Baltic, 3rd Belorussian, 2nd Belorussian, 1st Belorussian and 1st Ukrainian Front. The size of these fronts was larger than a Western army formation and could vary from 500,000 to 800,000 troops.[39]

So what was the calibre of the Red Army soldier? At least the planners had a healthy respect for the potential enemy:

The Russian Army has developed a capable and experienced High Command. The Army is exceedingly tough, lives and moves on a lighter scale of maintenance than any Western Army and employs bold tactics based largely on disregard for losses in attaining a set objective. Security and deception are of a high quality at all levels. Equipment has improved rapidly throughout the war and is now good ... The facility the Russians have shown in the development and improvement of existing weapons and equipment and in their mass production has been very striking.[40]

Nowhere was this re-galvanising of the Soviet military machine more evident than in engineering and communications. There was a marked improvement in Red Army wireless capability, while their engineering skills had improved their river-crossing operations, recovery of damaged vehicles and the swift restoration of bombed railway tracks. As for the soldiers themselves, there was high regard for their stoicism. It was an honour to be a Red Army soldier, and the armed forces were credited with saving the country, as well as winning the war for the US and Britain. Its soldiers had extraordinary self-reliance and were excellent night-fighters compared to the British or Americans. The Red Army soldiers were also physically and emotionally tough and could survive extremes of weather and battle conditions with low rations and poor clothing. Furthermore, they could accept death in combat and show extreme brutality towards their enemies. Many Allied soldiers who came into contact with Soviet soldiers at the end of the war found them 'primitive and chaotic' and when fuelled with copious quantities of vodka they could be capable of appalling and bestial acts. Witnesses described not-infrequent 'cases of thirty or forty Soviet soldiers raping one woman and then killing her'. The concept of the individual was not relevant.[41] Well trained in deception and camouflage, the 'Ivan' was taught to utilise captured enemy equipment and to use enemy weapons.[42]

The Red Army had emerged from the war with plenty of combat experience. When fighting in the snow, Red Army units had learned to be remarkably mobile and advance across fields, easily outflanking their enemy, while Allied forces would have to progress only on cleared roads. This Soviet talent for advancing through snowdrifts in open country remained a mystery for a long time, until their secret was exposed:

They would form up their columns of men twenty or more abreast, pressing into service any civilians who happened to be in the neighbourhood and these columns would be sent out across the trackless snow. The first few files of men would flounder through the drifts, and fall to the rear exhausted. But the column would be driven onwards, and by the time the human steam-roller had done its work, a path would have been pressed hard in the snow.

Marching feet of the following formations compacted the snow-ice farther, and then the light lorries and equipment were sent over the track, followed by the heavy vehicles and guns.[43]

If the Unthinkable advance became bogged down in freezing conditions in the East, convoys would be crippled. Oil would become waxy, and metal on both transports and weapons would turn brittle and break apart. Wheeled vehicles would slide off the roads, and more than 2ft of snow on level ground would create problems for tanks. The frozen ground would also inhibit the digging of supporting artillery gun pits, and hard snow would crack mortar base plates. So, such 'arctic' conditions would favour a defender, and especially one who was experienced and clothed to withstand severe temperatures. Then, when the spring thaw came, slush and mud would render many routes impassable and the trapped convoys would be easy targets for enemy aircraft.[44]

Yet, for all his formidable qualities, the Red Army soldier was suffering morale problems due to heavy casualties and war-weariness. The British planners comforted themselves with the belief that the standards of training and tactics were lower in the East than in the West:

> Due to the comparatively low standard of general education in the Red Army, the Russians have been forced to reserve their best manpower for specialist arms; i.e. the Air Force, Armoured Troops, artillery and engineers. This has left their infantry greatly deficient in the type of soldier who could be trained to any standard comparable to the infantry of a Western Power … There is widespread evidence that the Russian Command is finding considerable difficulty in maintaining discipline in the Russian Army abroad. Looting and drunkenness are prevalent.[45]

Because of such weariness and indiscipline, the planners assumed that any new conflict would place an unbearable strain on the Red Army. Not only would they be fighting outside the Soviet boundaries, but their high command would have a real problem in maintaining morale, especially among the 'low-grade' infantry formations. Allied propaganda would play its part in exacerbating the problem.[46] Nevertheless, there is little doubt that the Red Army would have fought wholeheartedly for Stalin. In the euphoria surrounding 9 May (Soviet V-Day was a day later than in the West), Stalin seemed to be forgiven by many for his 1930s collectivisation disasters, as well as his purges. Such was the relief at the end of the war that many soldiers, at least in the short term, readily accepted the blatant Soviet propaganda.[47]

One of the climactic events of Unthinkable would be a massive and decisive armoured clash inside Poland – an engagement even larger than the Second World War tank Battle of Kursk. So, with the Allied infantry so heavily outnumbered by Red Army troops, how would the respective armoured strengths compare? It was anticipated that on 1 July 1945 the Allies would be able to muster a minimum of twenty armoured divisions with some additional 'equivalent divisions' scratched together from armoured brigades. Travelling across the plains of northern Europe, the attack speed of tanks was only about 8mph on the level and down to 3mph on uphill stretches. They would be vulnerable to Soviet artillery or air attack as they were being unloaded from tank transporters, or as they were being refuelled every 100 miles during their advance.

Against this force the planners calculated that the Red Army could muster the equivalent of at least thirty-six armoured divisions, which equated to a Soviet superiority of nearly two to one. When the actual Soviet armoured formations were examined, they appeared as a bewildering mix of heavy and light units, sometimes combined with infantry. The total Soviet strength included 113 Soviet-sized Shock Tank Brigades and 141 Ordinary Tank Brigades, and it was estimated that each of these Ordinary brigades comprised more than fifty T-34 medium tanks together with 1,000 infantrymen.[48] In addition to the brigades (though not accounted for by the planners) the Red Army also had Independent Heavy Tank Regiments, each containing twenty-three heavy KV or JS (Stalin) tanks, as well as Independent Assault Gun or SU regiments. In all, it has been estimated that armoured units represented about one-third of all Soviet forces in the field, and although Soviet operational doctrine had traditionally inclined towards tanks being tied to the mass of the infantry, by 1945 Red Army tacticians were experimenting with a more independent role for armoured units.[49]

The Allied armoured strength boasted a mix of experimental and outdated machines. By the end of the Second World War, the Sherman M4A3E8 tank, with its 76mm gun, was already becoming dated, but there were new, more powerful machines starting to come off the production lines.[50] Although only 2,000 units of the latest Firefly tanks had been produced, they promised to be a worthy opponent of the main Soviet T-34 battle tank. The Firefly, which was developed from the Sherman tank, packed a considerable punch with its 17lb gun, but its armour was barely superior to its Soviet adversary. Fortunately, there were other new Allied tanks becoming available, such as the M-26 Pershing heavy tank, which was comparable to the German Tiger. But with only three months' combat service in the Second World War, the M-26 was still prone to breakdowns and was underpowered.

The Soviets, meanwhile, were using the JS-1, JS-2 and the later JS-3 tank, which came into service in March 1945. They also utilised the older but faithful T-34 tank, with its solid armour, which the Germans had found so hard to penetrate with their early anti-tank guns.[51] The T-44 had even thicker armour, but the latest Soviet T-54, with a larger 100mm gun, had only just finished its trials in February 1945 and would not be in full production for two more years. The brief of the planners did not allow for detailed analysis of the composition of Soviet armour, but the fact that nearly 15 per cent of Soviet armour in 1945 comprised tracked self-propelled guns, known as Tank Destroyers, surely added to the Soviet advantage. The latest model, the SU 100, had first come off the production lines in late 1944 and, with its 100mm high-velocity guns, was a first-rate defensive weapon that could penetrate tank armour at 1,640yds.[52] With this daunting Soviet numerical superiority in armour, as well as infantry, the only bright spot for the Allies was that their network of repair workshops had been supplying the Soviets with parts and engineering for their tanks, and in the event of hostilities, this would obviously cease.[53]

Logistics would prove to be a huge consideration for the Allies. Although their advance through eastern Germany and the immediate area in and around Berlin would drive through scenes of very heavy destruction, much of the countryside in the Soviet-occupied area was only lightly war damaged. However, the subsequent Soviet occupation had wrought greater destruction. In March 1945 the Soviets had carried out a stocktake of German assets and some 70,000 Red Army 'experts' had already descended on east German cities and towns and begun a systematic stripping out of materials and industrial equipment, for return to the Soviet Union. During the spring and summer of 1945 it was recorded that 1.28 million tons of 'materials' and 3.6 million tons of 'equipment' were removed and 4,500 factories were dismantled and removed.[54] This would present a problem for an incoming Allied army if it stayed for any length of time.

What was even more alarming was the quantity of food, livestock and vehicles that were removed from the eastern sector – a deficiency that would be laborious for the Allies to make good. Nonetheless, the Soviets had made sure that most of the railway system was still working in their occupied territory, and although the Germans had destroyed a number of railway bridges during their retreat, Soviet engineers were working around the clock to repair them.[55] But the main problem confronting the Allies involved the actual railway track, for the standard-gauge, which would carry Allied supplies and troops from Western Europe, would only continue up to the Oder River. Beyond that, Red Army engineers were believed to have laid broad-gauge track inside Poland to marry up with the broad track already in use throughout the Soviet Union. Changing from Western standard-gauge to broad-gauge would necessitate lifting all railway carriages and trucks and changing the bogeys underneath. It would take hours every time and hinder any Allied advance through Poland.

In their own rear lines, the Allies would also face considerable logistical problems; their territory in western Germany had seen heavy fighting in the last months of the war and destruction was widespread. The major concern was that large numbers of engineers, transport and administrative troops would have to be allocated to repair the infrastructure of the country, and bring some sort of order out of the chaos.[56] In addition to troops allocated to repair work inside Germany, there was also the necessity of policing the Allied sectors of Germany. At the time when Churchill had ordered the Unthinkable report, stability in Germany was far from assured and there was every possibility that renegade Nazi units, operating out of traditional strongholds in Bavaria, could cause problems. Consequently, the planners calculated that the Allies would need to station at least ten infantry and one armoured division within their own German sectors to dispel potential trouble.

It was not only western Germany that needed policing. Allied-occupied Austria was another territorial headache. Indeed, it was vulnerable not only to unrest, but also to a Red Army offensive. There was every likelihood that when Soviet forces were attacked in East Germany and Poland, they would retaliate by attacking Allied forces in Austria in an attempt to drive them out of Salzburg and the western sector of the country. However, it was thought that with the three armoured and twelve infantry divisions available to him, the Supreme Allied Commander, Mediterranean, could hold on to Salzburg. Furthermore, the mountainous nature of Austria would certainly stall any Soviet advance. But north of Salzburg the Allies would have to deploy larger forces to deter Red Army incursions, especially along the line of the Bohmer Wald mountains, running from Salzburg up to Zwickau. Since this 250-mile line guarded the southern extent of the Allied offensive, it would require a further five armoured and twenty infantry divisions to defend.

As the Allies advanced through the territories of Silesia and Pomerania in July, roads would have been choked with refugees, hindering the progress of military columns. Millions of Poles had fled westwards in the face of the Soviet advance, together with large numbers of East Prussian Germans heading for the British- or US-controlled sectors of Germany. Then there were over 1.5 million Polish forced labourers and prisoners leaving Germany and heading for their homes in Poland, while large numbers of Poles from the centre of the country were also moving west, attracted by the wealth of the Silesian region.[57] To add to the misery and mayhem, the Polish borders were due to be redrawn when a new Polish government was installed, but within weeks of VE Day, the Lublin Poles were already drawing new boundaries, forcing out ethnic Germans from Silesia, Pomerania and territory up to the Western Neisse river. The British estimated that up to 8 million ethnic Germans might be expelled when the Poles occupied this new land.[58] But some Poles were too impatient and during June and July 1945, before the official boundaries had come into existence, more than a quarter of a million Germans were unlawfully pushed westwards across the River Oder. Astonishingly, the planners ignored the effect of this massive human tide flooding back through territory earmarked for the Allied advance.[59]

One of the most contentious issues in the Unthinkable plan was the use of German forces within the Allied camp. It was anticipated that ten German divisions could be utilised for offensive operations, but because it would take time for them to be re-equipped from Allied sources, the units would not be ready for 1 July and would only become available in the autumn; that they should be used at all was likely to be highly controversial.

Who would form the officers and NCOs of a post-war German army to fight the Soviets? It was true that in the last months of the Second World War, new, much younger officers and NCOs had emerged from the ranks of the Hitler Youth to form the backbone of resistance as the Allies closed in. These highly indoctrinated young tigers had surfaced above the older, exhausted and more cynical NCOs. Often it was fear that drove these youngsters on. Fear of being strung up by the military police for not continuing the fight, or fear of capture and a horrible death at the hands of Soviet soldiers. Would they still fight without that fear and without the all-enveloping world of National Socialism in which they had been raised? Allied intelligence certainly thought so.

In a report on German forces prepared for Field Marshal Montgomery, it was noted that senior Wehrmacht officers were disappointed that they would not be required in a 'Third War' and younger officers were talking 'openly of the next war'. And it was not just officers who anticipated another conflict. The German ranks were reported to 'think only in terms of world war'.[60] Even before the Second World War was over, there were

Germans who volunteered to fight the Japanese, and Lord Halifax reported that General Marshall had confirmed that a good number of German POWs were willing to enlist in the fight against Japan. 'It might be good,' he argued, 'to give a force of them a selected task, eg., clearing Marshall Islands and letting them and the Japanese kill each other over there.'[61]

Another, deeper incentive for Germans to engage in a fight with the Soviets was the fact that, with Allied agreement, they were set to lose half their country to Soviet domination. There was also the motivation of revenge. In Soviet-occupied areas of Germany Red Army soldiers had carried out a comprehensive policy of rape against German women as well as atrocities against German POWs, and Soviet destruction of German property was widespread. If that was not enough incentive for German soldiers to relish another fight, there remained the unpalatable question of race: the Germans were more likely to fight alongside US and British forces against the Slav Russians. Hitler's war in the East had always been pursued with more vigour because of its primary purpose: to defeat and crush the Slav race. There remained an element within the Wehrmacht who felt there was a job still to be completed.

However, despite the keenness of some German individuals, the Germany army itself remained very fragmented. Approximately 2 million German soldiers surrendered to the British in 1945, and from this haul the British government anticipated using 225,000 to work in Britain in part-payment for reparations. For this reason most German soldiers were not designated as 'prisoners of war' because if they were so labelled, they could not be used for labouring or reconstruction work. Furthermore, most fighting formations were split up as soon as the fighting finished; the remains of the 2nd *Waffen SS* Panzer Division *Das Reich* surrendered on 9 May 1945 and some members were swiftly transferred to the former concentration camp at Flossenburg, in Germany, while others were sent to Regensburg Civilian Internee Camp.

The size of the German army was another concern, for their numbers had been seriously depleted by the war. In particular, the *Endkämpfe*, or the last few ferocious weeks of fighting, had claimed the lives of over 1.25 million German soldiers. Even the armed force, or *Waffen SS*, were no longer the tight, cohesive unit they had once been. As Robert Koehl has concluded, by the spring of 1945 the near half-a-million-strong SS force now comprised

> ... rag-tag units of grounded Luftwaffe and sailors; the sallow starchy complexioned boys of sixteen and seventeen; the confused and frightened eastern Europeans with only a dozen words of halting German; the grimy, tired *Kampfgrupen* of thirty or forty veterans of too many winter campaigns.[62]

Some of these SS men could be singled out as they hid in columns of POWs because (at least in earlier years) SS soldiers had their blood group tattooed under their right arm. Even if the Allies were short of manpower, it is hard to imagine that the *Waffen SS*, or indeed any Wehrmacht units that had been involved in atrocities on the Eastern Front, would be tolerated by British, US or Polish troops. However, the Wehrmacht soldiers who had fought in the West were more likely to be accepted, though begrudgingly, as brothers in arms and it was not long after VE Day that US troops began fraternising with both German civilians and soldiers alike. If and when the decision was taken to mobilise German forces, it would advertise the Allies' intentions, since Soviet agents would report any large or unusual troop movements. Any German mobilisation could only take place at the last moment and large numbers would have to be released from POW camps. They would need to be retrained and possibly re-armed with British or US small arms to ensure continuity of ammunition supply, and for this reason they would not enter the conflict until a later stage.

The deployment of German troops would create some interesting dilemmas for the Allies. Would the Nazi leaders still be executed? Would the brutish ex-governor of Poland, Hans Frank, declare at his war crimes trial that he was merely defending Poland against the Soviets – just as the Allies were now doing? Those senior German figures condemned for 'waging war' might be freed as the Allies were now 'waging war'. There was also the thorny question of who would command German forces. By 1 July 1945 Hitler's successor, Admiral Dönitz, would already have been dismissed by the Allies, but a 'good German' such as a survivor of the 20 July bomb plot conspiracy might have proved acceptable.

During the summer of 1945, as details of the Holocaust began to emerge, there might well be horror and outrage from British and US public opinion that the Allies were now siding with Nazi 'mass murderers' against their former ally, the Soviet Union. Whether such public opinion would be galvanised by 1 July 1945 is a moot point. When the plan was first devised at the end of April, the planners made the bold assumption that German troops could be used, if retrained, alongside the Western Allies. Although reports of atrocities in the concentration camps were published in British and American newspapers during 1944 and 1945, it was not until 15 April 1945 and the liberation of the Belsen camp that the wider public began to hear the graphic details.[63] The BBC commentator Richard Dimbleby gave a harrowing, first-hand account of what he witnessed at Belsen and by the end of April British cinemas were showing images of the thousands of unburied dead and skeletal survivors. It would take months, if not years, for the full scale of the Holocaust to become apparent, but certainly by the autumn of 1945, when Unthinkable had predicted German troops would be in action, British public opinion had hardened towards the German military. Contemplating a new alliance, Hastings Ismay was horrified about the effect on the democracies should Unthinkable take place:

> Should they [Britain and US] have forgotten all that they had said about their determination to destroy Nazism, taken the Germans into their fold, and proceeded, with their help, to crush their recent allies? One is forced to the conclusion that such a reversal of policy, which dictators could have taken in their stride, was absolutely impossible for the leaders of democratic countries even to contemplate. [64]

If the use of German troops would be anathema to the British public, what would the Poles think about having German troops back on their soil? It seems inconceivable that they would tolerate German soldiers in their country, especially with the approval of the Allies, and such an action would undoubtedly risk derailing the whole operation. The planners of Unthinkable were either deliberately underplaying the effect of German inclusion or were unaware of the depth of Polish suffering under the Nazis. It is true that they only anticipated the German contribution taking place in the autumn of 1945, by which time one of the scenarios envisaged a Red Army defeat. In such circumstances the Wehrmacht might not be required in Poland and it is conceivable that there would be a sufficient role for them in any newly Allied-overrun territory in East Germany.

The nightmare for the Allies would be an inconclusive outcome from the massive armoured battle inside Poland. The planners feared that even if such a contest brought Stalin back to the bargaining table, 'the military power of Russia will not be broken and it will be open to her to recommence the conflict at any time she sees fit.'[65] Undeterred by the terrible odds, the planners pressed on with the actual logistics of invading, first East German territory and then Poland. On 1 July 1945 the first Allied waves would make initial contact with large concentrations of Red Army troops in the Soviet-occupied zone (SBZ) of Germany. In the two months since May 1945, when this area came under Soviet occupation, the NKVD had set about organising the beginnings of a local police force, made up of imported German communists. But since this area was the last to be occupied by the Soviets, little headway could be made in the time available and internal security was almost totally in the hands of NKVD officers. They also supervised a number of new 'special internment camps' set up to imprison not only captured Nazis but anyone who might oppose the new regime and was guilty of 'crimes' against the Soviet occupying power. These camps would, no doubt, be swiftly overrun by the Allies and their liberated inmates would be a useful source of intelligence.[66] But beyond that, the Allies would find a desecrated country, for Stalin had wasted no time in stripping out German assets, as he had done in Poland and Austria.

Berlin would be an early target for the Allies. In the Soviet-occupied sector of Berlin, the communist-backed administration had tightened its grip on the population. Since April German communist organisers had been returning in droves to Germany after their wartime exile, and since the fall of Berlin were helping to identify opponents. Marshal Georgy Zhukov, the Supreme Commander of Soviet forces in Germany, turned a blind eye to the hard-line, pro-Soviet KPD party, which was already hard at work removing these opponents to communist rule.[67] By the time Unthinkable was launched, Stalin would have had only two months' occupation of eastern Germany, but the two most prominent members of the German Communist Party (KPD), 69-year-old Wilhelm Pieck and 52-year-old Walter Ulbricht, made sure that their takeover of East Germany was going to be stealthily executed. 'It's got to look democratic,' warned Ulbricht, 'but we must have everything under our control.'[68] Such a steady takeover would mean that by 1 July there would be no local State Security Police established or any organised local communist resistance to take on the Allies. The East German Sector would be totally under the control of the Red Army.

The area of Poland that the Allies initially hoped to overrun – up to a line running from Gdansk down to Breslau – was a region that had seen minimal Polish underground activity during the Second World War. Much of the area had, after all, previously been incorporated into the German Reich, and repopulated with *Volksdeutche* (people of German extraction). Consequently, without local Polish support, and with the iron-fisted security of the German police apparatus, any opposition in this region had been neutered. So, with little or no history of a resistance organisation, the Allies would certainly enjoy only local moral backing rather than armed support.

The Allies would most likely clash with units of the Polish People's Army (*Ludowe Wojsko Polskie*), known as the LWP or Berling's Army, so named after its original commander.[69] This army was the main local instrument of Soviet control in Poland, but how formidable or reliable was the LWP? Originally formed in the Soviet Union in July 1944, out of an old Left-leaning resistance group and a nascent military unit, the LWP comprised Poles and Jews from eastern Poland who had been absorbed into the Soviet Union after the area was taken over in 1939. When the Red Army advanced into Poland in 1944, the LWP came with them and by the end of the Second World War, the army was thought to number 200,000 men in ten divisions.[70]

However, from the outset the LWP suffered from a lack of competent Polish officers. The elimination of a large number of the pre-war Polish officer caste at Katyn, combined with the evacuation from the Soviet Union of General Anders and his pro-West army in 1942, meant that the pool of educated and technically able Polish officers and NCOs was small. Consequently, nearly 50 per cent of LWP units found they were commanded by Soviet officers from Belorussia or the Ukraine.[71] There were many committed communists among the ranks, but there was also a sizable minority in the ranks of Poles who had been captured by the Red Army in 1939 and saw that the LWP was their only hope of escape and return to Poland. They may have been happy to fight to remove the Germans from their soil, but they were far from committed to enforcing Soviet rule. In August 1944 the Soviet-sponsored PKWN ordered a call-up of local men from all Polish territory under Soviet occupation, but the response was lukewarm and desertions were commonplace.[72]

The LWP, comprising the 1st and 2nd Polish armies, had seen action in the Soviet sweep across Poland and in the battles around Warsaw. They were also deployed in the fight for the ports along Poland's Baltic coast, before joining the final assault on Berlin and the drive south towards Prague. But from May 1945 many of the LWP units moved back to the eastern borders of Poland to deal with the continuing conflict with Ukrainian partisans, or were moved north to supervise the expulsion of ethnic Germans from the old East Prussian territory. The LWP were also pushed forward to help implement land reform, which the Provisional government was banking on to gain peasant support. Consequently, it was unlikely that the Allies would be confronted by a large LWP presence along Poland's western border.

As far as the Soviets were concerned, the LWP would be unreliable in any conflict with the West. The Army had its own Polish political commissars to root out any nonbelievers, but even these apparatchiks failed to make their mark; in one intake only 100 out of 700 LWP soldiers were found to be 'sympathetic to the communist cause'. It has been estimated that by the summer of 1945 the Soviet Union could only rely on 60 per cent of the LWP

1st Army and perhaps only 40 per cent of the 2nd Army. Desertions were rife and whole units could disappear in the run-up to an operation. Indeed, it was the prospect of a Third World War that kept up the desertion rates.[73] Even among the party faithful, there were many who were clueless about what the communist party stood for, or the direction it was taking. Such a lukewarm endorsement of the creed was also apparent in areas where the new government felt it was strongest – in rural areas where land reform was proposed. Most rural peasants remained resolutely anti-Soviet, even though many were tempted with offers of parcels of land from broken-up estates.

While the Soviets could not rely on their Polish army, they could be sure of fomenting trouble behind the Allied lines. If the Unthinkable conflict progressed through the summer of 1945, so the incidents of Soviet sabotage behind Allied lines would increase. This would become critical as the Allied lines of communication became stretched and Soviet 'sleeper' cells in France and the Low Countries were activated. French loyalty was not investigated by the planners, but her inclusion in the Allied cause was imperative, otherwise it would be impossible to resupply US and British forces. There were already large cadres of communist sympathisers within the Second World War European resistance movements, especially within the French *Maquis*. Many still held arms in May 1945 and they could be organised and activated by Red Army co-ordinators. A number of these Soviet co-ordinators were ex-POWs who had been used as forced labour or held in prison camps in Germany or France, and were familiar with the territory. They were repatriated to the Soviet Union at the end of the Second World War, but not all ex-POWs were thrown into gulags or executed on the pretence of their 'corruption' in the west. A minority were selected to be trained in sabotage and then filtered back into France or Germany during May and June, hidden amongst the vast columns of refugees sweeping across Europe.

These were all military considerations, but there was a major political obstacle for Churchill to overcome. How could British and US public opinion possibly back another major war against a former ally? For years the British public in particular had been fed a diet of pro-Soviet propaganda. Lord Beaverbrook, as a former Minister of Supply, was particularly energetic in promoting aid to the Soviet Union. 'Stalin is a great man,' he boomed, 'I could feel the pulsating power of the man ... I put my faith in the man's leadership, and I believe in the Russian resistance.'[74] Beaverbrook constantly lobbied for a second front in the west to relieve the Red Army in the east, and argued passionately for recognition of Stalin's claim to the Baltic States. During a trip to New York in April 1942 he delivered a speech, sanctioned by Roosevelt, in which he lavished praise on Stalin and the communist system. 'Communism under Stalin has produced the most valiant fighting army in Europe,' he argued in an address that was broadcast coast-to-coast. 'Communism under Stalin has won the applause and admiration of all the western nations.'[75] With such a ringing endorsement of Stalin and his methods, it would indeed be hard to turn around public opinion within months of the war ending. Hastings Ismay believed it would be quite impossible:

> For over three years, public opinion in America and Britain had been led to believe that Russia was a brave and faithful ally who had done the lion's share of the fighting, and endured untold suffering. If their governments had now proclaimed that the Russians were untrustworthy and unprincipled tyrants, whose ambitions must be held in check, the effect on national unity in both countries would have been catastrophic.[76]

And those elements of the British press that urged a benevolent attitude towards the Soviet threat were not just to be found among the political left. The *Daily Express*, *Evening Standard* and *The Times* were all prominent in providing pro-Soviet articles and comment columns. There were other, well-established supporters of the ties between Britain and the Soviet Union. The British ambassador in Washington, Lord Halifax; the standard-bearer of the Left, Sir Stafford Cripps; and even those in the Conservative Party, such as R. A. 'Rab' Butler, all voiced approval.[77] Consequently the British public had no idea about the depth of savagery committed by the Red Army as they swept across Eastern Europe. If the Allies were to launch an attack against the Soviet Union on 1 July, Western public opinion would have to be rapidly 're-educated' about the new enemy between VE Day, on 8 May, and 1 July.

Moreover, after nearly six years of war, British public opinion was numbed by the fate of Eastern Europe, and when Romania succumbed to a new communist regime in the early spring of 1945, it caused barely a ripple. Despite the huge Polish contribution to the Allied cause, would British public opinion be so different if the Poles suffered a similar fate? Ironically, the British might still be pro-Soviet, but Stalin was making sure that this friendship was not reciprocated. Ralph Parker, the communist-leaning *Times* correspondent in Moscow confirmed that since April 1945, 'lecturers' in Soviet factories had been agitating against the Western Allies. They were reported to be taking the line that it was 'fortuitous' that the Soviets had fought alongside Britain and the US, but the Soviets could have just as easily sided with the Axis powers; the Western powers were now to be treated as 'capitalist adversaries'.[78]

Soviet public opinion, then, bracketed the US with Britain, and increasingly saw both as potential enemies. But how did the US view events? Unthinkable made a huge assumption that the United States would be a full and willing partner in the enterprise to attack the Soviet Union. But this was against all evidence of US actions and deliberations. Even before Yalta, the US Joint Intelligence Staff had assessed post-war Soviet intentions as 'benign', largely because the war had materially dented Soviet manpower and destroyed 25 per cent of her industry, thereby limiting ideas of 'foreign adventures'. Furthermore, the US felt that there was little chance of the Soviets making military incursions into Greece and the Dardanelles, or even penetrating into the British-controlled southern portion of Iran; before contemplating aggressive moves, the Soviets would first have to build up their economy, which, the US analysts believed, would take until 1952, and even then they would need substantial assistance from the US.[79] The American Joint Chiefs of Staff took the view that the Soviet Union would not embark on any adventures that might cause a rift with the emerging United Nations. This was, perhaps, a hopeful vision of a new world order in which the major powers as well as the smaller countries were beholden to the UN – but it was not a vision shared by Stalin.[80]

As for British post-war military adventures, the US planners clearly perceived the country as too economically weak to seek further expansion. So, just days after VE Day, Britain stood accused of an 'irrational fear of the Bolshevik menace', that could lead them into war against the Soviets. But, the US advisors cautioned, the Soviets were unlikely to push the British to such extreme action over Greece, Turkey or Iran. Strangely, in May 1945 the more volatile European flashpoints of Germany, Austria, Venezia Giulia or indeed Poland did not warrant much concern for the US Joint Intelligence Committee.[81]

There is no evidence that the British chiefs of staff ever consulted with their American counterparts over the 1945 Unthinkable plan to attack the Soviets. Until the plan had the approval of the British chiefs of staff, there was no need to involve the Americans – to do so would have meant violating the strict circulation list that was imposed on the planners. Anyway, by the early months of summer 1945 there were fewer opportunities for representatives of the British and US chiefs to meet and discuss plans. The Combined Chiefs of Staff Committee, which was the forum for such meetings, and which had proved to be one of the most successful innovations of the Second World War, was falling into disuse.[82]

5

THE PLAN – 'TOTAL WAR'

If Britain, US and Polish forces attacked the Red Army and a 'quick success' eluded them, then the only outcome was a Third World War, or as the planners expressed it, 'total war'. In this nightmare scenario the Allied forces would be drawn deeper into Poland and then into the Soviet Union. To counter the huge disparity between Soviet and Western manpower, victory in such a 'total war' could only come about after a massive mobilisation of forces in the United States. They would have to be trained, equipped and shipped over to Europe to join additional reserves, drafted from all the 'Western European Allies'. The Americans could survive large losses of equipment due to their industrial base, but their dependence on mechanisation meant that lines of communication were critical.[1] Even if the deployment of US forces could take place within months, the odds were against an Allied victory and the planners believed that nothing short of another Russian Revolution would cause the Soviet regime to implode. The enemy could only be 'eliminated' by the Allied conquest of large 'metropolitan' areas, which would deprive the enemy of its manufacturing base for weapons and ammunition. There would also have to be a simultaneous and wholesale defeat of the Soviet forces in the field.

Such destruction on this scale was extremely unlikely, for it was quite possible that the Red Army would withdraw across Eastern Europe and back into their homeland without suffering a major defeat. The planners used the salutary example of Hitler's invasion of the Soviet Union in 1941, which generated swift results in the first year but was then followed by defeat in 1942, as the German lines of communication became extended. During that invasion, the Soviets had withdrawn their manufacturing equipment to the interior and employed it in the massive Red Army counter attacks the following year. The planners now paled at the thought of the enormous distances that the Allies would have to penetrate to secure victory; even then, the appalling state of the 'roads' across the Soviet heartland was probably underestimated.[2]

The details of the direction of an Allied thrust into the Soviet Union were not contemplated in the plan, but the Allies might have followed Hitler's 1941 'Barbarossa' campaign and driven straight towards the Minsk-Smolensk region. Stalin had then made the huge strategic error of believing that the main German advance would come into the south-west of his country and, against the advice of his commanders, fatally transferred a large number of his divisions away from his Western Front. He had forecast that an invading army would initially head for the grain-rich Ukraine as well as the Caucasian oilfields. But by 1945 the Soviet Union was in a stronger defensive position; Stalin had bolstered the weak fortifications in former Polish eastern territories, and to the south he had firmed up his flanks by his occupation of Romania and increased troop concentrations around the top of the Black Sea. Furthermore, much of the Soviet oil production had been moved further out of the Allies' reach, towards the Volga and Urals.[3]

If the Allies were able to penetrate deep into Poland, their lines of communication would be stretched and the marshy terrain beyond Warsaw would slow down the advance. But at least the Allies would enjoy friendly support from the local Poles. This was the heartland of the recently disbanded Polish underground state and its military wing, the AK, which had mainly operated in the 'General Government' territory, in the centre of the country. This area had been run by a Nazi governor, Hans Frank, and since it was administered with appalling brutality, the AK could count on near total local Polish support. The AK had launched the heroic but doomed Warsaw Rising against the Germans in the summer of 1944 and although the rising had lasted for several months, its eventual defeat had meant the end of the AK. In January 1945 the resistance movement was formally disbanded, yet despite mass arrests by the NKVD, the AK legacy remained strong in the countryside and any number of organisations, notably 'Nie' and its successor, DSZ, took on the mantle of opposition in the spring of 1945.[4]

With much of the countryside ruled by anti-government splinter bands, be they ex-AK, nationalist NSZ, or, in the south-east, the Ukrainian Insurrectionist Army (UPA), any invading Allied forces would find plenty of support outside the towns. Although underground leaders felt that further armed resistance would cause needless bloodshed and called on their fighters to lay down their arms in April 1945, probably more than

30 per cent of their number did not comply. Despite the efforts of Polish Communist Party (*Polska Partia Robotnicza*, or PPR) stooges planted in every village and town to report on underground activists, the number of underground fighters who remained at large after the spring of 1945 remained stubbornly high. Probably 20,000 fighters and more than 200,000 reservists and supporters were still in circulation, many hiding in the forests in the north or surrounding Warsaw. Weapons were still scarce, though quantities of anti-tank weapons had been picked up from fleeing German soldiers. The Poles showed huge resourcefulness; many households had small hidden caches of weapons and ammunition that had been squirreled away but never used because the countrywide call to arms had never come.[5]

Although there were still many willing Polish resistance fighters, their networks and communications had seriously deteriorated.[6] Disillusionment, exhaustion and Soviet infiltration would further reduce their numbers throughout the summer and autumn of 1945, and unfortunately the more organised 'WiN' movement would not evolve until September 1945, by which time it would be too late for Unthinkable.[7] Yet, despite the declining fortunes of the underground during 1945, most Poles believed, or hoped, that an armed conflict between the Western Allies and the Soviet Union was imminent.

While the plan for Unthinkable widened to accommodate the possibility of the Allies being sucked deeper into Soviet territory, little analysis was carried out of the strength of the Soviet Union, and her power to resist an invasion. The country was certainly poor and her low gross domestic product (GDP) had dogged her throughout the Second World War. Unlike the wealthier West, she had struggled when called upon to mobilise a much higher proportion of her scarce resources. This was especially critical since the Soviets had never been able to devote sufficient funds to their engineering and metallurgical industries – vital to the production of modern armaments. So while the country had a huge advantage in military manpower, the Western Allies had more than six times the Soviets' industrial capacity.[8] Consequently, Stalin had taken steps to rectify this deficiency. Not only had he received $9,000 million in Lend-Lease from the US during the Second World War, including 15,000 aircraft, 7,000 tanks and more than 400,000 trucks and jeeps, but he had also expropriated vast quantities of equipment from his occupied territories in Eastern Europe. In May, Stalin made further requests for US aid in the form of credits, perhaps hoping that he could trade these for a future pull-back of Soviet forces.[9] Stalin also knew his other weakness was his country's reliance on food imports. In the event of another war, these imports from the West would cease, though they would be partly offset by compulsory imports from the occupied countries in Eastern Europe.

British and US leaders had never quite understood Stalin's paranoia and his obsession that his Stalinist–Leninist creed would be corrupted by influence from the West. This fanatical belief led to his order to filter out traitors who he believed were lurking among the host of Soviet citizens now returned from the West. This group included large numbers of POWs who had fought for their homeland, and many even believed in Stalin's policies. Yet no sooner were they liberated from German prison camps than they found themselves imprisoned, tortured or murdered by their own side. As soon as the Allies handed them over, they were dumped into any one of more than 100 Soviet prison camps, which each held a minimum of 10,000 prisoners. Former Red Army members were then screened by military counter-intelligence, or SMERSH (Death to Spies), and civilian prisoners were interrogated by agents from NKVD. This culling included senior army officers, so there remains the question – how competent was the Soviet high command to resist an invasion?

The most high-profile Soviet commander was Marshal G.K. Zhukov, who, despite some tactical errors, was recently hailed as one of the architects of the capture of Berlin.[10] In a bizarre way, any temporary setbacks for commanders such as Zhukov suited Stalin, for his overriding concern was competition from any other powerful and successful figure. Consequently, when Zhukov vied with Marshal I.S. Konev for leading the entry into Berlin, it unsettled the former and caused him to make rash manoeuvres, resulting in heavy troop losses. Stalin was prepared to accept such setbacks, as long as they reduced Zhukov's popularity.[11]

The planners also had to anticipate Stalin's subsequent moves once the Unthinkable conflict had spread. It was expected that the Soviets would open up new fronts across the world. In Scandinavia they would attempt to steamroller across northern Finland, cross into the top of Norway and advance as far south as Trondheim. The planners did not elaborate on the strength of local resistance in Finland, but if demobilisation had already started and the Finnish army had been materially reduced, the peacetime force could offer only very token resistance. Furthermore, due to recent Soviet invasions, some of their best farmland had been requisitioned and the Finns may not have had enough food to feed themselves, forcing them to swiftly sue for peace. Because the advance was likely to take place in the summer months, the Red Army would find the Northern Cape free of ice, but the many rivers would be swollen with rainwater, causing the ground to be saturated. Crossing into Norway and traversing the many natural hazards using teams of horse- and reindeer-driven transport would require all the skill of their engineers. Nonetheless, they could swiftly capture the key northern ports and the nickel mines near Petsamo, before moving down to secure Narvik – a vital port for the export of Sweden's iron ore. But first they would have to negotiate the choke point between Lyngen fjord and the mountains, which could be easily defended by Allied Special Forces and the Norwegian resistance. Should the Soviets be able to pass these obstacles, they would then hope to capture the large port of Trondheim, assisted by an amphibious assault, backed up by airborne troops. Consequently, with passage for their surface and submarine fleets into the North Atlantic now protected, the Soviets might well halt their advance.[12]

Elsewhere, Stalin would strike out and invade Greece and Turkey. If the latter was secured, he would most likely close the Dardanelles Straits, thus blocking Allied access to the Black Sea. But if access remained open, it is conceivable that the US Marine Corps, which numbered approximately 500,000 men, could be deployed in a diversionary attack on the southern flank of the Red Army, perhaps in amphibious operations in the Black Sea. Even assuming a passage could be forced through the Dardanelles, landings would be fiercely opposed and there would be sizeable marine casualties. Surprisingly, the planners did not see these possible moves as very alarming and there was a belief that the Soviet conquest of Greece and Turkey would not affect the overall strategic balance. However, Iran and Iraq were another matter; should these fall to the Soviet Union – and there was every likelihood they would, since only three Indian Brigade Groups stood in the way of eleven Soviet divisions – then Stalin would have cut off one of the West's main sources of oil. Fortunately for the Allies, the planners believed that because of Red Army commitments in Europe, the Soviets would not advance as far south as Egypt, or indeed into India.

As the Red Army swept through Finland, Norway, Greece and Turkey in response to the Allied offensive, Britain's Special Operations Executive (SOE) would be activated. After VE Day, SOE could no longer warrant its own independent ministry, and so its organisation was passed over to the Foreign Office. Lord Selborne retired as minister, and the charismatic Lord Lovat took on overall responsibility, while a good many of the SOE country section heads became absorbed by the Secret Intelligence Service (SIS).[13] Nonetheless, SOE would enjoy a new brief for the last six months of its life. It would still 'serve the clandestine operational requirements of His Majesty's Government', but now its actions were to be aimed at the new enemy, as an autumn directive confirmed:

In carrying out these tasks, SOE have been directed to accord priority to those countries which are likely to be overrun in the earliest stages of conflict with Russia, but which are not, at present, under Russian domination.[14]

As SOE resources were directed to countries in the frontline, notably Germany and Austria, SOE personnel in the British-controlled zone of Germany actually increased after VE Day. This was partly to combat any embers of the Nazi regime, but also, more ominously, for 'longer-term tasks'; these efforts would be directed towards preparing and equipping operatives for clandestine operations in the event of conflict with the Soviet Union.[15]

As the conflict widened attention would move from northern Europe towards likely Soviet targets in Asia. Turkey had been a goal for Soviet expansion for some time – the return of the Kars and Ardahan regions were early war aims for Stalin; a barrage of criticism of the Turkish government by Radio Moscow had been building since March 1945. This reached a peak in June, when the Soviets made a claim on the Dardanelles Straits, demanding the establishment of bases in this strategically important area. The Soviet foreign minister, Molotov, 'asked the Turkish Government to accede to the Soviet desires', but no one was under any illusion that this was not an outright threat. Consequently, there was no rush to disband the existing SOE offices in Turkey, or indeed in Iran or Norway. As far as Norway was concerned, SOE units would still be on standby during May and early June.[16]

In the Far East the planners decided that the most likely consequence of the opening of hostilities would be an immediate alliance between the Soviet Union and Japan. This would be a startling about-turn for Stalin, who was still neutral in the war with Japan and, after the Yalta agreement, was in fact due to open hostilities against her in August 1945. However, it was conceivable that with Japanese encouragement, Stalin could turn. After all, it would give Japan some breathing space and allow her to reinforce her troops in the Home Islands, as well as return to the offensive in China. With the cancellation of the Operation 'Downfall' plan to invade the Japanese mainland, the Allies would face a stalemate in their war with Japan. Fortunately, it was unlikely that the 1 million-strong Red Army in the East would engage in any offensive operations in the Far East.[17]

However much the planners discussed the likely Soviet response, they could never know at which point in the conflict Stalin would raise the stakes by invading new territory. Would the tripwire be the initial Allied advance into Germany and Poland during the strategy of 'quick success'?

Or would it require the escalation to 'total war' in the winter of 1945–46, before he struck out across the world? The planners gloomily concluded that 'the result of a total war with Russia is not possible to forecast, but the one thing certain is that to win it would take us a very long time.'[18]

If the Unthinkable war was not won by the winter of 1945, what then? As the Allied armies fought their way farther into Polish territory, they could certainly rely on more organised local support, at least in the centre of the country. In the north and along the Baltic coast, they would be entering the former territory of East Prussia, an area that formed part of the old German Reich. This was now Soviet-occupied but something of a wasteland and would not offer much sustenance to an invading army. After all, as the Germans retreated, they had demolished most of the country's infrastructure, but there was worse to come. The territory was the first part of the German Reich to be occupied by the Red Army and its soldiers set about terrorising, raping and looting the local inhabitants. Any property that the Germans had left standing was ransacked, and crops and livestock were widely pillaged. As in Silesia, there was no organised resistance network in the north that could co-ordinate sabotage or provide high-grade intelligence for the Allies; this would inevitably hamper Allied amphibious landings along the Polish coast.[19]

Despite the difficulties in the north, farther to the south the Allied advance would make faster progress, since they would be entering the heartland of Polish resistance. The towns and cities, though, could offer little sustenance to an advancing army. The capital, Warsaw, was still in ruins and although the streets were cleared of rubble, organised rebuilding would not start for another year. After the Warsaw Rising in the summer of 1944, Hitler had ordered that the remains of the city should be razed before the German army retreated westwards. Dedicated teams of German sappers had worked their way through the skeletons of buildings dynamiting everything, so that when Stalin eventually allowed the Red Army to cross the River Vistula and enter the western part of the city, in January 1945, they occupied a vast mound of bricks and masonry. The population in this part of the city had dwindled to fewer than 1,000. By 1 July 1945 some of the 60,000 residents from the eastern suburb of Praga (which had not been involved in the Rising) might have drifted across, but otherwise it remained a ghost city.[20] Other towns did not suffer this ferocity, but few had escaped either German retribution or Soviet vengeance.

Once the Allies were deep into Poland, they would also have to contend with sabotage from communist Poles operating behind their lines. Since their occupation of Poland in 1944, the Soviets had been able to invest more time in organising covert groups as well as in destroying anti-communists. The Red Army had brought with them units of SMERSH, who in turn used NKVD troops to round up, disarm or dispatch underground fighters. The NKVD were also used to train the local Polish communist security service under the direction of the ruthless General Ivan Serov. He remained in Poland until May 1945 and, after dealing with the survivors of the AK, had set about organising the local Polish secret police, known as the *Urzedy Bezpieczeństwa* (Security Offices, or UB). This unit, headed by Stanisław Radkiewicz, was still in its infancy in the summer of 1945, and it would take another year for this force of 2,500 raw recruits, who were poorly led by inexperienced officers, to grow into a force of 10,000 men. The UB were still a rag-tag outfit, enjoying little co-operation with the Soviet-backed Polish army, and in May 1945 Władysław Gomułka, one of the leaders of the PPR, even admitted 'it will come to pass that the UB shall be the NKVD's worst agency.'[21] Nevertheless, some 50 per cent of the original UB civilian recruits were replaced with military men and there were now more Soviet intelligence officers commanding them. They had the capacity to terrorise local communities, but in the event of an Allied invasion no doubt the NKVD would co-ordinate counter-intelligence operations behind Allied lines and round up potential supporters of the Allies within central and eastern Poland ahead of any fighting.

More horrors would lie in wait for Allied troops if they managed to advance beyond Warsaw, as the Napoleonic and German armies had found to their cost. The German offensive of 1939 had shown how easy it was, at first, for foreign armies to penetrate Polish territory. For an Allied army advancing from the west, there were no mountain ranges to cross and the terrain did not become difficult until the boggy marshes to the east, or the dense forests of the north-east. And it was these obstacles that invading infantry feared the most. The vast deciduous forests often contained stinking and glutinous floors, and where vegetation had grown, the ground was impenetrable. Flies and mosquitoes would cloud around every struggling foot soldier, and there would be no drinking water to quench his thirst. Food and medical supplies for the Allied infantry would decrease as the lines of communication stretched – and this was only the summer.[22] The bitter winter was worse and the German infantry knew this only too well. Advancing onwards towards Moscow was fraught with danger. Heinrich Haape was one of the most decorated German army doctors on the Eastern Front; his 3rd Battalion of Infantry Regiment 18 was part of the epic advance in 1941 that reached the gates of Moscow, only to be beaten back by the weather and disease. Of his battalion of 800 men, only 28 survived the first desperate winter, yet he still believed the outcome of Operation Barbarossa could have been different:

> If only the battle for Moscow had started fourteen days earlier, the city would now have been in our hands. Or if the rains had held off for fourteen days. If – if – if. If Hitler had started 'Barbarossa' six weeks earlier as originally planned: if he had left Mussolini on his own in the Balkans and had attacked Russia in May; if we had continued our sweeping advance instead of stopping at the Schutsche Lake; if Hitler had sent us winter clothing. Yes, if, if, if.[23]

For any army contemplating an invasion of the Soviet Union, the lessons of Barbarossa were indeed important. Once Unthinkable was enacted, it was a very real possibility that the Red Army would withdraw and suck in the invader, just as they had done in 1941. Then Hitler had believed that the Soviets would not withdraw from the Baltic States or back towards Moscow and that he could defeat them in the field, without being drawn too far in. It was a fatal miscalculation.[24] In the three months between June and September 1941, the German army had made extraordinary gains of Soviet territory, reaching the outskirts of Leningrad to the north and capturing Kiev to the south, but this was against a Red Army and Air Force that was in shock and was unprepared. It was not the battle-hardened and better equipped Red Army of 1945. In Unthinkable the Allies would have faced a more formidable foe, and the climate would have proved just as implacable.

As autumn gave way to winter, and the Allies found themselves advancing into the Soviet Union, they would find their daylight operating hours severely reduced. Compared to when they had started out from Germany on 1 July, they would have lost two and a half hours of daylight in the morning, while darkness would fall three and a half hours earlier in the evening. By mid-November temperatures would start to plummet. In the clear blue skies, the sun might appear in the morning but it would have lost its strength towards midday and the atmosphere would sharpen. The icy wind from Siberia would blow across the Steppes and the frost would come by early evening as the thermometer fell to -15°. Any army sentries with exposed flesh would suffer frostbite to their extremities. Then as December came, the temperature would fall even further. Minus 24, -36 and then -48°; it would be like walking through a deep freezer, except it would be four times colder. This unimaginable cold would paralyse everything and the casualties from frostbite and hypothermia would completely overwhelm any medical services.[25]

Napoleon's troops had fared no better. In the terrible winter of 1812 only 90,000 of the 600,000 French soldiers who set out for Moscow made it to the city. Then, during their retreat, all but a handful perished. It was not only the frostbite that killed them, but also the 'spotted fever' caused by lice. In 1945 a younger soldier might survive the fever, but any older soldier who was not inoculated against this scourge would perish. Even with American medical advances, the Western Allies would not have enough serum to treat their troops.

If the climate and disease were not bad enough, the Soviet terrain would prove just as formidable. The sheer scale of the Soviet Union was awesome and although large areas were without population or strategic targets, the distance that any Allied force would have to travel was vast. Taking the contemporary frontiers in 1940, the Soviet Union measured nearly 8.5 million square miles, compared to Britain's mere 100,000 square miles. The gap between populations was not so large; with Britain registering a quarter of the USSR's 194 million.[26] Such vast distances meant that Soviet equipment suffered constant wear and tear and when it had to be replaced, the parts or equipment had to be transported from the main industrial regions in the Urals, or east of Moscow. Furthermore, the country lacked good road and rail communication that could link industrial output to military deployments. The war had destroyed much of Soviet industry, though this was mitigated by moving many factories beyond the Urals.

If the Soviet Union could count on such natural defences, who or what could the British and US rely on? One of the main assumptions of Unthinkable was that Britain had the support of not only the US, but also the British Empire. This was far from assured, especially since another assumption of the plan was that Japan would ally herself with the Soviet Union and this would have serious repercussions for Australia. At the time when the plan was concocted in the spring of 1945, Australia was still locked in a grim war against the Japanese in Borneo. John Curtin was the Australian Prime Minister, but as an Irishman and resolute Labor Party man, he had little time for Churchill. Their relationship had never recovered from a stand-off in 1942, when Churchill had ordered the legendary Australian 9th Division to divert to Ceylon and India on their way back to Australia, after a gruelling campaign in North Africa. Curtin had also made clear his determination to see the United States, rather than Britain, as Australia's guarantor in the fight against the Japanese in the Pacific theatre.[27] Consequently, it is hard to see the Australian government, let alone their population, supporting the Unthinkable war – a conflict which would only add succour to the Japanese as well as bringing in the Soviets as a new enemy of Australia. Ultimately though, Australia's fate in 1945 was largely influenced by the US Supreme Commander for the South-West Pacific Area, General Douglas Macarthur. His close and dominating relationship with Curtin would mean that if Macarthur was enthusiastic about Unthinkable – and there are many reasons to believe he would have been – then Australian military forces would have to follow his lead.[28]

Canada, notwithstanding the support for Churchill from its premier, Mackenzie King, might also be reluctant to participate, especially if the US took against the plan. And it was not only Canada that was tilting markedly towards the United States. Australia, and to a lesser extent New Zealand, had become increasingly concerned at the priority Britain had given to defeating Germany over the defeat of Japan. Even Premier Smuts, whose relationship with Churchill was described by the latter as 'two old love-birds moulting together on a perch but still able to peck', was facing increasing pressure from his country's National Party for a more independent line.[29]

Because Unthinkable was mooted in the spring of 1945, before the US testing of an atomic device, there is no assumption in the report that such weapons would be used. However, by the time 'total war' had erupted, the US atomic program would be well under way and if there was a US will to use the weapons, the whole scenario would alter if Soviet, instead of Japanese, targets were selected. Even then the only targets considered were civilian or industrial centres. It was not until 1951, for example, that the British army developed the concept of using nuclear weapons 'tactically' on the battlefield. Nonetheless, even before then it was thought that an atomic bomb could be dropped on an aggressor army and then conventional forces would be unleashed on the shocked and devastated survivors. The main tactical effect of an atomic explosion was blast, particularly against fortified structures, but such a blast diminished rapidly; so at 1 mile away, a 1 kiloton bomb would only inflict damage equal to a full gale. Consequently, bombing enemy formations in the vast open plains or Russian Steppes would have limited value. Even if these areas were subject to saturation atomic bombing, the radiation fall-out would be so severe that friendly forces could only operate in the area for hours, in exhausting anti-radiation suits.[30] The concept of 'total war' was terrifying to contemplate.

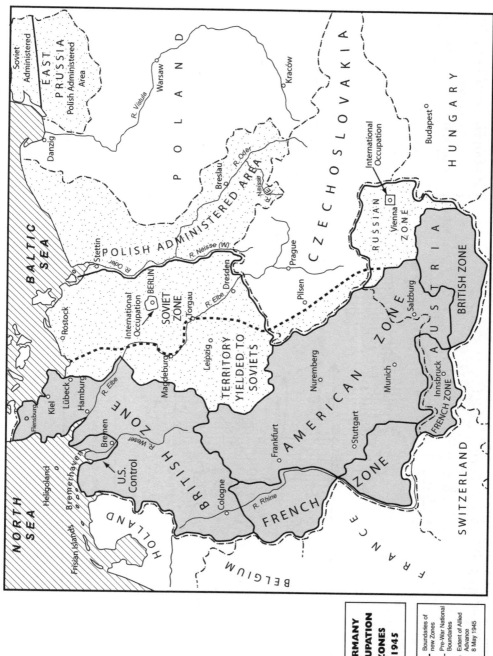

**GERMANY
OCCUPATION
ZONES
1945**

——— Boundaries of
new Zones

–·–·– Pre-War National
Boundaries

■■■■ Extent of Allied
Advance
8 May 1945

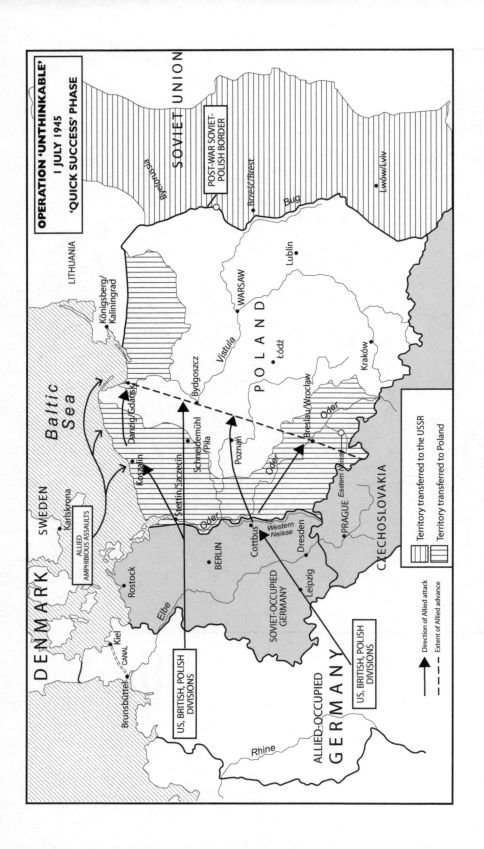

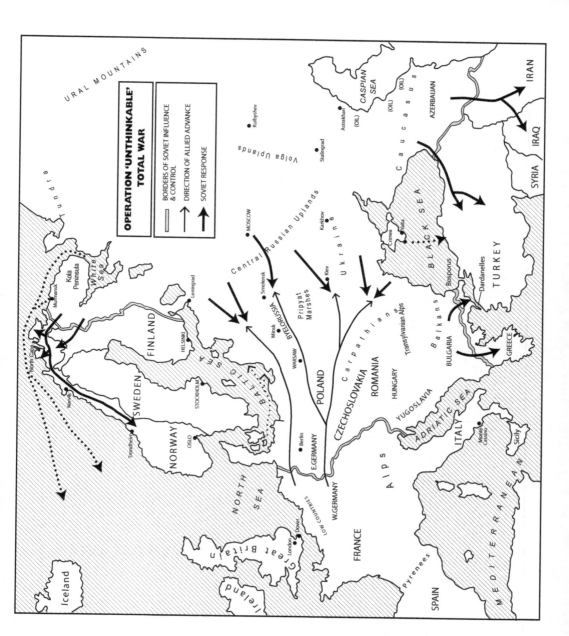

OPERATION 'UNTHINKABLE'
TOTAL WAR

BORDERS OF SOVIET INFLUENCE & CONTROL
DIRECTION OF ALLIED ADVANCE
SOVIET RESPONSE

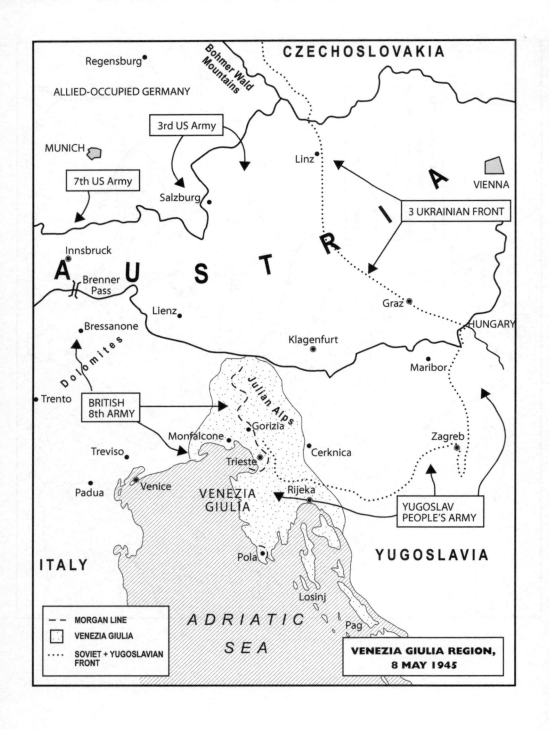

CZECHOSLOVAKIA

Regensburg

ALLIED-OCCUPIED GERMANY

3rd US Army

MUNICH

7th US Army

Linz

VIENNA

AUSTRIA

3 UKRAINIAN FRONT

Salzburg

Innsbruck

Brenner
Pass

Lienz

Graz

HUNGARY

Bressanone

Klagenfurt

Dolomites

Maribor

Trento

Julian Alps

BRITISH
8th ARMY

Gorizia

Monfalcone

Zagreb

Treviso

Cerknica

Trieste

Venice

VENEZIA
GIULIA

Rijeka

Padua

YUGOSLAV
PEOPLE'S ARMY

ITALY

Pola

YUGOSLAVIA

Losinj

- - - MORGAN LINE

VENEZIA GIULIA

········ SOVIET + YUGOSLAVIAN
FRONT

ADRIATIC
SEA

Pag

VENEZIA GIULIA REGION,
8 MAY 1945

'All aboard'. Churchill and Roosevelt. *(63-534 Harry S Truman Library)*

The Big Three at Yalta. Churchill, Roosevelt, Stalin (standing, from left: Cunningham, Portal, Leahy). *(US262-7449 Library of Congress)*

General Anders
at Monte Cassino.
(*37-639-3 Narodowe
Archiwum Cyfrowe*)

'Monty'. Pressing
on. (*208-PU-138LL-3
NARA*)

East meets West at
Torgau. (*111-SC-
205228 NARA*)

'Splitting Berlin'. Zhukov, Montgomery and Rokossovsky at the Brandenburg Gate, Berlin. (*TR2913 Imperial War Museum*)

Eisenhower, Patton and Truman in Berlin. (*64-386 Harry S Truman Library*)

'A burden for the Allies'. German POWs. (*260-MGG-1061-1 NARA*)

WAR CABINET

JOINT PLANNING STAFF

OPERATION "UNTHINKABLE"

Report by the Joint Planning Staff.

We have examined Operation UNTHINKABLE. As instructed, we have taken the following assumptions on which to base our examination:-

(a) The undertaking has the full support of public opinion in both the British Empire and the United States and consequently, the morale of British and American troops continues high.

(b) Great Britain and the United States have full assistance from the Polish armed forces and can count upon the use of German manpower and what remains of German industrial capacity.

(c) No credit is taken for assistance from the forces of other Western Powers, although any bases in their territory, or other facilities which may be required, are made available.

(d) Russia allies herself with Japan.

(e) The date for the opening of hostilities is 1st July, 1945.

(f) Redeployment and release schemes continue till 1st July and then stop.

Owing to the special need for secrecy, the normal staffs of Service Ministries have not been consulted.

OBJECT

2.   The overall or political object is to impose upon Russia the will of the United States and British Empire.

Even though "the will" of these two countries may be defined as no more than a square deal for Poland, that does not necessarily limit the military commitment. A quick success might induce the Russians to submit to our will at least for the time being; but it might not. That is for the Russians to decide. If they want total war, they are in a position to have it.

-1-

'Operation Unthinkable'. (*CAB 120/691 National Archives*)

Churchill and his Chiefs of Staff Committee (sitting from left, Portal, Brooke, Churchill, Cunningham. Standing from left, Hollis, Ismay). (*H41834 Imperial War Museum*)

'Right then, who's ready for World War Three?' Exhausted British troops near the frontline. (B10292 Imperial War Museum)

Amphibious landings. 'Using Allied Naval supremacy in The Baltic'. (26-G-2326 NARA)

'Bombed to smithereens'. Europe in ruins. (*208-AA-207L-1 NARA*)

Belarus partisans. 'Danger in the East'. (*Public Domain*)

Not the result of bombing. A German factory stripped out by Soviet engineers. (*CL3220 Imperial War Museum*)

River crossing under fire. (*208-YE-132 NARA*)

'Advancing through the wilderness'. (*111-SC-205778 NARA*)

French Resistance. 'Unpredictable allies'. (*531322 NARA*)

VE Day, 8 May 1945. Churchill addresses the nation. (*H41846 Imperial War Museum*)

Harry Hopkins. (*LC-USZ62-135306 World Telegram Palumbo*)

Joseph E. Davies. (*LC-DIG-hec-29262 Library of Congress*)

'The problem of logistics'. (26-G-3056 NARA)

The Red Army. 'A formidable foe'.   'Our new allies'. (242-GAP-286B-4 NARA)
(613474 Novosti Archive)

US Tuskegee aircrew, Spring 1945. 'Next mission – Moscow?' (*LC-DIG-ppmsca-13260 Library of Congress*)

Post-war Warsaw. (*LC-DIG-ppmsca-19261 Library of Congress*)

Potsdam, July 1945.
Attlee, Truman and
Stalin. (63-1453-24
*Harry S Truman
Library*)

Nagasaki. 'No
words can
describe it'.
(A61763D *Library
of Congress*)

6

WAR CLOUDS

As the planners continued their work on Unthinkable, events were moving quickly. Government policies were changing, and there was a new occupant in the White House. Within days of arriving, President Truman was exhibiting a bullish attitude towards the Soviet Union. Just before he met the Soviet foreign minister, Vyacheslav Molotov, for the first time, Truman told his advisors that if the Soviets didn't appear at San Francisco for talks on the formation of the United Nations, 'they can go to hell'. There were now others in the US State Department who reflected Truman's tough stance, including Secretary of the Navy, James Forrestal. 'If the Soviets continue to be intransigent,' he argued, 'the United States would be better off having a showdown with them, now rather than later.'[1] But there were others who urged caution. The US secretary of war, Henry Stimson, was keen for the US to 'get tough' on the Soviets over what he considered were 'smaller' issues, such as the handover of Soviet citizens, but he was wary about the wisdom of 'too strong a policy' over Poland.

Stalin used Molotov to continually block British and US approaches about Poland. On 23 April 1945 the British ambassador to the US, Lord Halifax, was unable to report any progress with the Soviet foreign minister. 'It proved impossible,' he told Churchill, 'to move Mr Molotov on any point. He was completely stubborn and unaccommodating.'[2] The 55-year-old Molotov had long since hitched his career to that of Stalin, and had enthusiastically supported his master's collectivisation policy and brutal purges before the war. He was unequivocal about his role. 'My task as Minister of Foreign Affairs,' he declared, 'was to expand the borders of our Fatherland.' He felt that the alliance with the West was expedient for the duration of the war, but by 1945 he, and a good number of the Soviet leadership, believed that war with the West was inevitable.[3] Molotov's icy moods did little to endear him to Western diplomats. 'He has the grace and conciliation of a totem pole,' lamented the Foreign Office mandarin Sir Alexander Cadogan, but Molotov was just the sort of implacable front man that Stalin required.[4]

On 25 April the Allied diplomats briefly turned their attention away from the strife in Europe to matters of world government. The San Francisco United Nations Conference was heralded by orchestras and the undeniable showmanship of the host, the US secretary of state, Edward Stettinius.[5] But Stettinius's charisma and the opening jollity soon subsided as the delegates from forty-six nations which had declared war on Germany and Japan started arguing about procedures. The one notable absentee was Poland, whose government-in-exile was still recognised by the West, but was pointedly denied an invitation to attend for fear of antagonising Stalin. The leading delegates at the conference were the foreign ministers of the Big Four nations (the US, Britain, the Soviet Union and China), while the secretary-general of the conference was an American diplomat, Alger Hiss. However, it transpired that Hiss, who had been an assistant to Stettinius at the Yalta Conference, was not just a prominent liberal, but also a closet communist. Critically, Hiss had been involved in the preparations for Yalta, and it was later revealed that decrypted telegrams from Soviet agents to their KGB handlers confirmed that there was a Soviet spy operating inside the US delegation at Yalta. Post-Cold War investigations, though not absolutely conclusive, pointed to Alger Hiss.[6] Yet Hiss was not the only mole inside Washington. The Assistant Secretary of the Treasury, Harry Dexter White, was one of several NKVD agents lobbying for US subsidies for the Soviet Union towards the end of the war.[7]

On 28 April 1945 the subtle diplomatic language between West and East ended. Churchill's frustration at Soviet stalling tactics over Poland finally boiled over and he sent a blunt telegram to Stalin. In his cable, no. 450, the prime minister accused Stalin of going back on the whole spirit of Yalta by refusing to discuss the names of the democrats put forward by the West for inclusion in a future Polish government:

> I certainly went to Yalta with the hope that both the London and Lublin Polish Governments would be swept away and that a new government would be formed from among Poles of goodwill … But you did not like this plan, and we and the Americans agreed, therefore, that there was to be no sweeping away of the Bierut government but that instead it should become a 'new' government, 'reorganised on a broader democratic basis with the inclusion of democratic leaders from Poland itself and from Poles abroad' … we British feel that after all this time absolutely no headway has been made towards forming a 'new' government.[8]

It was not only Poland that grieved Churchill; Yugoslavia was also a worry. Recalling his 1944 'naughty document', he reminded Stalin about their deal over agreed spheres of influence in Europe. 'I must say the way things have worked out in Yugoslavia certainly does not give me the feeling of a 50:50 interest as between our countries.'[9] Then, for the first time, Churchill broached the question of the sixteen-man Polish underground delegation, which had been missing for more than four weeks. Rumours abounded that they had been arrested, but there was no confirmation from the Soviets and, surprisingly, the normally acute Polish intelligence networks had failed to track their whereabouts. During April the Polish government-in-exile in London, as well as the British Foreign Office had received sporadic reports and rumours about the sixteen, yet it had taken until 28 April for Churchill to raise the issue directly with Stalin. Over the next few days Stalin continued to ignore Churchill's enquiries. His silence was ominous.[10]

The possibility of an imminent conflict was sustenance to those Germans and their supporters who believed that an alliance could be forged with the British and Americans against the Soviets. William 'Lord Haw-Haw' Joyce, the British traitor and broadcaster, was about to send out his last transmission from Germany; on 30 April, while his master, Adolf Hitler, committed suicide in a bunker in the Reich Chancellery, Joyce scuttled out of Berlin. He continued broadcasting from Hamburg, and the weary, but still polished, voice declared that 'the horrible war through which we have just been passing is but the prelude to a struggle of a far more decisive kind.' Furthermore, he claimed that Western Europe would be defenceless against Stalin, 'without the help of the German legions'.[11] Joyce was, of course, totally unaware of Allied post-war planning, but his bizarre prophecy about the German legions was an integral part of the Unthinkable plan, which was taking shape as he uttered his final broadcast.

Elsewhere in Europe, German forces were rapidly capitulating. In the north of Italy and the south of Austria they signed an unconditional surrender on 29 April, as armies from the Western Allies and the Soviet Union raced to consolidate their gains. The actions of the Red Army had already reinforced Churchill's belief that possession of strategic areas was essential for bargaining over post-war settlements. But while the US military clearly appreciated this, the US State Department wanted to rein back Allied troops as they approached Stalin's forces. A spearhead of American units had already made their first contact with the Red Army at Torgau on the River Elbe on 25 April. This meeting, just north-east of Leipzig, was as far as Stalin was prepared to allow the Western Allies, while he completed the conquest of Berlin, barely 60 miles to the north. However, to the south of Germany the border between East and West was more contentious. Austria was being hotly contested, though the Soviets had already taken possession of Vienna by 13 April, while another particularly dangerous confrontation was brewing over the north-eastern segment of Italy, bordering Yugoslavia. Churchill was desperate to allow the Supreme Allied Commander in the Mediterranean theatre, Field Marshal Alexander, to occupy Trieste, a key city in the region, but he still needed US sanction. On 30 April Churchill rushed off a cable to Truman:

> We are as much entitled to move freely into Trieste, if we can get there, as were the Russians to win their way into Vienna. We ought if possible to get there first and then talk about the rest of the Province. After all, the basic principle on which we have been working is that territorial changes must be left for the peace or armistice settlement ... we shall try to take possession of Trieste from the sea before informing the Russians or Yugoslavs.[12]

In order to stake a claim in Austria, Churchill was impatient for Alexander to push the British 8th Army, already advancing swiftly through northern Italy, up onto the plains of the Danube towards Vienna and, at the same time, peel off on his right flank into the farthest north-east corner of Italy. There were concerns that the bulk of SS troops, fanatical Nazis and war criminals were seeking a last redoubt just over the border in Austria. Furthermore, this hard core had large numbers of prisoners of war under their control and there were fears that they would slaughter their captives unless sufficient Allied forces could overwhelm them. But a thrust up from Italy into Austria relied on safe routes through the Alps and there were major obstacles in the way.[13] One serious problem for those forces pushing up into Austria from the south was the presence of large communist bands, particularly Tito's Partisans, who were contesting the city of Trieste and the adjacent Venezia Giulia region, an area of great strategic importance, but one that would swiftly became a new flashpoint between East and West.

Historically, Venezia Giulia, otherwise known as the 'Julian March', had belonged to the Austro-Hungarian Empire but was ceded to Italy at the end of the Great War.[14] During the Second World War, after the fascist Italian government had fallen in September 1943, German forces moved into the 3,000-square-mile region but were confronted with a guerrilla war with Yugoslav partisans. By the spring of 1945 most German forces had retreated and Yugoslavia, together with most of Venezia Giulia, was in the hands of Tito's Partisans. The area, like the rest of Yugoslavia, had a Slav majority with sizeable Italian populations in urban areas and along the coastline, but it was riven with factional and racial conflicts and widespread atrocities were carried out. Tito wanted Trieste, the most important prize in the region, for much the same reasons as the Western Allies. It was a sizeable port, which offered access to the Adriatic, and the promise of large trading revenues. For the West, Trieste offered an outlet for all the regions of the Danube basin, and this north-eastern segment of Italy also provided vital military lines of communication between the Adriatic and southern Austria. Churchill was determined to wrest Austria from Soviet control and, to this end, Field Marshal Alexander needed to keep Venezia Giulia in Allied hands, by force if necessary. His brief was then to set up an Allied military government in the interim and await a decision, at a subsequent peace conference, as to which country should incorporate the region.

However, Tito was ready to try his luck and, despite his agreement with Alexander some months before, the Yugoslav leader instructed his forces to overrun large areas of Venezia Giulia, including Trieste and the towns of Pola, Gorizia and Monfalcone, all of which had large Italian populations. Churchill was equally prepared to go to the brink and needed confirmation that the US would back an eviction of Tito's forces. But Truman, who had until now pleased Churchill with his tough rhetoric, changed his position. His response to the prime minister's request for support was lukewarm; he replied that he wished 'to avoid having American forces used to fight Yugoslav forces or being used in combat in the Balkan political arena'. These words alarmed Churchill, for they were early signs that the Roosevelt creed of opposing the extension of British influence in Europe was alive and well in the US State Department. There were still too many advisors around Truman who were determined to believe that any attempts to stem Soviet influence in Europe were all about British empire building. [15]

Despite the lack of appetite in the US for a showdown with Tito, Alexander's forces managed to enter Trieste on 2 May and take the surrender of the German garrison, but there remained an uneasy stand-off between the British 8th Army and elements of the Yugoslav army. To add legitimacy to his actions, Alexander cabled Tito to remind him that this operation had already been agreed by the two parties back in February, but the Supreme Commander was still worried that Tito might not back off. Reporting to Churchill, Alexander voiced concerns about conflict with an erstwhile ally:

If I am ordered by the Combined Chiefs of Staff to occupy the whole of Venezia Giulia by force if necessary, we shall certainly be committed to a fight with the Yugoslav Army, who will have at least the moral backing of the Russians. Before we are committed I think it as well to consider the feelings of our own troops in this matter. They have a profound admiration for Tito's partisan Army and a great sympathy for them in their struggle for freedom. We must be very careful therefore before we ask them to turn away from the common enemy to fight an Ally. Of course I should not presume to gauge the reaction of our people at home, whom you know so well.[16]

By 6 May Alexander had successfully managed to secure some of Tito's prime objectives, including Trieste, Gorizia and Monfalcone, and Churchill was delighted, but reminded Alexander that 'Tito, backed by Russia, will push hard, but I do not think they will dare attack you in your present position.'[17] Although the Allies had made good progress, Alexander faced the problem that if he was ordered to impose a border line with force, he might not have the military strength to do it. He cabled the premier with an alarmingly long list of the Empire and US troops to be shortly demobilised or redeployed to the Far East.[18] It was not long before he wished he hadn't bothered, for Churchill responded with a barrage of criticism against Alexander. 'What alarmed me most in your telegram,' Churchill chided, 'was that you seem to be agreeing to all this and assuming that the troops that you have left after December will be enough ... I was not made aware of what was happening.' Alexander was quick to reassure Churchill that all was not lost in the contest against Soviet influence, since he had the support of senior US figures, such as Ambassador Kirk, for keeping a strong military presence in Europe. This was reassuring, especially since a stocktake of US forces was made in the region and it was confirmed that General Patten, who would need little encouragement, could move five armoured divisions up to the Brenner Pass if necessary. Furthermore, if a conflict did arise, the US Mediterranean fleet was warned to move into the Adriatic and US aircraft were also on standby. However, for all the precautions, Truman remained adamant, declaring that 'unless Tito's forces should attack, it is impossible for me to involve this country in another war.'[19]

Churchill was on his guard against this crisis, but military advisors felt their chief was better at handling the much bigger strategic disputes than dealing with more regional territorial feuds. Using a cricket analogy, 'Pug' Ismay thought that 'the PM can be counted on to score a hundred in a Test Match but is no good at village cricket.'[20] Nonetheless, Churchill's incredible stamina seemed to always outlast his subordinates and his ability to snatch deep, untroubled sleep undoubtedly kept his sturdy constitution going.

He admitted later that only the sinking of the *Repulse* and *Prince of Wales* or the fall of Crete had kept him awake during the war. At all other times, he disclosed, 'I just turn out the light, say bugger everybody, and go to sleep.'[21]

As the war entered its last week, concerns moved on to the occupation of Germany and there was mounting pressure for the Poles to take part in the Allied occupation. Field Marshal Brooke, with the end of his stressful mission within sight, was weary of being harangued by General Anders:

> This afternoon Anders again came to see me having returned from visiting his Corps of Poles in Italy. He says there are at least one million Poles in Western Europe which he can (and wishes to) get hold of to swell his forces. He wishes to take part in the occupation of Germany, and then has wild hopes of fighting his way home to Poland through the Russians! A pretty desperate problem the Polish Army is going to present us with![22]

Although Brooke bemoaned the size of the Polish army, Churchill must have realised its use to the Allies if war erupted. He was also conscious that the West should not willingly give up its bargaining chips. To this end, on 1 May he warned Truman that the Allies should not withdraw to the previously agreed East–West line, thereby sacrificing valuable territory that they had recently captured. The following week, he stressed much the same argument to Anthony Eden:

Personal and Top Secret.

I fear terrible things have happened during the Russian advance through Germany to the Elbe. The proposed withdrawal of the United States Army to the occupational lines which were arranged with the Russians and Americans in Quebec ... would mean the tide of Russian domination sweeping forward 120 miles on a front of 300 or 400 miles. This would be an event which, if it occurred, would be one of the most melancholy in history. After it was over, and the territory occupied by the Russians, Poland would be completely engulfed and buried deep in Russian-occupied lands. What would in fact be the Russian frontier would run from the North Cape in Norway, along the Finnish-Swedish frontier, across the Baltic to a point just east of Lübeck.

Thus the territories under Russian control would include The Baltic Provinces, all of Germany to the occupational line, all Czechoslovakia, a large part of Austria, the whole of Yugoslavia, Hungary, Roumania, Bulgaria, until Greece in her present tottering condition is reached. It would include all the great capitals of middle Europe including Berlin, Vienna, Budapest, Belgrade,

Bucharest and Sofia. The position of Turkey and Constantinople will certainly come immediately into discussion.

This constitutes an event in the history of Europe to which there has been no parallel, and which has not been faced by the Allies in their long and hazardous struggle. The Russian demands on Germany for reparations alone will be such as to enable her to prolong the occupation almost indefinitely, at any rate for many years, during which time Poland will sink with many other States into the vast zone of Russian-controlled Europe ... these matters can only be settled before the United States Armies in Europe are weakened. If they are not settled before the US Armies withdraw from Europe and the Western world folds up its war machines, there are no prospects of a satisfactory solution and very little of preventing a Third World War.[23]

Stalin now saw fit to release information about the missing sixteen-man Polish delegation. During the San Francisco Conference, both Eden and Stettinius had asked Molotov to find out what had happened to the Poles, but nothing transpired. Then, on the evening of 3 May, Molotov invited some of the delegates, including Eden and Stettinius, to dinner at the Soviet Consulate in San Francisco. Charles 'Chip' Bohlen, an interpreter with the US party, witnessed the extraordinary revelation:

I walked in with Stettinius, who greeted Molotov with his usual ready smile. As they were shaking hands, Molotov said, 'Oh by the way, Mr Stettinius, about those sixteen Poles; they have all been arrested by the Red Army'. He immediately turned away and said, 'Hello Mr Eden'. Stettinius was left standing there with a fixed smile on his face.[24]

Having interrogated their Polish prisoners for more than three weeks in the hope of extracting intelligence on the remains of the underground movement, the Soviets had now decided to answer the West. There were suddenly announcements from all quarters. On 4 May Churchill received the following cable from Stalin, and it was far from conciliatory:

General Okulicki himself is charged with preparing and carrying out subversive activities behind the lines of the Red Army, subversion which has taken a toll of over a hundred Red Army soldiers and officers; the group is also charged with keeping illegal radio-transmitters in the rear of our troops, which is prohibited by law. All or part of them – depending on the outcome of the investigation – will be tried.[25]

On 5 May the official Soviet communist party mouthpiece, *Tass*, alleged that the Polish party had operated an 'illegal wireless station' behind the Soviet lines and would be put on trial.[26] Stalin himself reserved most of his bile for the commander-in-chief of the disbanded Home Army, General Okulicki, whom he branded an 'especially odious character'. Known as 'Kobra', Okulicki was the last C-in-C of the resistance movement and although he had ordered the disbandment of his army to save lives in January 1945, he was still a most valuable prize for the NKVD, who were seeking to tighten their grip on Poland.[27] Radio Lublin, the mouthpiece of the Soviet-sponsored Poles, then weighed in with a broadcast about accusations of 'high treason' by 'Okulicki and his accomplices' against the Polish state.[28] The capture and imprisonment of these Polish leaders was a critical move in the Soviet Union's control of Poland, for at a stroke it removed a generation of resistance leaders and stunted the growth of new organisations.

The main resistance body, the Home Army (AK) had been disbanded the previous January and ex-AK members were trying to regroup. A new movement known as *Niepodległość*, or 'Nie' ('No'), had recently been formed, but its commander, Colonel Jan Rzepecki, soon found that attempts to weld together a new organisation of anti-Soviet politicians and underground fighters was doomed. Another successor resistance movement, the Delegation of Armed Forces (*Delegatura Sil Zbrojnych*), or DSZ, suffered a similar fate, but the existing nationalist NSZ (*Narodowe Siły Zbrojne*) managed to fight on, vowing to destroy communist and pro-Soviet forces inside Poland. They achieved some successes but it was difficult for the West to determine how much support this nationalist movement enjoyed within Poland. However, by the early summer of 1945 there were moves to create another political/military organisation that would offer new hope to the resistors of Soviet rule. 'Freedom and Independence' (*Wolność i Niezawisłość*, or 'WiN') aimed to not only maintain ties with Mikołajczyk's democratic Peasant Party, but also to keep up the military pressure on the Soviet authorities.[29]

Although Churchill's concern over Poland was mounting by the day, his intelligence on what was happening inside the country remained weak. It always had been. Despite the efforts of the SOE to drop agents into the country, few had survived and even during the climactic events of the Warsaw Rising in the summer of 1944, Britain's monitoring of the crisis was too little and too late. They had relied almost exclusively on the efforts of a British ex-POW, Sergeant John Ward, who, by his own initiative, had escaped to join the AK and regularly relayed the plight of his Polish comrades back to London. But there were British attempts in early 1945 to gauge the level of Polish resistance. Operation 'Freston' was a largely unsuccessful attempt by SOE to place a military mission inside the country, but the operation had ended in farce in January 1945, when the members of the mission were bundled into a cattle truck by the Soviets and dispatched to Moscow. The much delayed operation had been intended to extract first-hand intelligence from ex-AK resistance leaders, but since the mission members arrived too late, their task was futile. However, intelligence was collected on the state of Poland's road and rail networks, which might have proved useful to the Unthinkable planners.[30]

The turmoil generated by the end of the war and the movement of large numbers of refugees did actually help the collection of intelligence, since the confusion often covered operations. There were also more overt attempts to gain intelligence in Poland. A combined British Secret Intelligence Service (SIS) and SOE operation sought to enter Poland under the guise of a 'Foreign Office Observers Mission' to gauge the political mood in the country. But it was bound to fail, since it depended on NKVD co-operation. Nonetheless, the exercise did highlight the dovetailing of the two secret British organisations. Many of SOE's 'assets' would be transferred to SIS in the summer of 1945, so, as the war ended, SOE made strenuous efforts to prevent their agents dispersing. After all, these men and women possessed a valuable bank of intelligence on European countries that SIS would find extremely useful for a future conflict with the Soviet Union:

> Contact should be maintained with them, if possible without heavy expenditure, to form a nucleus of tried and experienced agents, capable of rapid expansion in the event of another war. Many of these agents will need help to set themselves up again in civil life ... such help may take the form of finding agencies for the sale of British goods abroad, assisting former agents to obtain travel facilities in the immediate post-war period when travel is restricted.[31]

At the beginning of May the threat of the Red Army continuing their advance into Denmark was uppermost in Churchill's mind.[32] He received reports from the British Naval Attaché in Stockholm that the Soviets had dropped parachutists near Copenhagen and that local communist activity was being ramped up inside Denmark. With all haste, Montgomery's forces raced towards Lübeck to try and cut off the Soviet advance into the Danish peninsular. On 2 May the British 11th Armoured Division finally reached Lübeck, and a day later the 6th Airborne Division met up with the Red Army at the coastal town of Wismar. It was a close-run thing, for although US forces had helped the British as they advanced, Montgomery had managed to reach Lübeck with only twelve hours to spare.[33] All along the coast German units desperately tried to surrender to Western forces, rather than face the wrath of the Red Army, a state of affairs that only fostered Stalin's obsession that the Nazis were in league with the Western Allies. Yet Eisenhower went out of his way to placate the Soviet high command (*Stavka*) by confirming that all German units captured in disputed areas by US or British forces would be handed over to the Red Army, to suffer an uncertain fate.

Fighting effectively ended on all fronts on 7 May and there was frantic behind-the-scenes activity to co-ordinate the official declaration between the US, British and the Soviet governments. Much to Stalin's anger, the German caretaker regime, headed by Admiral Dönitz, officially surrendered to Eisenhower at Reims, rather than to the Red Army.[34] The surrender officially came into force in the very early hours of 8 May, so that Churchill could broadcast that day to announce to the British people that their struggle was over. Stalin then insisted on another 'unconditional surrender' in Berlin, and shortly before one o'clock in the morning of 9 May, Marshal Zhukov, in the presence of US and British commanders, took the surrender of Field Marshal Keitel. Hours later the news was announced in Moscow, and at daybreak on 9 May the city awoke to the celebrations of 'Victory Day'. By the evening several million Muscovites had gathered in Red Square.

All hostilities ceased at midnight 8 May, and the day was designated VE (Victory in Europe) Day. There were joyous celebrations throughout Britain but they were not universal, for the war in the Far East was far from over and many families had servicemen in training for the assault on Japan. Celebrations in Britain continued for days afterwards but again depressing news arrived that dampened spirits. Increasing information was coming in of the atrocities discovered in the Nazi concentration camps, which only served to generate further hostility in Britain and the US towards Germany and its servicemen. If Allied troops were expected to go into action, within months, alongside this erstwhile enemy, scores would be settled. It was hard to see how units could possibly co-operate.

But co-operation between the Western Allies and their erstwhile enemies would have to take place. By VE Day Hitler's appointed successor, Grand Admiral Karl Dönitz, was still operating the skeleton of the Reich government from the town of Flensburg, on the German–Danish border. On taking office, he had dismissed many top Nazi officials, including Heinrich Himmler, and cobbled together a provisional government he thought would be more palatable to the Western Allies. In the immediate aftermath of the war, Churchill decided that it was expedient to use this German administration to govern the stricken Western-occupied sector, albeit under orders from the Supreme Allied Commander. The prime minister reasoned that initially there had to be some force with which he could communicate, and order the remaining belligerent German units to lay down their arms. And in the forthcoming months a strong, Western-backed Germany would be a vital bulwark in the defence against Soviet encroachment. But Churchill reckoned without the 'loose cannons' in the German administration, such as Field Marshal Busch, who rushed to broadcast on Radio Flensburg; he announced that it was Dönitz who was still issuing the orders, and an almighty press row erupted. The days of the last chancellor of the Reich were numbered.

While Britain and America were celebrating VE Day, there was no such delight in Poland. Indeed, it is hard to overestimate the suffering and trauma that the country had endured under the Nazi occupation, and continued to bear under Soviet domination. A whole educated layer of society had been largely eliminated: army officers, lawyers, teachers, doctors, scientists, clergy – in fact anyone who could offer any sort of leadership in communities, or offer any challenge to the occupiers, had disappeared. Between 1939 and 1946 the wider Polish population declined from 35 million to fewer than 24 million, while the country's territory shrank from 150,000 square miles to some 120,000 square miles.[35]

Farther to the east, a triumphant Stalin had arranged victory celebrations for 'The Great Patriotic War', to take place in Moscow. In Red Square there were riotous scenes as hordes of jubilant Muscovites charged around the vast centre. A British diplomat witnessed a 'pink bald head circled with flowing white locks and a body in frock coat and gaiters' squealing as he was playfully tossed up into the air.[36] This was none other than the Dean of Canterbury Cathedral, Dr Hewlett Johnson, who was visiting the Soviet capital. Known as the 'Red Dean' for his pro-Soviet views, he was in the middle of a three-month visit to the country at the invitation of the Soviet organisation VOKS, which was supposed to foster cultural links between the Soviet Union and other countries; Johnson had been an ardent supporter of such links, but VOKS had a more sinister agenda as an agency of Comintern, the communist body tasked with spreading revolution in the West, by all means, including propaganda.[37] The extent of the cleric's knowledge of such subversion is not clear, but there was nothing untoward about his appearance in Red Square on 9 May. After all, he had been in Leningrad several days before, and was called down to Moscow by the British Embassy to conduct a thanksgiving service.

Other luminaries attending the service included Churchill's wife, Clementine, who was visiting the country on behalf of the British Aid to Russia Fund. However, she studiously avoided any meetings with her hosts that could be compromising. Churchill had warned his wife that 'Uncle Joe was behaving badly', but such warnings would never have been heeded by the Dean of Canterbury.[38] Indeed, several months later Johnson engaged in a bizarre meeting with Stalin and Molotov – a meeting that lasted nearly an hour and was a privilege extended to very few, especially to those outside the very tight diplomatic inner circle. According to Johnson, the meeting involved much mutual admiration and agreement over the failure of the British press to celebrate the Soviet military success. Perhaps Stalin believed that Johnson had more influence in Britain than he actually enjoyed, but the Soviet leader was eager to stress that 'we have no wish whatsoever to hurt England'. However, he also delivered the veiled threat that a peaceful relationship 'will depend largely on your politicians. If they have the will, we have the will'.[39]

Once the war was over, one of Churchill's main concerns was demobilisation, and the risk that it would leave the West at Stalin's mercy. He discussed with Eden what was going to happen when the US forces withdrew from Europe and British forces were demobilised – a much more important issue to him than the formation of the United Nations, still being discussed in San Francisco. Eden was able to report the encouraging news that US troops would not be withdrawn from Germany immediately, but the US government was still suspicious of British motives. The Americans understood Churchill's concerns but in Washington there seemed to be a greater fear of the expansion of the British Empire than fear of any communist takeover of Europe. Indeed, it was a view widely held among US servicemen, as well as US civilians and their politicians. A young veteran of the Pacific war, John F. Kennedy, wrote a comment for the *New York Journal*, declaring that 'Russia needs peace more than anything else'. In the article he did not seem to question the right of sovereignty for Soviet neighbours, declaring that 'no governments hostile to Russia will be permitted in the countries along her borders.' The future US president then concluded with the chilling warning that the Soviets 'feel they have earned this right to security. They mean to have it, come what may'.[40]

US opinion was also conditioned by the belief that Stalin seemed a more important ally in defeating the Japanese than the British – in the weeks before a confirmed atomic test, Truman needed Stalin more than he needed Churchill, and within a month of assuming office Truman was confiding to his wife that he found Churchill as 'exasperating' as the Soviets.[41] But Truman had foibles of his own, not least his obsession with the legacy of Roosevelt, as his biographer conceded:

> Truman developed an almost obsessive desire to leave no decision untaken – another area where he believed he could improve upon Roosevelt – and this meant that he left himself inadequate time for reflection and discussion. It was not that he was ill-briefed. He read his papers meticulously and impressed those around him with the thoroughness with which he mastered facts. But he was so determined to be decisive on the issues of the day ... that he was in danger of not fully considering the options, and not seeing one decision's impact upon another, or indeed its relation with a coherent general policy. A classic early example was his acceptance of a recommendation to cut-off Lend-lease within a few days of the end of the war in Europe.[42]

So with mistrust still prevailing between Britain and America, Foreign Secretary Eden ordered a stocktaking of the respective strengths of East and West. The report was certainly a depressing prospect for Britain. It warned that the Soviet Union, like all totalitarian governments, could afford to conduct a persistent and tough foreign policy, since they were not subject to the pressures of public opinion. However, the report stated that Stalin had fewer illusions than the Western Allies about how quickly Germany could regenerate – politically, economically and, ultimately, militarily. And to protect the Soviet Union against a resurrected and powerful Germany, the report surmised that Stalin had occupied Eastern Europe by proxy. But such occupation would become permanent, unless the West acted swiftly, and kept a foot firmly in Poland, Finland, Austria and Yugoslavia.[43]

In an attempt to break the Polish impasse, Churchill believed that another Big Three conference might just pin down Stalin. Even Truman was showing signs of 'wobbling' over his commitment to holding elections in Poland, suggesting that the Yugoslavia model might be adopted in place of the Yalta provisions. Churchill was appalled and felt that the best chance of a unified front lay in further discussions.[44] Writing to Truman on 11 May, he spelled out the vision that lay ahead:

> I consider that the Polish deadlock can now probably only be resolved at a conference between the three Heads of Government in some unshattered town in Germany, if such can be found. This should take place at latest at the beginning of July.[45]

The other problem that weighed heavily on Churchill was the future of his own government, for as soon as the war was over he knew that the coalition's days were numbered. The Labour Party had agreed to support the coalition until October 1945, but it was tempting for Churchill and his Conservative Party strategists to go to the country in June, tap the end-of-war euphoria and cut off the growing support for the Labour Party. But international events could easily overtake domestic matters and the risk of a conflict with the Soviet Union could erupt over Poland, the Balkans, Vienna or Trieste. On 12 May the West gave up some valuable leverage when US forces retired from their front on the Elbe River to an agreed line behind Eisenbach. This massive void would, no doubt, be filled by the Red Army within weeks, adding to their already huge territorial gains. In a telegram to Truman, Churchill made his first warning that 'an iron curtain is drawn down upon their front. We do not know what is going on behind.' And he feared the consequences. 'It would be open to the Russians,' he continued, 'in a very short space of time to advance, if they choose, to the waters of the North Sea and the Atlantic.'[46]

Despite early reassurances to the contrary, US troops were due to be withdrawn from Europe. The chief of staff of the US army, General George Marshall, told Lord Halifax, in Washington, that 50,000 troops would be withdrawn each month from Europe, and there would, no doubt, be increasing pressure from US public opinion to speed up the process. But there was one glimmer of light for Churchill. On 12 May Truman did a volte-face and supported his stance on the threat of force. 'We must decide now,' Truman said, 'whether we should uphold the fundamental principle of territorial settlement by orderly process.'[47] The president's Secretary of War, Henry Stimson, also waded in with the warning that the Western Allies and the Soviets were 'getting into a head-on collision'. He felt that the Americans had already given too much ground to the Soviets:

It is a case where we have got to regain the lead and perhaps do it in a pretty rough and realistic way. They [the Soviets] have rather taken it away from us because we have talked too much and have been too lavish with our beneficences to them. I told him [General Marshall] this was a place where we really held all the cards. I called it a royal straight flush and we mustn't be a fool about the way we play it. They can't get along without our help and industries and we have coming into action a weapon which will be unique. Now the thing is not to get into unnecessary quarrels by talking too much.[48]

News coming from the atomic, or 'Tube Alloys', project had buoyed up Stimson, but his president was more aroused by Tito's threat to the Italian border than the problem of Polish democracy. Cabling Churchill, the president stressed his belief that Tito was not going to peacefully give up Venezia Giulia and if the US and Britain allowed him to go unchallenged, it would set a dangerous precedent:

> It seems that Tito has an identical claim ready for South Austria, in Carinthia and Styria, and may have similar designs on parts of Hungary and Greece if his methods in Venezia Giulia succeed ... the problem is essentially one of deciding whether our two countries are going to permit our Allies to engage in uncontrolled land grabbing or tactics which are all too reminiscent of those of Hitler and Japan.[49]

Churchill was delighted by the president's new-found ebullience, though it was a development that alarmed Field Marshal Brooke. Writing in his diary that evening, Brooke recorded Churchill's reaction:

> Winston had a War Cabinet to discuss the Yugoslav situation. He had received a telegram from Truman, full of bellicose views and ready to be rough with Tito. Winston delighted, he gives me the feeling of already longing for another war! Even if it entailed fighting Russia![50]

Churchill was still elated the following day and a rather weary Admiral Cunningham witnessed a vintage display from his prime minister. 'It is much harder to make peace than war,' Cunningham wrote in his diary. 'Cabinet meeting at 1800 hours. PM treated us to long diatribe until 1940 hours before starting agenda.'[51] While such senior commanders as Cunningham were becoming weary of Churchill's persistent warnings, others were happy to add their vocal support, even though it was not always welcomed. Field Marshal Alexander alarmed the Americans as well as the British with his public remarks about Tito, comparing his methods to those of Hitler and Mussolini.[52] Similarly, the notoriously maverick US general George Patton was holding forth in the Hotel Majestic, in Paris, about the European security situation. 'It's all a God-damned shame,' he barked. When someone asked what he meant, he elaborated:

> Day after day, some poor bloody Czech or Austrian or Hungarian, even German officers come into my headquarters. I almost have to keep them

from going down on their knees to me. With tears in their eyes they say, 'In the name of God, General, come with your Army the rest of the way into our country. Give us a chance to set up our own governments. Give us this last chance to live before it's too late – before the Russians make us slaves forever.'[53]

Warming to his theme, Patton then declared that the Allied Third Army alone could 'thrash' the Red Army in combat. Indeed, he thought it better to take on the Soviet Union without delay, so that casualties would be smaller than in any future war. It was a view that may have chimed with Churchill's, but it was not the view of the American GI on the frontline:

> I didn't hear any anti-Russian talk. I think we were realistic enough to know that if we were going to fight them [the Soviets], we would come out second best. We hadn't even heard of the atomic bomb yet. We'd just have to assume that it would be masses of armies, and their willingness to sacrifice millions of troops. We were aware that our leaders were sparing our lives … In the final campaign down through Bavaria, we were in Patton's army. Patton said we ought to keep going. To me, that was an unthinkable idea. The Russians would have slaughtered us, because of their willingness to give up so many lives. I don't think the rank of the GIs had any stomach for fighting the Russians. We were informed enough through press and newsreels to know about Stalingrad.[54]

On 14 May Field Marshal Montgomery left Berlin and flew to London to see Churchill about the rapidly deteriorating situation in the Allied-controlled areas of Germany. But Montgomery was not only keen to discuss the problem of the vast numbers of German POWs; he was also hoping to lobby Churchill for the job of Military Governor. In the event, 'Monty' was disappointed. Churchill was not interested in talking about the governorship, for the premier had a far more pressing problem he wished to discuss, as Monty recalled:

> At our meeting in Downing Street the PM got very steamed up about the Russians and about the zones of occupation – which would entail a large scale withdrawal on our part. He ordered that I was not to destroy the weapons of the 2 million Germans who had surrendered on Lüneburg Heath on 4th May. All must be kept, we might have to fight the Russians with German help. This was Himmler's view.[55]

Quite how much Churchill told Montgomery at the time is not clear. His original order to Montgomery to halt the destruction of German weapons could not be found after the war, but it is quite possible that this document, like so many other sensitive papers, was routinely destroyed after reading. In any event, it seems that the retention of German equipment was not just confined to British-controlled areas. Churchill later confirmed that he also contacted the Military Governor of the US occupation zone, General Eisenhower, to make sure that there was a similar policy in US sectors. Churchill clearly coveted the vast quantities of German equipment, which would be useful to the West in a future conflict, but did not spell out the reasons for his request, giving the vague cover, 'we may have great need of these some day'. Eisenhower replied, apparently without questioning Churchill's motives, that any destruction of German equipment, including aircraft, was anyway a violation of the Act of Surrender and would not be tolerated.[56]

Instructions were certainly issued to Allied forces that German resources and weapons were to be preserved at all costs. All captured tracked or wheeled transport was to be preserved in good condition, while stocks of enemy fuel and oil were to be placed under armed guard. But it was the retention of German weapons that was of most interest. An extract from Allied orders covering conquered territory leaves no doubt those German assets were to be carefully preserved:

Anti-aircraft:
All anti-aircraft guns, heavy and light, under control of the Luftwaffe will be rendered inoperative by the removal of an essential part of the firing mechanism. The whole equipment will be safeguarded intact. All parts removed from AA will be properly prepared for storage, labelled with the number of the appropriate gun, segregated from guns, and safeguarded intact.

Searchlights:
All carbon rods will be removed from the projectors. The fuel pumps will be removed from the generators. The carbons and fuel pumps together with all carbon and fuel pump spares will be stored and safeguarded intact.

Small Arms:
All small arms will be collected and safeguarded intact.[57]

On 17 May Churchill went further. He advised the COS Committee that 'all reduction of Bomber Command is to be stopped. All reduction of the

Metropolitan Air Force, except Coastal Command, is to be stopped.' He followed this up with orders that the Royal Air Force in Italy was not to be demobilised and that all German aircraft under British control were not to be destroyed. He also gave instructions that demobilisation of the British Army was to be slowed down.[58] This was critical, since a cut in the numbers of an army unit would lower the effectiveness of that unit by far more than the actual percentage loss, so that if 10 per cent of a unit was demobilised (particularly if they were technical or highly skilled), the unit's fighting efficiency could fall by up to 50 per cent.[59]

But Churchill's insurance against a possible imminent conflict was countered by other new setbacks. Before Montgomery returned to Berlin, the embarrassing issue of the German Dönitz government had to be dealt with. An urgent meeting was held in London involving Churchill, Montgomery and Eisenhower and one of the items high on the agenda was the temporary German government, which was still in place more than a week after their surrender. Their transitory existence had offered the Allies a channel through which they could control the Wehrmacht, but Dönitz was now becoming an embarrassment. The British and American press were attacking the Allies' policy of keeping him in office while other top Nazis had been arrested, or committed suicide. Eisenhower saw his existence as an obstacle to better relations with the Soviets and it was decided that the Grand Admiral had to go. On 23 May troops surrounded the German HQ in Flensburg and arrested the occupants, who had, until recently, been operating with the consent of the Allies. Himmler simultaneously committed suicide in Allied custody.

At least Churchill was not alone in sensing the Soviet military threat to Britain. His coalition partner, the Labour leader, Clement Attlee, complained that the Soviets were 'behaving in a perfectly bloody way, telling us nothing, but setting up puppet governments all over Europe as far west as they could'.[60] And in a hardening of his rhetoric, Churchill told the Soviet ambassador in London, Feodor Gusev, that the British 'refused to be pushed about'. He complained of an 'iron screen' coming down and warned Gusev that he was going to postpone the demobilisation of the RAF, so that 'the British could discuss the security of Europe, backed up by military strength'.[61]

While the British prime minister continued on his dogged mission, his US allies were again veering away from confronting Stalin. Truman was now listening to the advice of Joseph Davies and his new secretary of state, James F. Byrnes, both of whom advocated restraining Churchill and accommodating Stalin. These US officials were influential men and were not inclined towards

Britain. Indeed, Davies had illustrated his anti-British credentials several years before when he told Stalin that after the war Britain would be financially ruined. Byrnes, despite being an appointed official, was heir apparent to Truman and it was generally agreed that his confidence in foreign affairs well exceeded his competence. Such was his sway with the president that it was no surprise when Truman later declared that 'I was having as much difficulty with Prime Minister Churchill as I was with Stalin.'[62]

However irritated the US president was with the harder British stance, he planned to make one last gesture to democracy in Poland. He would send his emissary Harry Hopkins to visit Stalin for private talks. Hopkins's brief would be to tell Stalin, in 'diplomatic language' that the US would carry out their obligations under the Yalta agreement and the US intended to see that Stalin fulfilled his side of the bargain. If Hopkins felt it was necessary, Truman told him, he could 'use a baseball bat if he thought that was a proper approach to Mr Stalin'.[63] But this was hardly Hopkins's style. Truman trusted him, though he described him as an 'advanced Liberal' rather than a 'parlour pink', yet Hopkins's close and sympathetic treatment of Stalin aroused enmity in some American quarters, and some were convinced he was a Soviet spy.

While US diplomacy plodded on in Moscow, the British were attempting to break the deadlock over the hotly contested region of Venezia Giulia. Ever since 7 May Alexander's representative, General Sir William 'Monkey' Morgan had been in tough negotiations with Marshal Tito over the territory, and by 21 May some progress had been made. Morgan had drawn up a provisional boundary between Yugoslavia and Italy, known as 'the Morgan Line', which Tito did not reject out of hand, though tensions rose as the British XIII Corps moved up to that line the following day.[64] The whole area remained a tinderbox.

These territorial and diplomatic crises would continue to erupt regardless of whether Churchill stayed in power. Having been so intimately involved with them, their solution was deeply personal to him, but what chance was there that he could survive in office? Senior Labour Party leaders in the coalition government, including Attlee, Bevin and Dalton, certainly entertained the idea of continuing the political alliance until the defeat of Japan, or possibly beyond, if certain social security and employment measures could become government policies. But they would have to win the approval of their party, which was probably impossible, given the mood of the rank and file of members, as well as their union colleagues. According to Lord Moran, the Labour members who met at the Blackpool Conference in mid-May were implacably opposed to continuing the coalition. 'They wouldn't look at it. Boiling with hate', he recorded. 'So the election will be in July.'[65] Consequently, the coalition broke up on 23 May and the Conservatives formed a caretaker government. The general election would be held on 5 July, but the result would not be declared until three weeks later when all the votes from troops in the Far East had been counted. At a stroke, the political consensus had vanished, as both the Conservative and Labour parties rushed to produce their own separate manifestoes. Even if Attlee and his senior party colleagues had warmed to the idea of Operation Unthinkable, it is inconceivable that they could have dragged along the bulk of their Labour parliamentary colleagues. The mood of the country was shifting and it was Churchill who was now in danger of being left behind. Lord Moran despaired at Churchill's combative mood:

No one agreed with the line that Winston had taken. He scoffs at 'those foolish people' who want to rebuild the world, but beneath this bluster he is, I believe, less certain about things. He has a feeling that he is back in the thirties, alone in the world, speaking a foreign tongue. And so he falls back on vituperation. He was brought up on that, and well it has served him in the Commons, where he could demolish the Stokeses and Shinwells. But now his blow seems to miss the mark. The war is over and the public are tired of strife, they do not want bickering. They want to get on with things.[66]

7

THE PLAN DELIVERED

The day after the coalition broke up, the Joint Planners finally presented their plan for Operation Unthinkable to the chiefs of staff. It was enclosed in a Ministry of Defence folder marked 'TOP SECRET – RUSSIA. THREAT TO WESTERN CIVILISATION '.[1]

On the morning of 24 May the chiefs had their regular meeting attended by the Joint Planners. The agenda involved operations in the Pacific, but at the end of the meeting the Planners left their file on Unthinkable with the chiefs for their consideration. In the evening the chairman of the Joint Chiefs, Field Marshal Sir Alan Brooke, settled down to read the plan and pondered its terrifying implications; he recorded in his diary:

> This evening I went carefully through the Planners' report on the possibility of taking on Russia should trouble arise in our future discussions with her. We were instructed to carry out this investigation. The idea is of course fantastic and the chances of success quite impossible. There is no doubt that from now onwards Russia is all powerful in Europe.[2]

Brooke later reflected on this diary entry and expanded on his thoughts:

> It may be remembered that a few weeks earlier, when examining the desirability of dismembering Germany after her defeat, the COS had then looked upon Russia as our future potential enemy. This paper had created a considerable stir in the Foreign Office, who considered it very remiss of us to look upon our present ally as our probable future enemy. We might even have been asked to withdraw this paper had we not asked for an interview with Anthony Eden, who approved our outlook. Now only a few weeks later [in fact it was months later], Winston had come to us expressing his anxiety at seeing 'that Russian bear sprawled over Europe', and instructing

us to examine from the military point of view the possibility of driving him back to Russia before the Americans and ourselves demobilized our forces! I asked him if he took charge of all the political aspects of launching a war on our ally! He said we could leave that aspect and concentrate on the military problem. Here I was on the evening of May 24th, a few days after VE Day, examining the results of the Planners' work on this problem. The result of this study made it clear that the best we could hope for was to drive the Russians back to about the same line the Germans had reached. And then what? Were we to remain mobilized indefinitely to hold them there?[3]

It was true that Brooke had reservations about many of Churchill's ideas. During the war, he had often held the balance between the four huge personalities of Churchill, Montgomery, Eisenhower and Marshall, who might otherwise have fallen out with each other. He did it not by tact but by being outspoken and direct. His umpiring was all the more credible because they all knew he had no desire for personal advancement. Brooke also harboured very mixed emotions about Churchill and his endeavours, and was bitter about his leader's lack of gratitude for all that the Joint Chiefs had achieved during the war. 'No recognition hardly at all for those who help him,' Brooke complained on the eve of VE Day, 'except the occasional crumb intended to prevent the dog straying too far from the table.'[4]

It was not just the Chief of the Imperial General Staff, who had an ambivalent relationship with Churchill. The First Sea Lord, Andrew Cunningham, known as 'ABC', respected his prime minister, but was never a wholehearted admirer, constantly fearing that many of Churchill's actions were motivated by a desire to gain closer control of the Admiralty.[5] The chiefs had seen plans instigated by Churchill before, and were understandably sceptical. Although they would diligently examine the report before them, their imagination was certainly not gripped by the prospect of Unthinkable. On 25 May Cunningham noted in his diary, 'drove to Broadlands Water on the Test. A lovely day, but no fish. CIGS caught a Chub!!' Brooke even went bird-watching the following day – not exactly the actions of a man who believed there was an immediate threat from Stalin.[6]

While Brooke and Cunningham deliberated on Churchill's plan, they were joined by the Vice-Chief of Air Staff, Sir Douglas Evill, who was deputising for the Air Chief, Air Marshal Sir Charles Portal. Evill had shared Portal's policy concerning not only the precision bombing of Germany but also the indiscriminate night-time bombing of her large population centres. If anything, Evill was more enthusiastic than Portal about the bombing campaigns as a means of causing widespread chaos in Germany. They had disrupted the passage of Wehrmacht reinforcements during the Second World War, but unfortunately, once the war was over, it would take years to shift the rubble from the streets of European cities and the destruction would seriously impede any advancing army. The sheer scale of the devastation, especially in the Soviet-controlled area of East Germany, may not have been fully appreciated by the Staff planners.

There was still no contact about Unthinkable between the British and US chiefs of staff. The US camp was wary of British intentions, a mentality encouraged by Hopkins when he returned on 6 June from his visit to Stalin. He reported that the American team had pushed for concessions over the make-up of the new Polish government and had received Stalin's agreement that four London Poles (Mikołajczyk, Grabski, Stanczyk and Kolodzei) would be 'invited to Moscow for consultation'. As for Stalin's imprisonment of the sixteen Polish underground leaders, Hopkins was assured by Stalin that 'they were apparently charged only with operating illegal radio transmitters.'[7] Truman was delighted with these results, but Churchill had heard it all before and reminded the president that 'we cannot cease our efforts on their behalf. These proposals are no advance on Yalta.'[8]

But Charles Bohlen, who witnessed Hopkins's discussions, concluded that Stalin and the Special Advisor had certainly agreed on one matter – that Britain was the irritant in the way of a deal over Poland:

> Marshal Stalin replied that the reason for the failure on the Polish question was that the Soviet Union desired to have a friendly Poland, but that Great Britain wanted to revive the system of *cordon sanitaire* on the Soviet borders.
>
> Mr Hopkins replied that neither the Government nor the people of the United States had any such intention.
>
> Marshal Stalin replied that he was speaking only of England and said that the British Conservatives did not desire to see a Poland friendly to the Soviet Union.
>
> Mr Hopkins stated that the United States would desire a Poland friendly to the Soviet Union and in fact desired to see friendly countries all along the Soviet borders.[9]

Furthermore, the president's Special Advisor remained 'sceptical about Churchill', and declared that it was 'of vital importance that we [the US] are not to be maneuvered into a position where Great Britain has us lined up with them as a bloc against Russia to implement England's European policy'.[10] Truman believed that he had fulfilled his commitments and now he saw the composition of any new Polish government as essentially a 'Russian–British–Polish' problem.[11]

At the same time that Hopkins was in Moscow, President Truman dispatched his emissary Joseph E. Davies to London. Truman's excuse for the visit was that he wished certain issues to be raised in person with Churchill rather than by cable. So, on the evening of 26 May, Davies visited Churchill at his official country residence, Chequers, but from the very start, it was an uncomfortable meeting. Davies was a bizarre choice to send to Britain. He had served as US ambassador to the Soviet Union before the war and was much taken with the Soviet 'experiment', revelling in their 'concepts of peace, justice and the brotherhood of man'. Needless to say his meeting with the prime minister, which lasted from 11.00 p.m. until 4.00 a.m., was a complete disaster. Davies began his pitch with the proposal that Truman should meet Stalin first, before any tripartite talks, because there was concern that the US and Britain should not be seen to be 'ganging up' against Stalin. Churchill was appalled that he should be squeezed out, but worse was to come. Davies then proceeded to play the old anti-Empire card:

> There are many who believe that England, finding now no great rival power in Europe to offset the new rising power of Russia, would try to use American manpower and resources to support the classic British policy of 'leading' Europe.[12]

It was a clear warning that Britain could not expect any support from the US for any Unthinkable-style adventures. Although Davies did not speak for the entire US administration, he represented the still-influential pro-Soviet, anti-imperial caucus in the State Department (among those could also be counted Stimson, Marshall and, to a lesser extent, Leahy). But Churchill retorted that, if needs be, England could stand alone to face the Soviet threat. 'She had done it before', Churchill warned an unrepentant Davies, who then left for further talks with the British foreign secretary, Anthony Eden. Again, this meeting was not a success. Eden was alarmed at the attitude of Truman's close advisor and thought that Davies was 'a vain amateur', but obviously a dangerous one. The pair met on 29 May, but according to Eden Davies's attitude 'didn't amount to more than an appeal for Russia'. Furthermore, Eden complained that Davies was 'a born appeaser and would gladly give Russia all Europe, except perhaps us, so that America might not be embroiled'.[13]

On 31 May the British chiefs of staff met, as they did on most days, at 1030 hours. Since the main part of the business was to discuss Unthinkable, the Joint Planners were also present. Brooke was quite clear in his diary about the conclusions reached. 'We again discussed the "Unthinkable war" against Russia at this morning's COS,' he noted. 'We became more convinced than ever that it is unthinkable!'[14] For the next few days, they would ruminate on their response to the prime minister.

Churchill was beginning to see the threat from the Left all around him, even in British domestic politics. On 4 June he gave a party political broadcast, a speech now constrained for the first time by a broadcasting time limit. But it failed to curtail his wild outburst against his Labour political opponents, who, he claimed, could only gain and hold onto power using a political police force, or 'some form of Gestapo'.[15] It was an unwise phrase and one that brought him much criticism. To many voters in the forthcoming election, it seemed that he could not let go of the war mentality, even though peace had now arrived. However, as far as Churchill was concerned, Britain and the free world were now facing a new enemy in the shape of encroaching communism.

While Churchill's alarm over Poland was not shared with the same intensity by Truman, the threat of communist encroachment into Italy did register with the US president. Truman was now prepared to endorse a British plan to keep Tito back by force. General Alexander had an operational plan for military action, which in Churchill's words would be 'sharp and short', and was sanctioned by the Supreme Commander, General Eisenhower. This would involve not only a move against Tito's inland positions but also an amphibious attack on the strategic port of Pola. Churchill contacted Truman on 2 June to prepare him for action:

It seems to me that unless Tito returns a satisfactory answer to your Ambassador and ours within three days of the presentation to him of the agreement we have drawn up, Alexander should be instructed to complete the occupation in force of such an area of Venezia Giulia as he may consider necessary for the protection of his lines of communication ... the fact that the Russians have so far remained quiescent is important. If we once let it be thought that there is no point beyond which we cannot be pushed about, there will be no future for Europe except another war more terrible than anything that the world has yet seen.[16]

Once more, in the face of a concrete battle plan, Truman changed tack again and qualified his support for the use of force. He declared to Churchill that he was unwilling to risk a war with Yugoslavia unless Tito attacked first and, even then, he could only tolerate a limited retaliation. Of course, foremost in Truman's mind was the forthcoming assault on Japan, and anything that could derail the massive build-up was to be evaded. 'I must not have any avoidable interference,' he warned Churchill, 'with the re-deployment of American forces to the Pacific.'[17] But Churchill feared that the Yugoslavs might think that the British combative stance was only bluff. So, to reinforce his case, he cabled Stalin to remind him of the help that Britain had given Tito during the war. 'We do not see why we should be pushed about everywhere,' Churchill complained, 'especially by people we have helped, and helped before you were able to make any contact with them.'[18]

The fact that the British, through SOE, had been assisting Tito's Partisans before the Soviets arrived on the scene clearly galled Churchill. And he would have been even more resolute had he known about the extent of the atrocities carried out by Tito's units since their occupation of Venezia Giulia at the end of April. The number of ethnic Italians murdered is hard to estimate, as many were shot and bundled into the *foiba* (natural wells and caves) that are found in the region. Croats and Slovenes were also eliminated by the Partisans. In fact anyone who opposed the communists was likely to be tortured or executed, even if they had previously opposed the fascists. There was also plenty of score-settling with former Mussolini supporters who had carried out the systematic slaughter of Slavs in the area. Whatever the ethnic make-up of those murdered, between 1,000 and 6,000 men and youths are thought to have perished in these *foiba*.[19]

While Churchill's attention was distracted by Tito, he could not afford to ignore developments in Poland. He was aware that if the Western Allies made the resolution of the new Polish government, and the fate of the imprisoned sixteen-man delegation, a prerequisite for talks at Potsdam, Stalin would simply ignore the talks. In his correspondence with Truman, Churchill despaired at the West's impotence in the face of Stalin. 'Renewed hope,' he reminded the president, 'and not rejoicing is all we can indulge in at the moment.'[20]

General Anders, ever mindful that Britain and the US might drop their support for the Western Poles, sought out Sir Alan Brooke in London. Anders took a hard line with Brooke, who was sufficiently battered after his encounter to note in his diary:

I had a difficult lunch with Anders at the Dorchester. He had just given up the appointment of Deputy Commander-in-Chief of the Polish Forces, and was about to return to the command of his old Corps in Italy. Just as fanatical as ever in his outlook on Russia, and determined if he can to increase the size of the Polish forces. He has no clear cut plans and just hopes for any further chance that may admit of his fighting his way back to Poland.[21]

There is no evidence that Anders knew Churchill had commissioned a contingency plan to attack the Soviet Union. But despite his recent row with the prime minister, Anders knew that Churchill was the only serious lifeline left for Poland. That lifeline was looking increasingly tenuous and it was about to be severely tested – the Chiefs of Staff Committee were just about to send their deliberations on the Unthinkable plan to Churchill. On 8 June, at the very moment that Anders was arguing with Brooke over lunch, the chiefs' report was dropped onto Churchill's desk. A covering letter from the secretary to the Chiefs of Staff Committee, Hastings Ismay, accompanied the top-secret papers:

Prime Minister

In the attached report on 'Operation UNTHINKABLE', the Chiefs of Staff have set out the bare facts, which they can elaborate in discussion with you, if you so desire. They felt that the less was put on paper on this subject the better.

HL Ismay.

There followed the report:

Prime Minister

In accordance with your instructions, we have considered our potential ability to exert pressure on Russia by the threat or use of force. We have confined ourselves in what follows to the barest outline of facts and figures. We could amplify these in discussion if you so desire.

And the 'barest outline of facts' meant a crushing superiority of Soviet manpower. The chiefs now summarised the details of the JPS Unthinkable report, but made an important change concerning the huge disparity of the size of the armies of East and West. While the planners had calculated

Allied forces available for the Allied offensive in 'Northern Europe' together with the Soviet forces that faced them in that region, the chiefs presented Churchill with the total estimated Allied forces in the European theatre on 1 July, as a whole (again, they converted Soviet divisions so they were comparable with Allied strengths). This swelled the Allied strength from 47 divisions to 103, and the Soviet strength from 170 equivalent divisions to 264. Looking at a conflict over the whole European theatre, the chiefs estimated an overall Soviet superiority of more than two to one, while their planners had calculated overall odds of nearly four to one in favour of the Soviets for the initial offensive in the north. There were no details given to Churchill of the numbers of divisions kept back for internal security, but the chiefs did provide a split, for the first time, of the make-up of Allied forces in Europe. On 1 July the US could field sixty-four divisions; the British and dominions, thirty-five divisions; and the Poles, four divisions.[22]

Again, when it came to air power, the chiefs elected to show Churchill the total aircraft strengths of the Allies and the Soviets in the whole European theatre. The allied Tactical Air Forces were reduced by 10 per cent, while their strategic aircraft numbers were increased by 10 per cent.[23] Meanwhile, the chiefs reduced their planners' estimates of Soviet aircraft by approximately 10 per cent. While Allied air strength appeared inferior to the Red Air Force, especially in fighter aircraft, it was reported that this advantage would be more than offset 'by the vastly superior handling and efficiency of the Allied Air Forces'. Despite that optimistic view, the allied air advantage could not be maintained, the chiefs argued, especially if losses mounted and could not be replaced quickly enough. This deficiency related as much to trained air crews as to actual aircraft. Meanwhile, the naval situation seemed assured. The chiefs merely stated, 'the Allies could, of course, achieve dominating superiority at sea.'[24]

The chiefs concluded:

It is clear from the relative strength of the respective land forces that we are not in a position to take the offensive with a view to achieving a rapid success. Since, however, Russian and Allied land forces are in contact from the Baltic to the Mediterranean, we are bound to become involved in land operations. In support of our land forces we should have our technically superior, but numerically inferior, tactical Air Forces. As regards Strategic Air Forces, our superiority in numbers and technique would be to some extent discounted by the absence of strategical [sic] targets compared with those which existed in Germany, and the necessity for using these Strategic Air Forces to supplement our Tactical Air Forces in support of land operations.

Our view is, therefore, that once hostilities began, it would be beyond our power to win a quick but limited success and we should be committed to a protracted war against heavy odds. These odds, moreover, would become fanciful if the Americans grew weary and indifferent and began to be drawn away by the magnet of the Pacific war.

A.F. BROOKE
ANDREW CUNNINGHAM
D.C.S. EVILL (For Chief Air Staff)[25]

Churchill pondered on the chiefs' decisive view that an attack on the Soviet Union was inconceivable. On 9 June he dictated his reply for the chiefs to Major-General Leslie Hollis, who delivered it to the Chiefs of Staff Committee the following day. Churchill's minute revealed an extraordinary about-turn:

I have read the Chiefs of Staff note on 'UNTHINKABLE' dated 8 June, which shows Russian preponderance of 2-1 on land.

If the Americans withdraw to their zone and move the bulk of their forces back to the United States and to the Pacific, the Russians have the power to advance to the North Sea and the Atlantic. Pray have a study made of how we could defend our Island, assuming that France and the Low Countries were powerless to resist the Russian advance to the sea. What Naval forces should we need and where would they be based? What would be the strength of the Army required, and how should it be disposed? How much Air Force would be needed and where would the main airfields be located? Possession of airfields in Denmark would give us great advantage and keep open the sea passage to the Baltic where the Navy could operate. The possession of bridgeheads in the Low Countries or France should also be considered.

By retaining the code word 'UNTHINKABLE', the Staffs will realise that this remains a precautionary study of what, I hope, is still a purely hypothetical contingency.[26]

Churchill was, more than ever, convinced about the Soviet threat but he heeded the advice of his chiefs that a military offensive was out of the question. The prospect of any sort of democratic representation in Poland was rapidly diminishing, and swift precautions were needed to ensure that

Britain, too, did not fall to Soviet domination. The chiefs swiftly ordered their Joint Planners to embark on a new report.

Meanwhile, on 11 June, Churchill called a Cabinet meeting to discuss the grave situation. A drained Field Marshal Brooke noted in his diary:

> At 5.30pm a Cabinet in which Winston gave a long and very gloomy review of the situation in Europe. The Russians were further West in Europe than they had ever been except once. They were all powerful in Europe. At any time that it took their fancy they could march across the rest of Europe and drive us back into our island. They had a 2 to 1 land superiority over our forces, and the Americans were returning home. The quicker they went home, the sooner they would be required back here again, etc, etc. He finished by saying that never in his life had he been more worried by the European situation than he was at present.[27]

At least there were some dividends from Churchill's tough foreign policy. On 9 June he breathed a sigh of relief when Yugoslavia signed the Belgrade Accord and Tito pulled his forces back from the disputed territory. Venezia Giulia was still a flashpoint but the immediate threat had receded and Truman could resume his commitment to the war in the Pacific. That was good news to many of his senior commanders, including Admiral King, the Chief of US Naval Staff, who was adamant that the American public would never accept that European operations should have priority over the Pacific theatre. Truman's desire to concentrate on the Pacific was also born out of his concern about the scale of casualties forecast for Operation 'Downfall', the plan for the invasion of mainland Japan. With this in mind, he sought the advice of ex-president Herbert Hoover, who advised Truman to end the war with Japan by negotiation rather than invasion. After all, the loss of up to one million US troops would not only be unacceptable, but also political suicide. It was advice Truman chose to reject and he decided that only the complete defeat and unconditional surrender of the Japanese would be acceptable. Downfall was back on, and even the US Chemical Warfare Service was consulted about the use of gas against the Kyushu defences prior to invasion. Japan remained a nightmare and Truman felt his problems were only exacerbated by his allies:

> Propaganda seems to be our greatest foreign relations enemy. Russians distribute lies about us. Our papers lie about and misrepresent the motives of the Russians – and the British out lie and out propagandize us both.[28]

Indeed, after the early hawkish weeks of the Truman presidency, advisors and commentators of American foreign policy were reasserting the importance of an independent US, free of pressure from the British, who were demonising the Soviet Union. The American left-wing publisher and war veteran Ralph Ingersoll spoke for an increasingly vocal lobby who did not want to 'antagonise the Russians on behalf of the British':

> Now in British eyes, the question of whether we will, if called upon, fight a war against Russia with them is crucial. There are not strong enough adjectives to describe its importance. The British are patently not strong enough to stand up to Russia by themselves and there is no one else but us, now, to win a war for their side. On the whole continent of Europe there are only the remnants of the beaten Fascists and Nazis, exiled Poles and starving Spaniards, for the British to recruit for war on Russia. During the war, the British attempted to manipulate our military policy so that we would fight the war the way they would like it fought – which was an anti-Russian way. They did not succeed. Now, with equal determination, they are attempting to manipulate American foreign policy to link our future irretrievably with theirs. If they succeed, and there is a third world war, we will surely fight it for them – against the Russians … I do not think this war would extinguish the human race. I think someone would win it first. It would however be a war to the extinction of either the Soviet Union or the British Empire and the United States.[29]

President Truman was ready to assert his independent line and troop withdrawals were a good place to start. In their advance into Germany in the closing weeks of the war, Allied forces had occupied ground beyond the agreed line and Churchill still wanted to retain that territory as a bargaining chip against Stalin. But Truman was no longer prepared to accept Churchill's stalling tactics. On 12 June he cabled the prime minister, informing him that 'I am unable to delay the withdrawal of American troops from the Soviet zone in order to use pressure in the settlement of other problems.' British chiefs of staff concurred with the American view and on 14 June a disappointed Churchill conceded, 'obviously we are obliged to conform to your decision.' He even dropped his condition that Allied withdrawal was conditional upon the resolution of the occupation of Austria. Consequently, British, American and French forces pulled back from their furthest positions into agreed zones.[30]

By mid-June, Field Marshal Montgomery, the Military Governor of the British-occupied German sectors, was finding himself overloaded with problems. He had 2.25 million German prisoners to guard and felt that he could do without the added responsibility of securing German weapons for what he thought was a precaution against any German resurgence. He could not fully understand the point of it all and sent an urgent memo to Field Marshal Brooke:

> I feel that I require some definite orders regarding the retention or destruction of German defences and weapons. At the moment there is a standstill order and nothing is being destroyed. Large scale coast defences and artillery weapons and ammunition create no immediate or urgent problem since the Germans could do little with them … I have many calls on my available manpower and am constantly trying to eliminate all guards and duties not absolutely vital. I recommend very strongly that I be given orders to destroy immediately the weapons.[31]

Montgomery was unaware at this stage, of course, of the true intent behind Churchill's order and he remained frustrated:

> On 14th June, I got fed up with guarding the weapons … the Coalition Government was coming to an end; it was impossible to get a decision, a firm one, on anything. I got no answer. I waited for one week. I then gave orders for all the personal weapons and equipment to be destroyed!! I did not tell the Prime Minister, nor the War Office, what I had done. I was, of course, in a very powerful position. I never heard any more about it.[32]

In fact he did hear more about it. Churchill was angry that Montgomery had been 'sounding off' to various newspaper reporters about the problems of holding German prisoners. The military government announced that all SS soldiers were being kept isolated from other formations and that they were likely to be kept locked up for at least 'twenty years'. He had also inferred that a similar fate awaited the German General Staff. These, the prime minister admonished, were matters to be dealt with by governments and not Field Marshals.[33]

While controversy mounted in occupied Germany, the 'other war' still raged in the Far East and its course had a material bearing on the likelihood of Unthinkable and the Japanese involvement. The early months of 1945 had proved to be extremely bloody for US forces trying to take Japanese-occupied islands. The Philippine-Luzon campaign in January had cost the lives of more than 8,000 Americans and seventeen US ships had been sunk by *Kamikaze* suicide bombers. The island of Iwo Jima fell the following month but at a cost of 29,000 US casualties, of whom 6,000 were killed. US air power enforced the pressure with a massive firebomb attack on Tokyo in March, resulting in the deaths of 100,000 Japanese inhabitants. But such actions had still failed to dent the will of the Japanese military to carry on the war. The battle for the island of Okinawa continued until June and again the US forces suffered terrible losses, with nearly 50,000 casualties. It was clear that this could not carry on, month after month, and contingency plans were well advanced for either a sustained and massive aerial bombing campaign against Japan, or for amphibious assaults against the Japanese Home Islands, or, indeed, a combination of both. On 18 June President Truman signed off the definitive plan, Operation Downfall, which allowed for a twin-phased invasion of Japan, starting in November 1945 with an assault on the southern Japanese home island of Kyushu. The main invasion near Tokyo Bay would follow.[34]

In the weeks following the end of the war in Europe, the US had instituted a huge reallocation of men and materials from the European to the Pacific theatre in preparation for Operation Downfall. The Combined Staff Planners (British and US) had calculated that 1,615,200 US troops and 396,400 British troops (including 42,700 dominion troops) would be moved from Europe to the Far East during the six months after VE Day. By 1 July 1945 perhaps a quarter of these forces would have been redeployed by surface ships and transatlantic air lifts and then if Unthinkable happened, all movements to the Far East would cease.[35] In addition to these changes, there were the demobilisations of US, British and dominion forces, which would further deplete the standing Allied forces in Europe. Whether it was the Allied forces which made the first move, or the Soviets, the massive reduction in US and British manpower looked critical for the West.

Meanwhile the controversy surrounding the composition of the Polish government showed no signs of a resolution. The West's main candidate for inclusion was Mikołajczyk, but his position was looking bleak. 'Mikołajczyk has great misgivings', Churchill reported. 'He feels that in the absence of Witos [a moderate ex-Lublin Committee member], he will be completely isolated in the conversations and that whatever he or Stanczyk say will be discounted, on the grounds that they are people who know nothing of what is happening inside Poland'.[36] Mikołajczyk was not keen to go to Moscow, since he was well aware the forthcoming election would be a sham. But Churchill pushed him, on the grounds that if he prevaricated, Stalin would announce that he had invited the Western Poles to join the government but they had refused to participate. Finally, on 16 June, much to Churchill's relief, Mikołajczyk, with five other democrats, finally agreed to join the Polish provisional government of National Unity. Churchill enthused to Mikołajczyk:

> The results that have been achieved seem to me to give the greatest hope of a reconciliation of the Polish National Power. This can only be done through friendship to Russia. The Soviets will, I am sure, appreciate kindly, action on your part as helping to bring them and the Western Democracies together. I think you have done very well indeed.[37]

But on 18 June Stalin showed how far his 'friendship' extended to Poland, when the show trial of the 'Polish Sixteen' opened in the Hall of Columns in Moscow. It was cynically timed to coincide with the announcement of the first Moscow meeting of the provisional Polish government, where Mikołajczyk and his colleagues were heavily outnumbered by the communist PPR members and their Soviet-leaning allies.[38] It would become the pattern for other Soviet-dominated governments of Eastern Europe, whereby the communists would control the key posts, including the police, justice system and interior ministries, while the 'democrats' would be handed the less significant portfolios. While the provisional government meeting was under way, the outcome of the trial of the exhausted sixteen was never in doubt, with trumped-up charges of 'planning armed action together with Germany against the USSR'. According to the communist party mouthpiece *Pravda*, 'The Polish-Fascist Bandits' were guilty of murdering hundreds of peaceful Red Army soldiers. With such a loaded case the outcome was obvious. All but three of the men were imprisoned, and several, including General Okulicki, would subsequently die in jail in suspicious circumstances.[39]

The Poles were not the only human fodder used by Stalin. According to Averell Harriman there had been nearly 5,000 Allied officers and men held in Soviet-occupied areas of Poland in March 1945. They were released piecemeal and despite attempts by the Western Allies to have the remainder freed, Stalin was hedging again. Many of the POWs were held deep inside Soviet territory and were useful leverage for Stalin in persuading the US to recommence Lend-Lease aid, which had been suspended in May.[40] Stalin, nevertheless, had sought to allay Western fears:

> As regards British prisoners of war, your fears for their welfare are groundless. They have better conditions than the Soviet prisoners of war in British camps

where in a number of cases they were ill-treated and even beaten. Moreover they are no longer in our camps, being on their way to Odessa, whence they will leave for home.[41]

The British were relieved that a face-saving operation had been reached over the new provisional Polish government. Of the twenty members, three came from outside the country, including Mikołajczyk, and three were selected as non-Lublin members from inside the country. It had the very thinnest veneer of a democratic government and no one can have failed to realise that it was a complete whitewash. But it offered a way out to the British Foreign Office and the American State Department, who were desperate to finish with the matter and move on. Even SOE were desperately grasping at straws, and seemed pathetically grateful for Stalin's 'concessions':

> It is certain that the Lublin Committee have been quite generous in their allocations, since Interior [Kiernik] and Agriculture [Mikołajczyk] are two key posts, and Social Welfare [Stanczyk] is of quite considerable importance.[42]

These sham posts held little importance in the future government, but Britain and the US were now able to say that the provisions of Yalta had been carried out and arrangements were put in hand to recognise the Soviet-sponsored provisional government. An urgent top-secret cipher from the British War Office to FM Montgomery confirmed this intention and Montgomery was ordered not to communicate this to any of the Polish troops under his command, especially since it meant that the London Polish government was to be abandoned. The posts of both the minister of defence (Kukiel) and commander-in-chief (Bor-Komorowski) would most likely disappear, but the immediate concern of the War Office was a possible split within the Polish armed forces over supporters and opponents of the new regime. It was also far from clear whether the British would prevent their former military allies from being forcibly repatriated to Poland.[43] According to Field Marshal Brooke, this was a problem that the Foreign Office had refused to face:

> We are now faced with difficulties ahead concerning future of Polish Forces! In a few days we shall be recognising the Warsaw government officially and liquidating the London one. The Polish forces then present a serious conundrum which the Foreign Office has done little to solve in spite of repeated applications for [a] ruling ever since May![44]

The British government was also thrown off-balance by the US decision to rush through recognition of the new Soviet-backed regime in Poland. Churchill reprimanded Truman:

> I was surprised at your No. 83 [telegram], giving me only a few hour's notice of your decision to recognise the new Polish Government. Our position is different from yours. The old Polish Government is seated here in London, with officials and very large staffs. It administers a Polish army of 170,000 men, whose attitude has to be carefully considered … We had been hoping to give the London Poles at least 24 hour's notice, which seems only reasonable.[45]

The US administration, and particularly the State Department, was unconcerned about British sensibilities. They portrayed Britain as the driving force behind a European Bloc as a counter to Soviet domination in Europe, as well as a belligerent imperial power that was out of its depth in the new order:

> It is apparent that any future world conflict in the foreseeable future will find Britain and Russia in opposite camps … In a conflict between these two powers the disparity in the military strengths that they could dispose upon that continent would, under present conditions, be far too great to be overcome by our intervention on the side of Britain. Having due regard to the military factors involved – resources, manpower, geography and particularly our ability to project our strength across the ocean and exert it decisively upon the continent – we might be able to successfully defend Britain, but we could not, under existing conditions, defeat Russia. In other words, we would find ourselves engaged in a war which we could not win even though the United States would be in no danger of defeat and occupation.[46]

It was a sober assessment, but within weeks the US administration could find it was dealing with a new British government with new foreign policies. On 5 July, after a gruelling election campaign, British civilians and servicemen abroad cast their votes. Although the results would not be heard for three weeks – to allow counting of the Far East votes – Churchill's doctor, Lord Moran, feared the worst for his patient. 'It is clear that the PM is on the wrong tack … for the first time the thought went through my head that he may lose the election'.[47] Churchill had not yet lost the election but he had certainly lost the battle over Poland. On 6 July the British government formerly recognised the new provisional Warsaw government and the London-based Polish government-in-exile had to act quickly to defend its members and its armed forces. There were vast quantities of II Bureau intelligence papers in their possession which could compromise anti-communist Poles and they were determined to put them beyond the reach of their opponents. In London large bonfires destroyed much of the intelligence material relating to the Soviet Union, as well as Polish personnel files, while the remainder of the papers were passed to the British authorities.[48]

Inside Poland many of the former II Bureau intelligence cells were now disconnected from their former diplomatic missions, their records were destroyed and transmitters were hidden for future operations against the occupying power. Recognition of the new Polish government by the other puppet governments of Eastern Europe was already assured, though not all ministers were happy.[49] Meanwhile, official British government policy attempted to smother Polish underground activities and to clamp down on radio contact between Polish bases in Britain and resistance cells in Poland. The Poles tried to circumvent this by the use of couriers, but their failure to establish a radio broadcasting system in Poland was a major setback for them.

The practical effect of the Western Allies recognising the pro-Soviet Polish provisional government was that General Anders and his Polish forces in the west were now free to pursue their own agenda. Since their previous masters, the Polish government-in-exile, had now been disowned by the British and American governments, individual Polish commanders feared for their future, and it was possible that the whole army would fracture. Although they were still financed by Britain, as the weeks went on it would be increasingly difficult for the British Army to incorporate the Poles in their future plans. Yet once the events of early July unfolded, it was elements of the Polish army who were the most keen to take on the Soviet Union. Ignoring the war-weariness of the West, they continued to believe that armed conflict with Stalin was inevitable. As early as August 1944 the Polish General Staff prepared a report anticipating that Britain would be at war with the Soviet Union within ten years. So with this in mind, General Anders had continued to sanction recruitment to the Polish Army, even accelerating the process in the immediate aftermath of VE Day, allowing his forces to balloon to an estimated 250,000 men by the late summer of 1945.[50]

Polish forces continued to swell, but what was the state of the British army and would it still be able to take on the Red Army in the summer of 1945? Whether by deliberate design or bureaucracy, demobilisation had slowed to a trickle. In the first two months of peace, only 200,000 men and women had been demobilised – just one-twentieth of all servicemen. There was a growing clamour to speed up the rate, especially from the press, and this impatience would grow even further once Japan was defeated. But there is no doubt that general security concerns among service chiefs played a part in this sluggish release, though there is no evidence to link it directly to Unthinkable. Churchill was now, at the very least, keen to release servicewomen. 'They do not mutiny,' he told his Cabinet, 'or cause disturbances, and the sooner they are back in their homes the better.'[51]

There was some hope that a future conflict could be averted, if only the three great leaders could meet in person. After some wrangling about venues and dates, Potsdam, just outside Berlin, was chosen for a conference and Churchill, Truman, Stalin and their retinues left for the last great meeting of the Big Three. On 8 July Truman sailed to the conference on board the warship USS *Augusta*. He was initially in good heart, enjoying a Technicolor Bob Hope film and warming to the sound of the ship's eight-inch guns practice-firing. Harking back to his artillery experience during the Great War, he lamented, 'I'd still rather fire a battery than run a country.' The artillery exercise was also witnessed by another of the president's advisors, Charles Bohlen, assistant to the secretary of state. Bohlen observed a scene that was sadly symbolic of Britain's position within the Big Three:

> Truman and Secretary Byrnes were standing on a three-gun turret when it fired a salvo. Two of the guns went off properly. The third gave a sort of belch, and a shell eased out of the muzzle and fell into the water a hundred yards or so from the ship.[52]

Truman was going to Potsdam unwillingly, and only on the condition that he could push America's own agenda. 'How I hate this trip,' he noted in his diary, 'but I have to make it – win, lose or draw – and we must win. I'm not working for any interest, but the Republic of the United States.' To this end, he turned down the possibility of visiting Britain before the conference so that there could be no accusations from Stalin about Britain and the US 'ganging up' against him. The Big Three were already going their separate ways.[53]

8

FORTRESS BRITAIN

As the president cruised towards northern Europe, an exhausted Churchill took the opportunity of a few days rest after the election and a chance to refresh himself before Potsdam. He and his wife, Clementine, stayed at the Château de Bordaberry, overlooking the Bay of Biscay in south-west France, painting and swimming, or, more accurately, floating. Churchill's private secretary, Jock Colville, recorded in his diary that 'the Prime Minister floated, like a benevolent hippo, in the middle of a large circle of protective French policemen who had duly donned bathing-suits for the purpose.'[1] When he was not bathing, Churchill painted coastal scenes at St Jean-de-Luz and Hendaye, using rich colours from his paint box to depict the dramatic Atlantic seashore.[2]

Meanwhile, on 11 July, as the prime minister enjoyed a brief moment of relaxation in France, his chiefs of staff in London received their first glimpse of the second report on Operation Unthinkable. It had taken a month for the same JPS team of Grantham, Thompson and Dawson to report back on 'what measures would be required to ensure the security of the British Isles in the event of war with Russia in the near future'. It was, of course, highly sensitive, even by the standards of national security and the normal staffs in the services ministries were not consulted. The premise was quite conceivable, for one of Stalin's cherished ambitions was to control a unified greater Germany, and his Red Army might not stop at the Rhine.[3] The report, however, assumed that the Red Army had overrun the whole of Western Europe and were poised to attack Britain, but there was no discussion as to how quickly and by what method the Soviets would conquer Europe.

There would have been some warning of a Soviet invasion, hopefully via British Intelligence, but the job of gathering intelligence on Red Army dispositions was never straightforward. Extracting information from German intelligence officers about Soviet movements caused a crisis of conscience for senior British intelligence officers, such as Dick White. 'I would have objected to the use of a Nazi as an agent,' he curtly noted, but 'the prospect never arose.' The Americans, however, had no such qualms and were not only using German *Abwehr* officers, but were even 'pinching' British agents. Britain's pre-eminent place in the world of espionage was slipping, as was the relationship between the British and US intelligence services.[4] The British Embassy in Moscow was obviously a conduit for local intelligence and debate about Soviet intentions. Staff spent endless hours poring over the Soviet press, such as *Pravda*, *Izvestia* or the English-language *Moscow Evening News*, as well as any number of technical journals for information about the strength of Soviet armaments. Then there were diplomatic trips to Kiev or Leningrad during April and May 1945, when the presence of the NKVD was not quite as claustrophobic as it would shortly become. There were gaps and opportunities, through which diplomats could talk to local people or glimpse 'off limits' areas.

Even if the West had some prior notice of a Soviet attack, it would only take the Red Army weeks to arrive on the French border. But what were the constraints on the Soviet operations? One major problem for the Red Army would be their long lines of communication, and once they had pushed their vast 'Front' units out of Eastern Europe they would no longer find themselves a majority force in their occupied territories, such as Poland, Ukraine and Germany. Resistance fighters in those countries could rise up in significant numbers and cause serious problems behind the Soviet lines.[5]

Nonetheless, the planners opened their report with the blunt scenario:

The following are the main methods by which the Russians might attempt to attack the British Isles after they had reached the shores of the North Sea and Atlantic:

– By cutting our sea communications
– By invasion
– By air attack
– By rocket or other new methods

It was believed that the Soviets were unable to mount a submarine or air attack on Allied shipping, at least nowhere near the capability of the German threat in the Second World War. Reassuringly, it would take some years for Soviet technology to catch up, especially in submarine design. So, if the Soviets could not cut British sea communications, could they launch a successful invasion of Britain? They were unlikely to rely just on airborne operations and if they came ashore by landing craft, they would need to land in very large numbers to establish a beachhead. But the Soviets would be severely handicapped by their inexperience in such amphibious operations, and, having little or no merchant navy of their own, they could hardly support them. Most Allied merchant shipping would have been already withdrawn from Atlantic ports or otherwise scuttled in advance of the approaching Red Army; the threat of an invasion was always present but because of Soviet limitations the planners decided that the threat of invasion was not imminent.[6]

Being overwhelmed by the Red Air Force was another possibility. Although their strategic bomber force was not rated by British advisors, the flying distance from coastal air bases in France or the Low Countries to Britain was short enough to bring industrial and military targets within easy range. Although Soviet tactical bombers were normally trained to support land operations, they could easily adapt for such an important mission and their sheer numbers could pose a threat. The RAF could expect to inflict very heavy losses on the Red Air Force, but its victory was by no means assured. However, it was the prospect of an attack by rockets or pilotless aircraft that posed the most concern:

> The Russians are likely to begin large scale production of these weapons at an early date. We must expect a far heavier scale of attack than the Germans were able to develop, and we do not at present see any method of effectively reducing this. This would be the main threat over the considerable period which must elapse before the Russians can contemplate any attempt at invasion.[7]

The planners were right to acknowledge this menace from the new weapons, for the Soviets were racing to develop copies of the German V-2, as well as 'pilotless aircraft'. But fortunately for the Allies, they were some way from manufacturing large rockets capable of crossing the Channel. It was true that they had acquired detailed plans and operational knowledge of the V-2 rocket when their forces overran the Blizna testing ground in south-east Poland in August 1944.[8] They were also due to receive the captured V-2 plant at Nordhausen from the Americans on 1 July 1945 (ironically the same date as Unthinkable had been due to start). But even then, the Soviets still did not possess any stocks of captured, complete V-2 rockets and neither did they have the services of enough German scientists. They did manage to secure some, but they were not even communist sympathisers. Helmut Gröttrup, a former assistant to the director of the Guidance, Control and Telemetry Laboratory at Peenemünde, had other motives, as his wife later confided:

> They [the Americans] grabbed Wernher von Braun, Hüter, Schilling, Steinhoff, Gröttrup and other leading rocket experts. We were housed at Witzenhausen and interrogated. After weeks had passed, Helmut was handed a contract offering him a transfer to the USA without his family, a contract terminable by one signatory only: the US Army. Since we wanted to remain in Germany, we moved back to the Russian Zone.[9]

It would be another year before scientists such as Gröttrup could begin to turn out Soviet V-2 rockets in sufficient quantity to endanger the West.[10] The planners did not detail the type of rockets that posed a threat, but it would not come from the smaller Katyusha type. After all, the closest distance between France and England was 26 miles and the most powerful existing rocket, the M-13 DD, only had a range of 7 miles. However, if the rocket threat materialised any earlier, the main British defence would depend on anti-aircraft batteries, rather than the RAF – at least as far as Churchill was concerned. He had already attacked Sir Archibald Sinclair over claims that it was the RAF which had defeated the V-weapons:

> You have no grounds to claim that the RAF frustrated the attacks by the V weapons. The RAF took their part, but in my opinion, their effort ranks definitely below that of the AA Artillery and still further below the achievements of the Army in clearing out all the establishments in the Pas de Calais. As to the V2, nothing has been done or can be done by the RAF.[11]

To reduce the threat from rockets, the possibility of retaining bridgeheads on the continent was considered. By holding on to coastal areas, the idea was to deprive the Red Army of launch sites. If they had to fire rockets from further inland, aimed at London, it would be beyond the range of a V-2 type. But it was out of the question to expect an Allied army to hold on to a continual stretch of continental coastline in the face of such massive enemy forces. However, peninsulas such as Cherbourg or Brittany could be considered, along with Denmark or Western Holland, though concentrating Allied troops in these compact areas would provide the enemy with an easy target. In the end, the planners came down against establishing bridgeheads for the following reasons:

The range of the present rocket would necessitate the holding of a continuous front well into France and the Low Countries, if the scale of attack by this method is to be seriously affected.

If used as bases for a return to the continent, we should be sacrificing surprise and would enable the enemy to build up against us at leisure.

Except in the case of Denmark, use of which is limited by way of lack of harbours on the north and west coasts, the air forces we could station in the bridgehead would be little greater than those required to support the troops defending it.[12]

Rockets were obviously an insoluble problem for the planners, who were more comfortable with the idea of conventional warfare and planning for the possibility of the Red Army sitting in captured French fortifications across the Channel. How would British commanders deploy their forces to defend the homeland? There would be the risk of a Soviet airborne invasion or amphibious landings, or both, and there would have to be mobile British units to deal with these threats – garrisons would need to be sent to defend urban and industrial centres, as well as ports. As for the defence of the rest of the country, that would be in the hands of some twenty British and US infantry and armoured divisions, deployed south of a line between the Severn and the Wash, with a concentration in the south-east of the country. The bulk of these forces were already in Britain, but they would have to be supplemented by troops withdrawing from Europe in the face of a Soviet advance. The speed of the retreat on the continent would mean a lot of their heavy equipment would be left behind. Indeed, the loss of equipment and the ability of British industry to replace it and keep its forces continually supplied would require industrial capacity to be substantially raised.[13]

There was no reference in the plan to the possibility of an actual Soviet occupation of the British mainland, or indeed the provisions to set up a British government-in-exile in somewhere such as Canada, Newfoundland or South Africa.[14] There was some reassurance, however, that the Royal Navy and RAF would provide a safe cordon around the country, with the local naval forces guarding the southern and eastern approaches and the Home Fleet protecting the northern waters. Depending on how the Soviet threat developed, convoy escorts would be required at a later date.[15]

If the planners had unbounded faith in the Royal Navy, they had even more confidence in the ability of the Royal Air Force to deal with the Red Air Force, but only if both RAF and USAAF squadrons could be recalled from Europe in time to operate from British bases. To this end, RAF aircraft and personnel would be held back from deployment in the Far East, though the effect this would have on the continuing war against Japan was not calculated. Even if these conditions were met, the combined Anglo-American air force would need to muster 230 fighter squadrons, 100 tactical bomber and 200 heavy bomber squadrons.[16]

The planners concluded:

> It is only by the use of rockets and other new weapons that the Russians could develop any serious threat to the security of this country in the initial stages. Invasion or a serious attack upon our sea communications could only be undertaken after a period of preparation which must last some years.[17]

While the chiefs of staff contemplated the JPS report, Churchill continued his long-overdue break in France, pending the start of the Potsdam Conference. 'I'm going to relax completely,' he informed his doctor. 'I'm not going to look at any papers.'[18] It was clear he was not going to digest any government documents, and that included any new papers on Operation Unthinkable. They would have to wait. On 15 July, without returning to London, he flew from Bordeaux to Berlin for the beginning of the Potsdam conference.

Churchill invited Attlee to join him at Potsdam, pending the results of the British general election and Attlee flew out to the conference on 15 July, much to the surprise of the Soviet delegation, who could not understand why the leader of the opposition party should be included. By the time of the conference Allied troops had been withdrawn to the agreed zones, and Eden, as foreign secretary, was preparing to 'tie up the loose ends' of the Polish machination. Although Churchill remained depressed at not achieving his goal over Poland, he entered the conference room at Potsdam knowing that the Allies still had a major card to play – a card that could change the whole strategic balance.

Even before the first atomic test in July, the British had given their consent in principle to its use against the Japanese. Churchill confirmed that support for the bomb was emphatic:

> The historic fact remains, and must be judged in the after-time, that the decision whether or not to use the atomic bomb to compel the surrender of Japan was never an issue. There was unanimous, automatic, unquestioned agreement around our table.[19]

Truman entered the rooms at the Cecilienhof Palace in Potsdam fully briefed about the impending Trinity atomic test.[20] The conference was due to start on 16 July, but Stalin had suffered a minor heart attack and the start of business was rescheduled for the following day. It was no wonder then that Major-General Leslie Hollis remarked 'in the eighteen months since I first saw him [Stalin] at Teheran, his hair had gone as white as the tunic he wore.'[21] Churchill used the spare day to visit Berlin and the ruins of the Reich Chancellery. Lord Moran, who accompanied the PM, noted that Churchill was strangely unmoved by the surroundings. He was not even excited by the prospect of seeing the entrance to the bunker and the scene of the last sordid days of his bitter enemy. He took a few steps down into the bunker and promptly came back up into the ruined gardens. 'Hitler must have come out here to get some air,' he ventured, 'and heard the guns getting nearer and nearer.'[22]

A battered chair, hastily rescued from the bunker, was brought forward for a photo opportunity, and the prime minister dutifully sat down. 'Churchill tries out Hitler's chair for size', trumpeted the subsequent headlines, but there was little triumph in Churchill's demeanour. He was, no doubt, thinking of the forthcoming meetings and his first real discussions with Truman. He had met the president fleetingly before and had spoken to him on the telephone, but this was the first time they had met as world leaders. The PM was impressed with Truman but the feelings were not entirely mutual. 'I'm sure we can get along,' Truman cautiously noted in his diary, 'if he doesn't try to give me too much soft soap.'[23] When Truman finally met Stalin the following day, he had no such reservations about the Soviet leader. 'I can deal with Stalin. He is honest – but smart as hell.'[24] Some of Stalin's pronouncements certainly chimed with Truman, especially when he mentioned he would like to divide up some of the old colonies and mandates.

Business got under way quickly, despite the constant interruptions caused by delegates leaving the meeting rooms – diarrhoea was rampant, due to pollution of the local water supply – while the main concern of three British chiefs of staff was the plague of mosquitos ever present around their lakeside villa. Brooke, Portal and Cunningham made time for the odd spot of recreation, though the British chiefs were disappointed to be told that the nearby Lake Griebnitzsee was polluted by dead bodies and the fish had been blown up by hand grenades. Nevertheless, the Chief of the Imperial General Staff could still be seen in a canoe, with fishing rod in hand, being paddled around the lake by the Marshal of the RAF.[25]

As the delegates prepared for their meetings, 6,000 miles away in a small military installation in the Jornada de Muerto desert in southern New Mexico, US scientists were about to experiment with a world-changing weapon. Just before dawn on 16 July, a truck arrived at the site bearing an innocuous-looking metal sphere. The ball looked simple enough, and, with a radius of 4ft 6in, it very much resembled a sea mine. The 4-ton load was hoisted off the truck and placed on the ground. Then, with due reverence, a canopy was placed over it, allowing technicians to adjust the device in complete and sterile privacy. The ball was then raised high up into a gantry, some 100ft above the ground. At precisely 5.29 a.m., 'Fat Man' was detonated. The plutonium bomb vaporised the gantry and eliminated all desert life within half a mile. Equivalent to the result of using 20 kilotons of TNT, the blast created an 'oven heat' that was felt 10 miles away, and its searing light was sufficient to cause temporary blindness at that distance.[26] J. Robert Oppenheimer, the scientific director of the Manhattan Project tasked with developing the atomic bomb, solemnly witnessed the Trinity test explosion:

> We knew the world would not be the same. A few people laughed. A few people cried. Most people were silent. I remembered the line from the Hindu scripture, 'Now I am become Death, the destroyer of worlds'. I suppose we all thought that, one way or another.[27]

On 18 July Truman informed Churchill about the results of the atomic test. Before he had left for Potsdam, Churchill had asked Truman to cable him as soon as the news came through as to 'whether it is a flop or a plop'. The telegram read 'It's a plop. Truman.'[28] At Churchill's request the president held off from telling Stalin until 24 July. Even then Stalin did not seem to be particularly impressed or surprised at the news. There is no doubt that he knew of the progress of the US Manhattan Project through such spies as Klaus Fuchs, whose information was 'of great value' to the Soviets and was later exposed in the Venona transcripts.[29] Stalin would also have been familiar with the earlier Anglo-American atomic co-operation, known as the Tube Alloys project, from Soviet agents inside Whitehall, London. However, he may not have understood the full implications until the bomb was dropped on Hiroshima several weeks later. Only then did Stalin and Beria break into a gallop with the development of a Soviet nuclear programme.

The explosion of an atomic bomb was also another massive jolt to Stalin's view of his future relations with the West. Together with Roosevelt's death, in April 1945, these two seismic changes in the international landscape reawakened Stalin's 'old demons of insecurity'. He would now have to deal with a material shift in the balance of military power, as well as a new host of diplomatic figures, including, shortly, a change in the British leadership. Such insecurity was also felt by Stalin's colleagues. Yuli Khariton, one of the early Soviet atomic designers, gloomily concluded that 'the Soviet Government interpreted Hiroshima as atomic blackmail against the USSR, as a threat to unleash a new, even more terrible and devastating war.' The Soviets were now well aware that the USAAF was capable of delivering atomic bombs, from their bases in Europe and the Middle East, to the very heart of Stalin's empire. The bomb also hammered home to Stalin that if Japan quickly capitulated, he could swiftly lose his chance to enact the Yalta agreement and capture strategic territory around Manchuria and Japan and thereby improve his security in the east.[30]

News on 16 July that the plutonium-based bomb was successful meant that the Americans might not need to worry about pushing the Soviets to enter the war against Japan – could they now finish off Japan on their own? At this stage the US military did not think that atomic bombs could ensure victory on their own, but would instead be a powerful addition to the mix of bombardment necessary to support the land invasion of Japan in the autumn of 1945. A much simpler uranium bomb, known as 'Little Boy', was also being developed, though this would not require a test explosion. Even so, little was known about the effect of radiation, and army commanders even discussed using the bombs tactically to soften up beach defences around the Japanese mainland.

The success of the Trinity test theoretically released the West from the obligation of courting Stalin and should have freed them to take a hard line with him over Poland and the other occupied Eastern European states. According to Field Marshal Sir Alan Brooke, Churchill was jubilant about the new bomb:

> He had absorbed all the minor American exaggerations and as a result was completely carried away. It was now no longer necessary for the Russians to come into the Japanese War, the new explosive alone was sufficient to settle the matter! ... Furthermore, we now had something in our hands which would redress the balance with the Russians.[31]

The Potsdam leaders issued a final ultimatum for a Japanese surrender, but this was swiftly rejected by the Japanese prime minister, who announced that his forces would fight on. He was secretly trying to obtain a peace agreement with the Chinese, so that large numbers of Japanese troops could be released for the defence of the Home Islands. The Japanese military were hell-bent on continuing the war, but US decrypts of telegrams revealed that some Japanese politicians were looking for someone to broker a peace deal with the Allies. They were in a minority, so the US bombing onslaught against the Japanese mainland and islands continued. Raids by up to 500 Superfortresses and 1,000 carrier aircraft blitzed Tokyo, Nagoya, Yokohama, Osaka and Kobe, together with numerous oil refineries and ports.

Despite his euphoria over the bomb, Churchill was by now physically, if not mentally, exhausted. And as the PM's health deteriorated, Eden increasingly took on the responsibility for the British delegation at Potsdam. 'The PM is not mastering his brief,' Lord Moran noted, 'he is too tired to prepare anything.' Yet Churchill was invigorated by the new military and political advantage that the bomb had given the West. 'He was completely carried away,' noted Field Marshal Brooke, 'and was delighted to think that the bomb could redress the power balance with Stalin. "Now we could say," Churchill enthused, "if you insist on doing this or that, well we can just blot out Moscow, then Stalingrad, then Kiev, then Kuibyshev, Karkhov, Sebastapol [sic]. And now where are the Russians!!!!"'[32] Brooke later conceded that Churchill was right to appreciate that the atomic bomb had shifted the balance of military power:

> Winston's appreciation of its value in the future international balance of power was certainly far more accurate than mine. But what was worrying me was that with his usual enthusiasm for anything new, he was letting himself be carried away by the very first and rather scanty reports of the first atomic explosion. He was already seeing himself capable of eliminating all the Russian centres of industry and population, without taking into account any of the connected problems, such as delivery of the bomb, production of bombs, possibility of Russia also possessing such bombs etc. He had at once painted a wonderful picture of himself as the sole possessor of these bombs and capable of dumping them where he wished, thus all powerful and capable of dictating to Stalin![33]

The atomic bomb had clearly reignited Churchill's hopes of Unthinkable, though as Brooke reflected, it was the US who had the bomb and controlled its use, and not Britain.[34] Even then, in 1945 there were great logistical problems in dropping an atom bomb. It was one thing for a B-29 bomber to pass through heavily depleted Japanese air defences, but quite another to attempt to penetrate a web of densely packed anti-aircraft defences across the Soviet Union. The aircraft bearing the bomb would have to fly at night, negotiate heavy ground fire and fighter inceptors, and then drop its bomb from a high altitude using radar, for which scope returns had to be prepared. Because at this stage US policy was still defiantly set on a course of accommodation with Stalin, there was little chance of a 'first-strike' against the Soviet Union. Anyway, the stock of atomic bombs was still extremely limited and until the development of rocket delivery, there remained the hindrance of enemy defences shooting down any bomb-laden aircraft.

Although Churchill had thrown in a number of Soviet city targets, such target data, especially east of Moscow, was very basic and few accurate maps existed. Even if these sites could be identified, factories manufacturing aircraft, ordnance and ball-bearings were heavily defended. The atomic bomb delivery aircraft, the B-29, had a radius of some 2,000 miles, so when it was operating out of US airbases only a limited number of Soviet targets could be attacked. The alternative was to operate from forward air bases in Europe, such as East Anglia, or Foggia, in Italy, but none of these had the necessary weapons pits for loading or facilities to store the atomic bombs.[35] At this stage no one knew the effect of an atomic blast on a city, but since most Japanese population centres comprised wooden buildings, it was assumed that the devastation would be complete. Conversely, a Soviet concrete-built city could expect to survive total demolition.

While Japan remained oblivious to its fate, Churchill would shortly know his political future. He had already discussed the outcome of the British general election with Stalin, and, as far as the Soviet dictator was concerned, Churchill would be returned with a majority of eighty seats. Stalin was adamant that an army always voted for a strong premier.[36] On 25 July the conference was suspended while Churchill, Eden and Attlee flew to London to discover the election results. They were due to return to Potsdam two days later, but there was a dramatic outcome. Remembering the pre-war shortcomings of the Conservative Party, rather than its leader's wartime record, the country gave the Labour Party a landslide victory. Churchill, exercising that extraordinary will and strength, refused to flinch at the electoral upset. Those around him were stunned, though his family, and particularly his daughter Mary, offered huge support. She recalled a weekend at the prime minister's retreat, Chequers, when, for the last time, the family entered their names in the visitors' book. It was a volume full of the names who had dictated the fortunes of war, but now the PM signed off with one word – 'Finis'.[37]

In Potsdam Stalin was staggered at the result and couldn't comprehend that Churchill couldn't 'fix' it. The result caused Stalin some concern, because now he had lost both his equals. First, in April, Roosevelt had died and now, in July, Churchill had disappeared. The loss meant that the old triumvirate had melted away and Stalin became even more paranoid now that he had to deal with untested replacements.[38] On the same day that the British contingent were away, Poland came up on the agenda. To Truman it seemed settled business. 'Russia helped herself to a slice of Poland,' he complained, 'and gave Poland a nice slice of Germany, taking also a good slice of East Prussia for herself. Poland has moved in up to the Oder and the west Neisse, taking Stettin and Silesia as a fact accomplished.' The Soviet-sponsored Polish provisional government had moved quickly to acquire this territory, and started to expel the millions of ethnic Germans, but it was a new boundary that neither Roosevelt nor Churchill had officially approved.[39]

Two new faces appeared at Potsdam – Clement Attlee, the Labour Prime Minister of Britain, together with his foreign secretary, Ernest Bevin. This caused the Soviets some consternation; Molotov was suspicious of the new British leaders, and repeatedly asked Attlee why he didn't know the result of the general election beforehand.[40] The new leaders' styles were totally different to Churchill and Eden. Attlee had little charisma but was technically master of his brief, whereas Bevin was the complete opposite of his suave, patrician predecessor and was only too happy to point it out. When returning from his first trip to America, waiting reporters were eager to record his experience. 'What are your first impressions of America?' they shouted. Bevin did not pause for a second. 'The newspapers are too big,' he replied, 'and the lavatory paper is too small.'[41]

Even though Bevin lacked the finesse of Eden, he continued much the same foreign policies, particularly the continued alliance with the US. He was anti-communist and had spent much of his political life fighting communist influence within the trade union movement. Indeed, Bevin arrived in Potsdam 'fully aware of the tensions that existed and with a shrewd assessment of the scope of Soviet ambitions, a much shrewder one at this stage, than most of the Americans'.[42] However, despite Bevin's undoubted talents, he was at odds with many in his own party who wished to see a 'Third Force' of socialists within Europe, unaligned with either the US or the Soviet Union. Bevin was essentially an imperialist and believed that the best way to defend the British Empire was by a military and atomic deterrent, whereas Attlee's hopes for security were largely vested in the emerging United Nations. Consequently, while Bevin and his immediate advisors might have agreed with the provisions of Operation Unthinkable, he would have faced an uphill struggle against Attlee and a large part of the Labour party.[43]

On 6 August 1945 a specially adapted Boeing B-29 Superfortress, *Enola Gay*, set off for Hiroshima to deliver the innocently named 'Little Boy' uranium bomb.[44] The target city was an important embarkation port, industrial centre and was also the site of a large military depot. The bomb took forty-three seconds to fall, burst at 2000ft above the city and destroyed 70 per cent of the buildings. Estimates of those immediately killed range from 70,000 to 90,000. It was devastating but Truman had no remorse over the use of the atomic bomb, and had little patience with those who did. J. Robert Oppenheimer, who had been a key figure in the Manhattan Project, afterwards expressed doubt about the morality of using the bomb, but was dismissed by Truman as a 'cry-baby'.[45] After the Hiroshima bomb the Japanese attempted to petition the Soviet Union for a treaty, but in response Stalin declared war on Japan and the Red Army invaded Manchuria. It was true that this Soviet action had been agreed at Yalta, but its timing was an example of Stalin's talent for opportunism.

On 9 August the US dropped a second, more powerful plutonium bomb on the industrial port of Nagasaki, killing in excess of 50,000 inhabitants. Still, the Japanese military refused to surrender, but it was the intervention, his only intervention during the war, of Emperor Hirohito that pressed them to surrender. Under his direction there was no loss of face. He declared the war over but never mentioned the word defeat, and Japan formally surrendered on 2 September. Unsurprisingly, this was a huge relief to the US military, for there would be only one more atomic bomb in stock until several more were produced the following month. Consequently, Churchill's idea that the West could threaten to obliterate the Soviet Union in 1945 was very wide of the mark.

Stalin had made some important strategic gains from his war with Japan, and he was not about to concede his territorial designs in the West. Barely a week after the Japanese surrender, his foreign minister, Molotov, was involved in bitter wrangling with his counterparts in the West over recognition of the Soviet puppet governments in Europe. It seems that at the same time as this deterioration in relations, Stalin had discovered some startling information about British intentions. Oleg Tsarev, an ex-KGB journalist, has alleged that in September 1945 Stalin received his first high-level intelligence on a British strategic post-war plan. 'The Security of the British Empire', dated 29 June 1945, was a memorandum prepared by the

British Post-Hostilities Planning Staff and had found its way onto Stalin's desk.[46] It was not as detailed as the Unthinkable plan, nor did it involve the US, but it was still a highly restricted document exposing British strategic thinking. There was a deluge of such documents coming into Stalin's possession, for by the end of the war Soviet agents, including such high-fliers as Kim Philby, were operating in the very heart of Whitehall. He was head of anti-Soviet operations (Section IX) within the Secret Intelligence Service (SIS) and probably procured the 'British Empire' document for the NKVD. One of his SIS colleagues later confided that Philby had 'ensured that the whole post-war effort to counter Communist espionage became known in the Kremlin. The history of espionage records few, if any, comparable masterstrokes.'[47]

As well as Philby, there were other well connected Soviet spies supplying intelligence papers to Stalin. John Cairncross, who had previously worked for the ULTRA operation at Bletchley Park, was another SIS officer who turned traitor – at the time of VE Day, Cairncross worked for Section I, devoted to Political Intelligence. Anthony Blunt, who had worked for MI5 during the war, also proved to be of great help to Soviet intelligence and, in the words of a senior figure in their Foreign Intelligence Directorate, 'had carried out such huge, titanic work for us'.[48] He had also successfully run a sub-agent, Leo Long, who served in military intelligence during the war and then continued to work as a mole within the British Control Commission in Germany, rising to the post of Deputy Director of Intelligence.

The NKVD had two further moles within the British Foreign Office: Donald Maclean was First Secretary of the British Embassy in Washington, a sensitive post which was often diplomatic cover for senior intelligence officers. Another was Guy Burgess, who had left the BBC in June 1944 to take up a post in the press department of the Foreign Office. According to the former KGB agent Vasili Mitrokhin, during the period January to June 1945, Burgess supplied copies of 389 FO documents classified as 'top secret' to his Soviet handlers. He would regularly take a holdall full of these sensitive papers out of his office and meet his Soviet contact in a park. On one occasion he and his handler were even stopped by the police, who thought his bulging case looked like the proceeds of a robbery, but Burgess promptly convinced the officers that he had no housebreaking equipment on him. They then apologised for troubling him and his silent friend.[49]

With the subsequent election of the Attlee government in July 1945, Burgess obtained even greater access to secret government papers, via his appointment as an aide to Hector McNeil, Parliamentary Under-Secretary of State at the Foreign Office. It is not known whether the details of the tightly restricted Operation Unthinkable ever reached Stalin, though he had certainly received details of earlier reports prepared by the British Post-Hostilities planners. Such information was passed on by Donald Maclean, known in secret Soviet transcripts as 'Homer'. He also regularly supplied his Soviet handlers with complete copies of telegrams between Churchill and Truman that often contained details of British tactics used in the argument over the composition of a Polish government. Consequently, Stalin knew all about the differences between Britain and the US over Poland, as well as their anxious exchanges about the fate of the sixteen Polish underground leaders.[50]

9

US HAWKS

By the autumn of 1945 it was the turn of the Americans to become the hawks in the stand-off with Stalin. The US finally began to outline plans for their post-war strategy, yet there was no presidential or 'top-down' directive as there had been with Churchill and Unthinkable. Instead, individual officers as well as the US Joint Planning Staff (USJPS) took the initiative in preparing reports on a post-war strategic plan. The plans did not, at this stage, detail operations but looked at overall US military capability and its requirements for worldwide bases and military reserves. 'New weapons and countermeasures' were discussed, with special consideration given to the potential of atomic bombs and guided missiles.[1] Experts concluded that these new weapons had limitations, which would not change US military strategy, for at the time the range of V-2-type rockets could not be extended beyond 1,000 miles, while atomic bombs could not be made small enough to suit artillery rounds or naval torpedoes. Consequently, the planners and their experts believed that these new weapons would supplement conventional weapons and the idea that atomic bombs could be used as a deterrent did not seem to enter the equation. However, the planners did determine that crippling a nation's industrial capacity would not affect the outcome of any atomic war, since the war would be over well before that could take effect. By late 1945 the strategic plan, which cloaked its objective with talk of 'maintaining world peace', was presented to the US Joint Chiefs of Staff and then the president for approval.[2]

The impetus for more detailed US operational plans for a major conflict with the Soviet Union would take months to build. The US planners had not consulted with their British counterparts at this stage, for as an ailing Harry Hopkins observed, 'to hear some people talk about the British, you would think the British were our potential enemies.'[3] But to some Americans, the British Empire was just that; when Major-General Francis

Davidson of the British General Staff was on a tour of the US in the autumn of 1945, he was accosted by a journalist who demanded to know about 'British imperialistic designs on Indonesia'. Such language might well have come out of the Kremlin, but at least Anglo-US military relations were on a more cordial level. During the autumn and winter of 1945 there was increasing co-operation between the two armies as well as a sharing of intelligence on Soviet deployments. Gradually, as a result of these constant and verifiable dossiers, corroborated by their own agents in the field, US intelligence began to take the Soviet threat seriously.[4]

During October and November 1945 the US Joint Chiefs examined reports that assessed current Soviet military capability at more than sixty offensive infantry divisions, 25,000 tanks and 60,000 large-calibre artillery pieces. They concluded that Soviet forces could easily overrun Western Europe and the Middle East any time before 1948; such an alarming prospect made the US Joint Intelligence Committee calculate the effect of 'blocking' that advance by unleashing nuclear weapons. In what was the first US outline plan to attack the Soviet Union, twenty Soviet cities were selected as targets for atomic bombs, to be delivered by heavy bombers, yet the American JIC were excluded from most of the US atomic secrets and would not have had accurate data on the number of available bombs.[5]

In November 1945 the US State Department was alarmed by news that Soviet troops in civilian clothes were assisting a tribal revolt in Iranian Azerbaijan with a view to annexing this adjacent province.[6] The US Joint Chiefs of Staff ordered 'a reassessment of US military capabilities in view of Soviet aggressive policies', which indicated the US themselves were now preparing contingency plans for a conventional war with the Soviet Union.[7] On 2 March 1946 the US Joint War Plans Committee (JWPC) produced a draft for Operation 'Pincher', the US broad equivalent to the British Operation Unthinkable. However, the *casus belli* was no longer Poland. It was assumed that the Soviet Union had already set up its ring of satellite states to protect its borders, and the conflict would arise from the Soviets attempting to infiltrate more countries beyond that ring. In particular, Pincher singled out the Middle East as a flashpoint, where US or British interests could be undermined. There might also be incidents in Turkey or Iran, which would compel the Western Allies to retaliate by military force, and thereby spark a Third World War. The original plan envisaged a war sometime between 1946 and 1949, but as tensions rose dramatically during 1946, the time span was drastically reduced. It looked to US planners as if they were staring into the abyss. Of course, they were unaware of the extent of the leaks by Donald

Maclean, and how much the Soviets knew about US plans for retaliation in the event of a hostile move against Turkey. It is possible that because of the knowledge that the US would retaliate, Stalin may have backed off from an invasion of Turkey in 1946, which diffused the crisis.[8]

Belatedly, President Truman talked of Stalin's tactics in Poland as an 'outrage'. This tough talking may have resulted from the new US atomic muscle, but their foreign policy hardened by the month.[9] In February 1946 George Kennan sent his famous 'Long Telegram' from the US Mission in Moscow to Washington. It was a seminal moment, for in Kennan's own words, 'these years had been a strain for me nearly all the way through, because I watched our government making concession after concession to the Soviets.' It seemed that both the US government and public opinion had needed a gestation period before they could readily address the Soviet threat.[10]

It was not just the US administration that was changing its policy towards Stalin. Churchill's fears about Soviet domination in the spring of 1945 had, by early 1946, become orthodox thinking in the British Foreign Office. The Mediterranean, Turkey and Iran were all vulnerable, and northern Italy had proved contentious. There were also concerns that the pro-Soviet French communist party might take power in France. If a conflict with the West erupted, Stalin would have no qualms about ordering a communist insurrection in France, to be followed by an attempted communist coup in Belgium and, after a civil war, a communist regime could follow in Spain.[11] The worst fear for Britain remained triumphant communism 'fuelled by German economic might', as the British JIC confirmed:

> Russia will no doubt give full weight to the fact that Great Britain and the United States are both war weary, faced with immense internal problems and rapidly demobilising their forces. By comparison, Russia's own forces and industry are still on a war basis. No further demobilisation has been announced, and Russian divisions are being rapidly re-equipped with the latest material.[12]

Churchill, now free of the political constraints on a prime minister, though still recognised as a world statesman, sensed a rising tide of realism in the West. On 5 March 1946 he used such recognition to full effect by giving a legendary speech during a tour of the US. At Fulton, Missouri, he uttered a solemn warning to Russia, and talked of 'an iron curtain' descending on Europe. He reminded the American people that the West could not afford to appease the Soviet Union, for such a policy had been disastrous before the war and now, in a post-war world, would be seen simply as weakness by Stalin.[13] Yet despite the dramatic tone of his speech, the British press and public were lukewarm in their support for the ex-premier. This was hardly surprising, since in Britain there remained an overwhelming feeling of gratitude to the Soviet Union for their undeniable sacrifice in the war. Such public goodwill was certainly fostered by the unrelenting diet of wartime pro-Soviet propaganda that emitted from the British government. It was unrealistic to suppose that barely a year later the public could absorb the 'justness' of an attack on the Soviet Union.

Regardless of any protests in the West, Stalin's suppression of Eastern Europe continued apace. In March 1946 alone the Soviet Ministry of the Interior recorded that '8,360 bandits were liquidated' in the Ukraine, while in the Baltic Soviet Socialist Republic (SSR) states of Latvia, Lithuania and Estonia nearly 100,000 people were deported to gulags 'forever'.[14] Even as the packed cattle trucks of 'bandits, nationalists and others' trundled eastwards, Stalin launched his own verbal repost to Churchill's Missouri speech, denouncing him as 'a firebrand of war'. But Churchill's views were no longer seen by the US as either extreme or as an impediment to better relations with Stalin. Just days before Churchill had delivered his Fulton speech, the US JWPC had finalised their Operation Pincher war plans. US policy was turning full circle in its attitude to the Soviet Union:

> It is wise to emphasise the importance of being so prepared militarily and of showing such firmness and resolution that the Soviet Union will not, through miscalculation of American intentions, push to the point that results in war.[15]

The US draft plan for their own Unthinkable war estimated that in the spring of 1946 the Soviets had fifty-one divisions in Germany and Austria, fifty divisions in the near or Middle East and twenty divisions in Hungary and Yugoslavia. This force of 121 divisions was supported by a central reserve of 152 divisions in the homeland, and a total of 87 divisions of pro-Soviet forces within the satellite states of Eastern Europe. A Soviet attack would most likely sweep across Western Europe and seize the channel ports and the Low Countries in little more than a month. Simultaneous attacks would be launched into Italy as well as the Middle East. In the midst of such overwhelming force (again, an estimate of three to one in favour of Soviet infantry), it was recommended that US troops would retreat into Spain or Italy to avoid being decimated by the Red Army on the continent. It was conceivable that the Red Army would even carry the invasion into Spain in an attempt to block the western Mediterranean, in which case US forces would swiftly withdraw and retreat to Britain. While Britain was considered a valuable base, Germany, Austria, France and the Low Countries would be sacrificed. Retreating Allied forces would also move across to the Middle East to bolster defences around the vital Suez Canal Zone. It was no surprise that the US chiefs of staff now accepted that an essential object of Stalinist policy was to 'dominate the world'.[16]

There would be a fight-back by the West, of course, but not until the Red Army had swept through Western Europe, the Balkans, Turkey and Iran; in the Far East, South Korea and Manchuria would also fall. Although Pincher did not go into further detail, the US and her Allies would launch devastating air attacks from remaining bases in Britain, Egypt and India, no doubt deploying their growing stock of atomic bombs, though the use of such weapons was still not seen as a 'war winner'. Meanwhile the US Navy would seek to blockade the Soviet Union and destroy her naval fleets, as attempts were eventually made to recover Western Europe by a southerly thrust via the Mediterranean.[17]

One old festering wound in Europe that looked like it could precipitate Operation Pincher was the dispute between Tito and the West over the Venezia Giulia region. It was also this scare that brought together the US and British Joint Chiefs of Staff for their first planning sessions for a Third World War. The first British Unthinkable plan, involving the attack on Soviet forces on 1 July 1945, had not been discussed beyond the tight circle of the prime minister, his Joint Chiefs and their Joint Planners. Similarly, the highly sensitive US Pincher plan was initially confined to the US Joint Chiefs, their Joint Planners and the commander-in-chief. But on 30 August 1946 Field Marshal Henry 'Jumbo' Maitland Wilson, representing the British Joint Chiefs, attended a lunch with his American counterparts. Reporting back to his JCS committee, Wilson was able to reassure them that at least both sets of chiefs were alert to the risk of an armed clash in Venezia Giulia, which could pull in both power blocs, whether they wanted war or not. There was agreement that in the event of a conflict in the Venezia region it was pointless having a plan for large reinforcements to be sent into the territory, since the fight would swiftly spread into central Europe. Poland, no longer seen as the tripwire by late 1946, would nevertheless find herself at the very centre of military activity.[18]

Ironically, the US chiefs were now discussing all the scenarios that Churchill had foreseen eighteen months before, when formulating his plan for Unthinkable. President Truman had even appointed a Special Counsel, Clark Clifford, to report on the growing Soviet menace, concluding that Stalin believed 'a prolonged peace' between the Marxist and capitalist societies was impossible and the only outcome was war.[19] At a top-level meeting between the US and Britain, even the new US chief of staff, General Eisenhower, was talking the Unthinkable talk of establishing Allied 'bridgeheads' in Europe. In the face of any Soviet onslaught he advocated withdrawing forces to bridgeheads in the Low Countries. As Churchill had earlier recommended, this would deny the enemy the use of bases from which to launch rocket attacks at Britain, as well as offering the Allies a short line of communication back to Britain. The UK would be of huge strategic value for the Allied air forces, though the Americans noted that longer airstrips would be required in British bases to enable more B-29 squadrons to be accommodated. The Naval representative also argued for a reoccupation of Iceland to broaden the reach of naval forces.

So, with a consensus reached, the meeting broke up, but not before it was agreed that the utmost secrecy should be imposed on the Combined Joint Chiefs of Staff outline plan, and that no one beyond the level of the chiefs and their immediate planners should be allowed access. The US chiefs were most keen to drive on and agree a command organisation for the US and Britain in the event of Soviet aggression, which they saw as 'imminent'.[20] However, it was not long before other senior British commanders became involved in the plans. On 16 September Field Marshal Montgomery, supposedly on a private visit to the United States, met with General Eisenhower and President Truman to discuss the war plan options for the West. Cabling Prime Minister Attlee to advise him of developments, Montgomery referred to the highly sensitive plan and stressed it was 'Personal and Eyes only for PM'. 'So far as I am aware, no (repeat) no one here knows anything about matter.' Montgomery was keen to add, 'all agree that secrecy is vital.' To cover their trips to meet US Joint Planning Staff, the British planners used the excuse of researching for a 'report on the strategical lessons of the recent war'. There was even concern within the British camp that the amply proportioned 'Jumbo' Wilson might have presented a large silhouette on board the yacht where he met with US chiefs. Furthermore, it was questioned whether British planners should wear 'uniform or mufti' when meeting with their American counterparts. Fortunately, the idea of 'cocktail parties' for visiting teams was hastily dispensed with.[21]

Yet it seemed that the tight security in the US was now unravelling. The British were horrified to learn that the secretaries to the US War

Department and Navy Department were also aware of the plan and it was only a matter of time before operatives in the US State Department heard of the details. British security operatives may well have been aware of the leaks to the Soviets from within the State Department and feared the worst. Attlee certainly did. Confiding to Field Marshal Wilson, he stated 'the issues now raised are of the utmost importance and potential value, but any leakage would have the gravest consequences.'[22]

During October 1946 the Canadian war planners were also introduced to the operation and a representative met with British and US planners for further meetings in London. Discussions included the intended bridgeheads and the capacity of Naval forces to evacuate US and British troops from mainland Europe, should the Red Army advance to the West. There was also the pressing problem of renewed Soviet threats to Greece and Turkey, as well as the issue of 'standardisation' of weapons and equipment between the US, Britain and Canada.[23]

Operation Pincher went through a number of modifications during the summer of 1946, and the US Joint Planners ensured that it remained relevant, but it still excluded specific reference to the use of atomic bombs by the strategic bomber force. As with Unthinkable the planners made little attempt to project beyond the initial stages of a conflict, since there were just too many variables. One of the constant worries remained the issue of demobilisation. For with peace came a great desire for 'bringing the boys home' as soon as possible and for reducing the huge cost of a vast army. Consequently, by June 1946 the US armed forces, which had numbered more than 12 million at the end of the war, were reduced to fewer than 3 million.[24] Secretary of State James Byrnes was frustrated with the whole process, 'The people who yelled loudest for me to adopt a firm attitude towards Russia,' he moaned, 'then yelled even louder for the rapid demobilisation of the Army.' So formidable was the strength of Soviet armour and infantry that once US troop reductions were under way, the planners concluded that Allied land forces would not be strong enough to drive into the Soviet interior for at least three years. Allied air power offered the only hope of victory, by employing massive strikes against 'the industrial heart of Russia'.[25]

It was unrealistic to believe that the Soviet Union could be threatened with oblivion in 1946. Even by the autumn of that year the US only possessed nine atomic bombs. There were two Mark III Fat Boys earmarked for testing off the US mainland, and seven Mark IIIs were held in secure housings on the mainland. They could only be delivered to the Soviet Union by the Silver Plate B-29, suitably modified to hold the weapon in place, but there was a lack of properly trained aircrews, as well as bomb assembly teams. Furthermore, scientists were returning to civilian life and the production of both uranium and plutonium was falling. However, production would be dramatically increased in the next few years, so that by the time of the first Soviet atomic test in 1949, the US would have a stockpile of some 400 atomic bombs. Despite the comfort of atomic superiority, senior commanders in the West were in no doubt about the consequences of an imminent world war. 'My part in the next war,' wrote Sir Arthur 'Bomber' Harris, 'will be to be destroyed by it.'[26]

While Britain and the US faced up to the Soviet Union, Poland, as a cause, had slipped off the list of priorities. During Christmas Eve 1946 the 'Polish Sixteen', who had been the hope of a future liberated Poland, were languishing in various Soviet prisons. One of the most prominent leaders, General Okulicki, passed his last hours in Moscow's Butyrka Prison. His disappearance, together with other leading members of the Polish underground, in April 1945, had done much to increase the climate of fear surrounding Soviet intentions. He was either murdered by the NKVD or died as a result of his hunger strike; it has been estimated that between 1944 and 1947 some 50,000 Poles, including many members of the AK, were deported to the Soviet gulags.[27] In the spring of 1946 the US Joint Chiefs declared that the Soviet Union was giving the highest priority to 'building up their war potential and that of their satellites so as to be able to defeat the Western democracies'. To combat Soviet plans for 'eventual world domination', the West would also have to provide military and economic aid to frontline states, such as Greece, Turkey and Iran.[28]

So the post-war Western governments continued their stand-off with the Soviet Union, a situation that became known as the Cold War. The 1947 elections in Poland were duly rigged and a communist government was returned. But the Polish government-in-exile in London continued its existence, despite the worldwide recognition of the communist puppet government in Poland. In fact, showing all the old stoicism, the London Poles continued their existence until 1991, when the old presidential seals were finally handed over to the first post-communist government in Warsaw. Throughout the late 1940s the Cold War festered with intermittent crises erupting, such as the Berlin Blockade, when the Soviets attempted to cut off Western access to Berlin. The West arranged an airlift of supplies to lift the 'siege' and, in 1949, the Soviets backed down. It was, however, a momentous year for other reasons – the Soviet Union developed its own atomic capability and the balance of power shifted again.

Operation Unthinkable might have been just another quiet footnote in the story of the Cold War, but in 1954 there was a bizarre incident involving Churchill and Montgomery that threatened to expose the whole plan. In a low-key speech at his Woodford constituency, Churchill suddenly announced that in 1945 he had ordered Field Marshal Montgomery to preserve captured German weapons and to be ready to reissue those arms to 'German soldiers whom we should have to work with if the Soviet advance continued'. An intrigued press tackled Montgomery for his comments and there ensued a wrangle over whether or not Churchill had ever formally issued the order. The Soviet press immediately seized on his comments, attacking 'Churchill's crusade', and there were critical articles in the British and the US press.[29] The *Chicago Tribune* attacked Churchill and his wartime policy with headlines that screamed 'Folly on Olympian Scale'. The whole episode blew up out of nowhere but more rational observers wondered why, at the height of the Cold War, the prime minister would casually disclose such controversial plans to attack the Soviet Union. Major-General Sir Edward Spears was wheeled out in defence of Churchill. 'The whole thing is absurd,' he countered. '*The Times* is behaving as if Sir Winston had called in Hitler for help against Russia. Hitler was out of business.'[30] But the prime minister still had to calm the storm by admitting that he could find no telegram in his records and that he must have issued a verbal order to Montgomery. Privately he confessed, 'I made a goose of myself at Woodford.'[31]

EPILOGUE

Churchill's Operation Unthinkable may have appeared 'fanciful' to his chiefs of staff when it first appeared in May 1945, but for Poland it could have represented a last hope of freedom. Militarily it could have been an open-ended disaster. However, a year later all military options were back on the table and both British and US foreign policies were alive to the Soviet threat.

As for the communist domination and subjugation of Eastern Europe, some Western leaders had certainly let Stalin believe that it was a 'done deal'. Winston Churchill's 'naughty document', showing percentage splits of influence, must surely have encouraged Stalin to believe his takeovers would go unchallenged. In the US, Secretary of State Byrnes did little to stand up to his Soviet counterpart, Molotov, and compromise rather than toughness was the hallmark of early US foreign policy. It was also a policy that showed signs of a post-war obsession with the dismantling of empires, rather than the resisting of dictators. Meanwhile, Churchill's plan for the Unthinkable war against the Soviet Union was part guilt over Poland and part frustration that Stalin had indeed duped his erstwhile allies at every turn. Even if Churchill was late in realising the threat from Stalin, he was still a good year in advance of his American Allies in arriving at that view. With the knowledge that the US did not see Europe as having the same strategic importance as the Pacific, Churchill was quite right to fear Britain's isolation in 1945–46. Furthermore, it was not until Stalin started making aggressive gestures towards Turkey and Iran that the US reacted to the threat. It seemed that Stalin was attempting to control these two countries as a buffer, in the way that he had used Eastern Europe.

It must have appeared to Stalin that Western Europe might not be too difficult to control. After all, the economies of Europe were in a parlous state, with weak governments and were ripe for communist takeovers. Yet, there was very little appetite in the West to remedy those weaknesses by military force. The planners could not have foreseen the scale of the problems that an invading Allied army would face in Europe in 1945, not least the vast tide of refugees sweeping westwards or the famines across Eastern Europe. This was largely because intelligence on the target territories was closed off to them by the suffocating communist security system.[1]

In recent years plans have come to light in the old Warsaw Pact countries of Eastern Europe, showing the Soviet Union's expected reaction to an invasion from the Western Allies. Probably the earliest detailed plans unearthed date from 1951 and show how the Czechoslovak army would have reacted to a Western invasion of its borders. It also details how the Czechs could mobilise and carry out offensive operations into West Germany, though, tellingly, only under Soviet command. Such early plans avoid the detail of nuclear warfare, but clearly assume that the Red Army and its allies could advance across a nuclear-wasted Europe.[2]

Operation Unthinkable's vision of a limited and punitive war against the Soviet Union was eventually ruled out. But what if they had no option but to attack? If one of the flashpoints had erupted in Poland, Austria or Venezia Giulia, and spilled over into Allied-occupied territory, then would the Allies have just stood their ground, or would they have counter-attacked and driven Soviet forces out of eastern Germany and beyond? But regardless of who started it, the modern reader can appreciate with hindsight the apparent madness of finishing one world war and then, several months later, starting all over again. A year later, though, the US was preparing contingency plans for conflict with the Soviet Union, and indeed continued in that state of alert throughout the Cold War. By then there was also the added element of atomic bombs, though they were still seen as an enhancement to a nation's conventional arsenal rather than the harbinger of a new form of warfare. Just how many atomic bombs it would take to destroy Stalin's will was never apparent. The success of the atomic test in July 1945 had briefly reignited Churchill's belief in vanquishing the communist Soviet Union by force. But his removal from office just weeks later finally put paid to his notion that he could ever direct the Unthinkable war. That particular baton was picked up by the Americans, who are still running with it — though the direction of the threat that faces them is no longer as clear as it was in 1945.

NOTES

Introduction

1. Winston S. Churchill, *The Second World War. Volume VI. Triumph and Tragedy* (Cassell, London 1954).
2. Ironically, in 1889, while still at Harrow School, Churchill had foreseen this conflict between East and West. He wrote an essay, with maps, about an imaginary war between Britain and Russia which would break out on 7 July 1914. At the time of his essay, Russia was Britain's main rival. See Harrow School records, Cabinet War Rooms, London.
3. James Leasor, *War at the Top. Based on the Experiences of General Sir Leslie Hollis* (Michael Joseph, London 1959), p. 284. Also James Schnabel, *The History of the Joint Chiefs of Staff. The Joint Chiefs of Staff and National Policy, Volume I, 1945–1947* (Michael Glazier, Wilmington 1979), p. 21.
4. Mark Harrison, *Accounting for War. Soviet Production, Employment and the Defence Burden 1940–1945* (Cambridge University Press, Cambridge 1996), p. 15. Official estimates varied widely, according to who was in power. Stalin cited 7 million deaths, Khrushchev reported 20 million and Brezhnev quoted in excess of 20 million. According to estimates gathered by Prof. Richard Overy, the most likely figure is in excess of 25 million deaths; see Richard Overy, *Russia's War* (Penguin, London 1999), pp. 287–9.
5. For the Soviet threat to the West see R.H. Bruce Lockheart, 11 April 1945, Char 23/14, Churchill Archive Centre, Churchill College, Cambridge (hereafter CAC); also Vladislav Zubok and Constantine Pleshakov, *Inside the Kremlin's Cold War: From Stalin to Khrushchev* (Harvard University Press, Cambridge MA 1996), p. 39.
6. Winston S. Churchill (hereafter WSC) to President Truman, 12 May 1945, PREM 3/473. See also Char 20/218, CAC.
7. Lord Moran diary, 6 September 1945, in *Winston Churchill. The Struggle for Survival 1940–1956* (Constable, London 1966), p. 299.

8. Martin H. Folly, *Churchill, Whitehall and the Soviet Union 1940–45* (Macmillan, London 2000), p. 138.

Chapter 1: 'An Unspoken Fear'

1. The US government has recently released files into the US National Archives and Records Administration (hereafter NARA), showing that US intelligence was aware of the crime and who had really committed it. Two American POWs who had witnessed the German discovery of the bodies had sent reports to the US. Roosevelt and his advisors remained silent on the subject for fear of upsetting Stalin. The original outcry came from the discovery by the Germans of the graves of 4,421 Poles at Katyn. It was later discovered that simultaneous executions of educated Poles took place at Kharkov (3,820), Ostashkovo (6,311) and in various POW camps (7,305); see Jonathan Walker, *Poland Alone. Britain, SOE and the Collapse of the Polish Resistance 1944* (The History Press, Stroud 2008), p. 47.

2. The Polish underground state comprised not only a military organisation called the Home Army, or *Armia Krajowa* (AK), but also a press, culture, education and welfare administration. For the origins and collapse of the AK see Jonathan Walker, *Poland Alone*.

3. FM Lord Alanbrooke diary, 27 July 1944, Alanbrooke Papers, ref. 5/1/9, Liddell Hart Centre for Military Archives, King's College, London (hereafter LHCMA).

4. 'Effect of Russian Policy on British Interests', 17 February 1944, FO 371/43384, National Archives, Kew, London (hereafter NA).

5. Alanbrooke diary, 2 October 1944, Alanbrooke Papers, ref. 5/1/9, LHCMA; see also 'Effect of Russian Policy on British Interests'.

6. See Cavendish Bentinck notes on JIC report, 18 December 1944, FO 371/47860, NA. Also Victor Rothwell, *Britain and the Cold War 1941–1947* (Jonathan Cape, London 1982), pp. 122–3.

7. Northern Dept., Foreign Office memorandum, 4 October 1944, FO 371/39414, NA. Also Clark Kerr to Foreign Office, 16 October 1944, FO 371/39414, NA.

8. For the 'Uncle Joe' factor see Martin H. Folly, *Churchill, Whitehall and the Soviet Union 1940–45* (Macmillan, London 2000), pp. 77–80.

9. James Leasor, *Op. cit*, pp. 280–1.

10. Richard Holmes, *The World at War. The Landmark Oral History* (Ebury Press, London 2007), p. 536.

Chapter 2: Yalta

1. Elliott Roosevelt, *As He Saw It* (Duell, Sloan & Pearce, New York 1946), p. 240.

2. Roosevelt, *As He Saw It*, p. 121. For an analysis of America's anti-Empire position see Chester Wilmot, *The Struggle for Europe* (Collins, London 1952), pp. 632–6.

3. John Lukacs, *1945. Year Zero* (Doubleday, Garden City NY 1978), p. 71.

4. The idea, of course, of Soviet domination of post-war Eastern Europe should not have surprised the US diplomats; the earlier Big Three conference in Tehran in November 1943 had already agreed to the ceding of Poland's eastern territory to the Soviet Union.

5. For percentage deal see PREM 3 66/7, NA; also David Reynolds, *In Command of History. Churchill Fighting and Writing the Second World War* (Penguin, London 2005), pp. 458–60. For the 'bargain' mentality see Fraser Harbutt, *Yalta 1945. Europe and America at the Crossroads* (Cambridge University Press, New York 2010), pp. 43–4.

6. Elizabeth Nel, *Mr Churchill's Secretary* (Hodder & Stoughton, London 1958), pp. 167–8.

7. For observations on the Yalta Conference see James Leasor, *War at the Top*, pp. 280–2.

8. Both Valentin Berezhkov and Sergo Beria have testified that they were involved in setting up and transcribing the conversations; see Gary Kern, 'How Uncle Joe Bugged FDR', at cia.gov/library/center-for-the-study-of-intelligence.htl. Also S.M. Plokhy, *Yalta. The Price of Peace* (Penguin, London 2011), pp. 78–9, 234–5.

9. Interview with Prof. George Kennan in episode 1, 'Comrades', of the documentary series *Cold War*, National Security Archive, George Washington University, www.nsarchive.org.

10. Kennan in 'Comrades'.

11. Winston S. Churchill, *The Second World War. Volume VI*, p. 308.

12. 'Interview with Viscount Portal', Alanbrooke Papers, LHCMA.

13. Frank Roberts, *Dealing with Dictators. The Destruction and Revival of Europe 1930–70* (Weidenfeld & Nicolson, London 1991), p. 75.

14. Frank Roberts, *Dealing with Dictators*, p. 76.

15. There was some initial confusion at the end of the war as to which Soviet client state should take Stettin. Although Stalin had indicated that it was to be given to Poland to compensate her for the loss of the port of Königsberg, East German authorities laid claim to it. It was not until 17 July 1945 that Stalin officially announced it was to become Polish. See R.C. Raack, *Stalin's Drive*

to the West 1938–1945. The Origins of the Cold War (Stanford University Press, Stanford 1995), p. 100.

16. Zygmunt Szkpjak (Ed.), 'Section VI Poland. Report of the Crimea Conference, Yalta, 11 February 1945', in *The Yalta Agreements. Documents Prior to, During and After the Crimea Conference 1945* (Polish Government-in-Exile, London 1986).

17. William Leahy, *I Was There. The Personal Story of the Chief of Staff to Presidents Roosevelt and Truman Based on his Notes and Diaries at the Time* (Gollancz, London 1950), p. 33.

18. 'Speeches at Dinner at Vorontsov Villa', 10 February 1945, Char 23/14, CAC.

19. Amy Knight, *Beria. Stalin's First Lieutenant* (Princeton University Press, Princeton 1993), pp. 131–5.

20. Norman Davies, *God's Playground. A History of Poland, Volume II. 1795 to the Present* (Oxford University Press, Oxford 1981), p. 489. For an exhaustive study of the borders see 'The Modern Polish Frontiers', pp. 492–535.

21. Importantly this gave Stalin railway access to the Manchurian ports of Dairen and Port Arthur, as well as allowing him to annexe the strategic Kurile Islands, to the north of Japan.

22. Richard Holmes, *The World at War. The Landmark Oral History* (Ebury Press, London 2007), p. 542. Soviet demands included the acquisition of the Sakhalins and adjacent islands, recognition of Soviet interests in the port of Dairen, restoration of the lease of Port Arthur as a naval base, acquisition of the Kurile Islands, joint Soviet-Chinese operation of the Chinese Eastern Railway and the South Manchuria Railway. See James Schnabel, *The History of the Joint Chiefs of Staff*, p. 26.

23. Victor Rothwell, *Britain and the Cold War 1941–1947* (Jonathan Cape, London 1982), pp. 17–18.

24. Stalin also obtained joint Sino-Soviet access to these areas. See WSC to Dominion Prime Ministers, 5 July 1945, Char 20/222, CAC.

25. Quoted in Jon Meacham, *Franklin and Winston. A Portrait of a Friendship* (Granta Books, London 2003), p. 317.

26. Portal believed that Admiral King was also determined that the US should not share the kudos with Britain for the defeat of Japan. See 'Interview with MC Long', Alanbrooke Papers, LHCMA; also Wilmot, *Struggle for Europe*, pp. 640–3.

27. John R. Deane, *The Strange Alliance. The Story of Our Efforts at Wartime Co-operation with Russia* (John Murray, London 1947), pp. 84–5.

28. Roosevelt, *As He Saw It*, p. 241.

29. Schnabel, *History of Joint Chiefs*, p. 28.

30. Quoted in Dmitri Volkogonov (Trans. Harold Shukman), *The Rise and Fall of the Soviet Empire. Political Leaders from Lenin to Gorbachev* (HarperCollins, London 1998), p. 128.

31. Jan Ciechanowski, quoted in Szkopiak, *Yalta Agreements*, p. 129.

32. Nigel Nicolson (Ed.), *Harold Nicolson Diaries 1907–1964* (Phoenix, London 2005), 27 February 1945, p. 344. For Roosevelt's concessions see Laurence Rees, *World War Two: Behind Closed Doors. Stalin, the Nazis and the West* (BBC Books, London 2008), p. 337.

33. Lord Alanbrooke diary, 22 February 1945, Alanbrooke Papers, LHCMA.

34. Lieutenant-General W. Anders, *An Army in Exile. The Story of the Second Polish Corps* (The Battery Press, Nashville 1981), p. 256.

35. Prof. Anita Prażmowska to author, 17 January 2013.

36. Anders was unaware at first of how far the US and British governments had drifted in their compromise with Stalin since the Tehran Conference at the end of 1943. See Joanna Pylat, Jan Ciechanowski and Andrzej Suchitz (Eds.), *General Władysław Anders. Soldier and Leader of the Free Poles in Exile* (Polish University Abroad, London 2007), pp. 44–5, 164–7.

37. Anthony Eden to WSC, 3 April 1945, FO 954/20 #521-6, NA.

38. Prof. Anita Prażmowska to author, 17 January 2013.

39. WSC to Roosevelt, 8 March 1945, FO 954/20 #433, NA. A Gallup poll conducted in March 1945 showed that only 15 per cent of the British public disapproved of the new Polish boundaries. The war-weary public, assailed from all sides by Second World War horror stories, did not appear too pre-occupied with the fate of Poland. See P.M.H. Bell, *John Bull & the Bear. British Public Opinion, Foreign Policy and the Soviet Union 1941–1945* (Edward Arnold, London 1990), p. 182.

40. John Colville, *The Fringes of Power. Downing Street Diaries 1939–1955* (Hodder & Stoughton, London 1985), 23 February 1945, p. 563.

41. Lord Alanbrooke, post-war reflections, Cf. 26 March 1945, Alanbrooke Papers, LHCMA.

42. For Eisenhower's conflict with Churchill over this issue see Lukacs, *1945*, pp. 60–2. Despite his 'relaxed' attitude to the Soviet threat in the spring of 1945, Eisenhower became avowedly anti-Soviet in the 1950s.

43. Colville, *Fringes of Power*, 7 March 1945, p. 570.

44. WSC to Roosevelt, 8 March 1945, FO 954/20 #432, NA.

45. Eden to WSC, 3 April 1945, FO 954/20, NA.

46. Quoted in Harbutt, *Yalta 1945*, p. 350.

47. WSC to Roosevelt, 11 March 1945, FO 954/20 #442, NA.

48. Henry Stimson diary, 2 April 1945, Stimson Papers, Library of Congress, Washington DC (hereafter LoC).

49. Ibid., 23 April 1945.

50. Roosevelt to WSC, 12 March 1945, FO 954/20 #450 & 453, NA.

51. WSC to Roosevelt, 16 March 1945, FO 954/20 #465, NA.

52. WSC to Roosevelt, 26 March 1945, FO 954/20 #478, NA.

53. British Embassy (Moscow) to Foreign Office, 3 April 1945, FO 954/20, #520, NA.

54. Memorandum, 6 May 1945, FO 954/20 #726, NA. Also Stefan Korboński, *Fighting Warsaw. The Story of the Polish Underground State 1939–1945* (Hippocrene Books, New York 2004), pp. 426–33.

55. WSC to General Ismay, 3 April 1945, JPS memorandum, CAB 84/71, NA.

56. Harbutt, *Yalta 1945*, pp. 282, 353.

57. Dominions Office to Anthony Eden, 9 April 1945, FO 954/20 #550, NA. Also Harbutt, *Yalta 1945*, pp. 36–7.

58. Stalin to WSC, 11 April 1945, FO 954/20 #561, NA.

59. Minutes of British War Cabinet, 13 April 1945, CAB 65/52, NA.

60. WSC to Stalin, 22 April 1945, FO 954/20 #623, NA.

Chapter 3: Three Fishermen

1. Churchill later regretted not attending Roosevelt's funeral. His motives are still not clear, but he may have been keen to tilt the power balance back towards Britain, since he later admitted to the king that he was hoping that Truman would see him in London, rather than vice versa.

2. Harry S. Truman diary, 12 April 1945, Harry S. Truman Library, www.trumanlibrary.org.

3. *New York Times*, 24 June 1941. For Truman and his advisors see John Lukacs, *1945. Year Zero* (Doubleday, Garden City NY 1978), pp. 133–69.

4. Peter Hennessy, *The Secret State. Whitehall and the Cold War* (Allen Lane, London 2002), p. 20.

5. JPS report, 19 April 1945, JPS Memoranda File, CAB 84/71, NA.

6. For a study of the systematic attacks on the Polish people see Bartholomew Goldyn, 'Disenchanted Voices. Public Opinion in Cracow 1945–46' in *East European Quarterly*, June 1998, Volume 32, #2. Also, Geoffrey Roberts, *Stalin's General. The Life of Georgy Zhukov* (Icon Books, London 2012), p. 241.

7. William Bader, *Austria Between East and West 1945–1955* (Stanford University Press, Stanford 1966) pp. 13–16.

8. WSC to President Truman, 12 May 1945, Char 20/218, CAC. Also James Schnabel, *The History of the Joint Chiefs of Staff*, p. 38.

9. FM Wilson to chiefs of staff, 21 April 1945, CAB 120/683, NA.

10. In an attempt by the Austrian communists to gain power by democratic means, they were defeated in a November 1945 election and contained by a four-powers occupation. A subsequent attempted communist putsch in 1949 failed and the country settled into decades of neutrality.

11. From December 1946 the Chiefs of Staff Committee and their sub-committees came under the responsibility of the Ministry of Defence instead of the War Cabinet Office.

12. Brooke was appointed CIGS in 1941. When Admiral Sir Dudley Pound stood down, Portal was due to succeed him but, at Churchill's insistence, Brooke was appointed. For the Chiefs of Staff Committee see 'Interview with General Lord Ismay', Alanbrooke Papers, LHCMA.

13. General Hollis memoir, p. 40, Hollis Papers, 86/47/1, Imperial War Museum, London (hereafter IWM). Ismay combined his role on the COS Committee with his post as Deputy Secretary (Military) to the War Cabinet.

14. The CCS was formed in 1942.

15. 'Interview with General Lord Ismay', Alanbrooke Papers, LHCMA.

16. See 'Sir James Grigg Interview', Alanbrooke Papers, LHCMA.

17. Foreign Office memorandum, 11 April 1945, HS4/145, NA.

18. The original brief from the PM is referred to in chiefs of staff memorandum to WSC, 8 June 1945, CAB 120/691.

19. 'Timing for Plans', File p. 3 G 4/3, Major-General F.H.N. Davidson Papers, LHCMA.

20. Memorandum, M.F. Berry, 6 April 1945, JPS Reports, CAB 84/71, NA. For end of war date see 'Planning Date for the End of War with Germany', 12 April 1945, and 'Employment of Turkish Forces', 9 April 1945, JPS Reports, CAB 84/71, NA.

21. When the file 'Operation Unthinkable: Russia and the Threat to Western Civilisation' was released into the public domain via the National Archives, the maps accompanying the report were not present. The four maps were titled 'Russian Strengths and Dispositions', 'Allied Strengths and Dispositions', 'Campaign in North East Europe', 'Vulnerable Points on Russian L of C'. Their omission from the file in the public domain is not necessarily significant, since the JPS was in the habit of destroying many of their supporting draft documents and maps; see CAB 120/691, p. 6.

22. For a history and analysis of the Chiefs of Staff Committee see Clement Attlee, 'Central Organisation for Defence', 11 September 1946, CAB 129/12, NA.

23. Sir Ian Jacob in Sir John Wheeler-Bennett (Ed.), *Action This Day. Working with Churchill* (Macmillan, London 1968), pp. 195–6.

24. During 1944–45, the PHPS comprised Captain C. Allen, Brigadier F. Curtis and Air Commodore P. Warburton. It had replaced the 'Post-Hostilities Planning Sub-Committee' in May 1944. For the succession of various planning groups see Julian Lewis, *Changing Direction. British Military Planning for Post-war Strategic Defence, 1942–1947* (Routledge, London 2003), pp. xxvi–xxvii.

25. Anthony Gorst, 'British Military Planning for Postwar Defence 1943–45' in Anne Deighton (Ed.), *Britain and the First Cold War* (Macmillan, London 1990). Also Martin H. Folly, *Churchill, Whitehall and the Soviet Union, 1940–1945* (Macmillan, London 2000), pp. 102–5, 129. In October 1944 the PHPS broke free of Foreign Office supervision and became purely a military sub-committee of the chiefs of staff; it produced its final paper, 'The Security of the British Empire', in the early summer of 1945. It then handed over its responsibilities to the Joint Planning Staff.

Chapter 4: The Plan – 'Quick Success'

1. 'Operation Unthinkable', CAB 120/691, NA. The first paragraph is unnumbered, but the second is numbered '2'. The extent of the plan runs to seventeen pages plus appendix, but is incomplete. The maps referred to in the body of the text are missing and it is not clear whether there were any previous drafts, though 'No. 15' is quoted on the copy. However, it must be presumed that copies of the plan were kept to an absolute minimum. The file also includes correspondence from the chiefs of staff and US Directors of Plans between 1945 and 1947.

2. 'Operation Unthinkable', CAB 120/691 109040, p. 3.

3. The JPS team were G. Grantham, G.S. Thompson and W.L. Dawson; see 'Report on War End', 12 April 1945, JPS Reports, CAB 84/71, NA. When the war ended, on 8 May, the JPS would have revised their estimates – the 1 July start date for Unthinkable may have accommodated this.

4. Later became Lieutenant-General Sir Geoffrey Stuart Thompson and was appointed Director Land/Air Warfare and Director of NATO standardisation at the War Office in 1952. He died in 1983.

5. The strategic importance of the Oder-Neisse line is studied in Debra Allen, *The Oder-Neisse Line: The United States, Poland and Germany in the Cold War* (Praeger, Westport 2003).

6. Victor Rothwell, *Britain and the Cold War 1941–1947* (Jonathan Cape, London 1982), p. 374; also 'Operation Unthinkable', p. 12.

7. 'Operation Unthinkable', p. 6.

8. Max Hastings, *Armageddon. The Battle for Germany 1944–45* (Macmillan,

London 2004), pp. 527–8; also Norman Davies, *Rising '44. The Battle for Warsaw* (Macmillan, London 2004), pp. 479–80.

9. Later Admiral Sir Guy Grantham. Appointed Commander-in-Chief Portsmouth and Allied Commander-in-Chief, Channel and southern North Sea in 1957. He died in 1992. For Cunningham's report, finally presented to COS on 5 June 1945, see AIR 8/798, NA.

10. Prof. Anita Prażmowska to author, 17 January 1945.

11. Dr Jacek Sawicki to author, 31 October 2012; also 'Operation Unthinkable', pp. 10–11.

12. Hugh Faringdon, *Confrontation. The Strategic Geography of NATO and the Warsaw Pact* (Routledge & Kegan Paul, London 1986), p. 237.

13. 'Operation Unthinkable', p. 14.

14. Later Air Chief Marshal Sir Walter Lloyd Dawson. Appointed Inspector-General of RAF in 1956. He died in 1994. For report see COS (45) 321, AIR 8/798, NA.

15. 'Operation Unthinkable', p. 7.

16. Ibid., p. 7.

17. Ibid., p. 5.

18. The report stated that four Polish squadrons stationed in north-west Europe would be used.

19. The USAAF continued to have problems with its jet Lockheed P-80, which had to be grounded during the Second World War.

20. 'Operation Unthinkable', p. 10. On 1 May 1945 the RAF possessed 3,182 bombers and 3,337 fighters, a total dwarfed by the US Navy's compliment of 22,000 combat planes. However, a large number of these aircraft were required for the war in the Pacific as well as home defence.

21. For the principal RAF bombers and fighters in use in 1945 see Hilary St George Saunders, *Royal Air Force 1939–1945, Volume III. The Fight is Won* (HMSO, London 1954), Appendix VIII. In the early summer of 1945 the B-29s were in the Pacific theatre and there were none in Europe. Their sudden appearance, in preparation for Unthinkable, would alarm the Soviet Union.

22. JPS memorandum, 25 April 1945, JPS Reports, CAB 84/71, NA.

23. The Mosquito, if operated from forward airbases in western Germany, could reach deep into Soviet-occupied territory. With an average range of more than 2,000 miles, it was an important component of the Allied strike force. Since it was mainly constructed of wood, rather than aluminium, it was easier to replace losses.

24. According to D.B. Tubbs in, *Lancaster Bomber* (Macmillan, London 1972), the range/loads of the Lancaster were 2,530 miles with 7,000lbs, 1,730 miles with

12,000lbs, 1,555 miles with 22,000lbs (Grand Slam). The author is grateful to Simon Tidswell for statistics.

25. In the Battle of Berlin, in the winter of 1943, German cities were pounded by waves of Lancaster bombers. In total 1,047 aircraft were lost, amounting to 5.1 per cent of sorties dispatched. In addition 1,682 were damaged. By comparison, the Mosquito losses amounted to just 0.5 per cent. See Tubbs, *Lancaster Bomber*.

26. 'Operation Unthinkable', pp. 12, 17.

27. The British-made GL Mk II radar system was supplied to the Soviet Union during the Second World War, under Lend-Lease. The British would withdraw support for this system once hostilities started, and the Soviets would have to rely on their own cloned copies, such as the Son-2a system.

28. Alexander Boyd, *The Soviet Air Force Since 1918* (Macdonald and Jane's, London 1977), p. 205; also 'Unthinkable', pp. 15, 17.

29. 'Soviet Capabilities to Launch Air Attacks Against the Soviet Union', JIC, 29 November 1946, 0000 Reel II, Records of Joint Chiefs of Staff Part II 1946–1953, GB 0099 KCLMA MF 1–70, LHCMA. Also Boyd, *Soviet Air Force*, p. 206.

30. Vasiliy Reshetnikov, *Bomber Pilot on the Eastern Front* (Pen & Sword, Barnsley 2008), pp. 169–70.

31. Boyd, *Soviet Air Force*, p. 215. These B-29 replicas were branded as the Tu-4.

32. Reshetnikov, *Bomber Pilot*, p. 63.

33. Ibid., pp. 171–2.

34. 'Operation Unthinkable', p. 13.

35. 'Operation Unthinkable', pp. 9–10. On VE Day the Allied forces amounted to nearly 4.5 million men deployed.

36. Keith Sword, Norman Davies and Jan Ciechanowski, *The Formation of the Polish Community in Great Britain 1939–50* (School of Slavonic and East European Studies, London 1989) pp. 62–3, 446. Joanna Pylat et al., have estimated total Polish forces in May 1945 at 201,160; see Joanna Pylat, Jan Ciechanowski and Andrzej Suchitz (Eds.), *General Władysław Anders. Soldier and Leader of the Free Poles in Exile* (Polish University Abroad, London 2007), p. 174.

37. For US demobilisation and the Soviet threat see James Schnabel, *The History of the Joint Chiefs of Staff*, pp. 212–26.

38. 'Operation Unthinkable', pp. 5, 11. Soviet divisional formations were smaller than Western divisions. Intelligence had determined that Red Army strength in Europe at the end of the war was 169 Shock Divisions, 347 Ordinary Divisions, 112 Shock Tank Brigades and 141 Ordinary Tank Brigades. Only a proportion of these units would face the Allied offensive.

39. When computing 'equivalent' divisions, the planners estimated that a Soviet Shock Division was worth two-thirds the fighting value of an Allied division, while an Ordinary Division was a third that of an Allied division. Similarly, a Soviet Ordinary Tank Brigade of fifty tanks and 1,000 men was worth a third of its Allied equivalent. For the size of other Red Army formations see David Glanz et al, *Slaughterhouse. The Handbook of the Eastern Front* (Aberjona Press, Bedford PA 2005), pp. 299–390.

40. 'Operation Unthinkable', p. 16.

41. Quoted from Robert Meiklejohn diary, 17 March 1945, in Frank Costigliola, 'After Roosevelt's Death: Dangerous Emotions, Divisive Discourses, and the Abandoned Alliance' in *Diplomatic History*, Volume 34, January 2010.

42. The Red Army had also benefited in the short term by the large quantities of captured German equipment and weapons, such as M.T. and anti-tank weapons.

43. Dr Heinrich Haape, *Moscow Tram Stop. A Doctor's Experiences with the German Spearhead in Russia* (Collins, London 1957), p. 332.

44. Faringdon, *Confrontation*, p. 39. Most of the Soviet Union has snow for more than a third of the year. See also 'The Influence of Climate' in James Lucas, *War on the Eastern Front* (Greenhill Books, London 1991), pp. 78–90.

45. 'Operation Unthinkable', p. 16.

46. For fatigue and morale in the Red Army see Catherine Merridale, *Ivan's War. The Red Army 1939–45* (Faber & Faber, London 2006), pp. 228–32.

47. Ibid. During the post-war communist era, 9 May assumed colossal importance in Soviet Russia, uniting the disparate factions within the country.

48. 'Operation Unthinkable', p. 11.

49. R.M. Ogorkiewicz, 'Soviet Armoured Formations' in *The Army Quarterly*, Volume LXXI, #1, October 1955.

50. The Sherman continued in service up to and including the Korean War.

51. Only later, larger-calibre guns, such as the 75mm, could penetrate the armour.

52. The SU100 was a turretless tank and consequently its weight was reduced and frontal armour was increased. Although it could only be fired by line of sight in one position, its hull was difficult to penetrate.

53. Albert Seaton and Jean Seaton, *The Soviet Army. 1918 to the Present* (The Bodley Head, London 1986), pp. 156–9.

54. For a study of the Soviet pillaging of their occupied sector of Germany see Anne Applebaum, *Iron Curtain. The Crushing of Eastern Europe 1944–56* (Allen Lane, London 2012), pp. 36–7.

55. Debriefing notes from security assets in Poland #V., HS4/145, NA.

56. 'Operation Unthinkable', pp. 8–9.

57. Such moves to Silesia were not always for the best motives, and many petty criminals headed west. Prof. Anita Prażmowska to author, 17 January 1945.

58. Dr Jacek Sawicki to author, 31 October 2012; also S.M. Plokhy, *Yalta*, p. 203.

59. Keith Lowe, *Savage Continent. Europe in the Aftermath of World War II* (Viking, London 2012), p. 233. Also Rafael A. Zagovec, 'Dances of Death: The Endkämpfe and the German Experience of Defeat' in *Everyone's War*, No. 11, Spring 2005. The starving and stateless may have been nearer to 11 million.

60. 'Notes by Field Marshal Montgomery on the General Intelligence Picture', ref. 12, Alanbrooke Papers, LHCMA.

61. Earl of Halifax to Foreign Office, 14 May 1945, PREM 3/473, NA.

62. Robert Lewis Koehl, *The Black Corps. The Structure and Power Struggles of the Nazi SS* (University of Wisconsin Press, Wisconsin 1983), pp. 221–2.

63. For a study of the British response to reports about the concentration camps see Jonathan Walker, *Poland Alone. Britain, SOE and the Collapse of the Polish Resistance 1944* (The History Press, Stroud 2010), pp. 128–39.

64. General Lord Ismay, *The Memoirs of General Lord Ismay* (Heinemann, London 1960), p. 392.

65. 'Operation Unthinkable', p. 3.

66. Krzysztof Persak and Łukasz Kamiński (Eds.), *A Handbook of the Communist Security Apparatus in East Central Europe 1944–1989* (Institute of National Remembrance, Warsaw 2005), pp. 202–5. Ironically the Soviets set up some of these prisons in some of the old Nazi concentration camps, such as Buchenwald.

67. John Koehler, *Stasi. The Untold Story of the East German Secret Police* (Westview Press, Oxford 1999), pp. 50–1.

68. Christopher Andrew and Oleg Gordievsky, *KGB. The Inside Story of its Foreign Operations from Lenin to Gorbachev* (Sceptre, London 1991), p. 360.

69. By May 1945 Colonel Zygmunt Berling had been demoted and exiled to Moscow. He fell foul of the PKWN, who affirmed that he was 'an enemy of Polish democracy'.

70. The strength of Berling's Army is very approximate, as estimates vary between 172,000 and 280,000. See Antony Polonsky and Bolesław Drukier (Eds.), *The Beginnings of Communist Rule in Poland* (Routledge & Kegan Paul, London 1980), p. 63.

71. Anita Prażmowska, *Civil War in Poland 1942–1948* (Palgrave Macmillan, London 2004), pp. 124–5; also Steven Zaloga, *The Polish Army 1939–45* (Osprey, Oxford 2005), pp. 26–7.

72. See Foreign Office memorandum 'Conditions in Poland', FO 371/476648, NA. Many local villages remained resolutely pro-Home Army and even the

land reform, promoted as a means to gain support for the Soviet-backed Poles received less than fulsome support. Prażmowska, *Civil War in Poland*, pp. 125–7; also W. Jurgielewicz, *Ludowe Wojsko Polskie 1943–1973* (MON, Warsaw 1974).

73. Dr Tomasz Łabuszewski to author, 31 October 2012.

74. Quoted in James Leasor, *War at the Top*, p. 174.

75. Anne Chisholm & Michael Davie, *Beaverbrook: A Life* (Hutchinson, London 1992), p. 434.

76. Ismay, *Memoirs*, p. 392.

77. Folly, *Churchill, Whitehall and the Soviet Union*, pp. 28–31.

78. Frank Roberts, *Dealing with Dictators. The Destruction and Revival of Europe 1930–70* (Weidenfeld & Nicolson, London 1991), pp. 90–1.

79. Nelson MacPherson, *American Intelligence in War-Time London. The Story of OSS* (Frank Cass, London 2003), p. 235; also JIC 250/1, 'USSR Post-war Capabilities and Policies', 31 January 1945, and 250/2, 2 February 1945, both reel 14, 95, RG 226, NARA.

80. On 25 June the United Nations Charter was finally signed, although individual countries still had to secure the approval of their parliaments or congresses.

81. MacPherson, *American Intelligence in War-Time London*, p. 236; also Joint Intelligence Staff (JIS), 161, 'British Capabilities and Intentions', 10 May 1945, reel 1, entry 190, RG 226, NARA.

82. With the death in November 1944 of FM Sir John Dill, communication between the Allied Chiefs started to slip and never regained that ease which he engendered. Co-operation, of course, continued with research and development as well as intelligence, but these were lower-level collaborations. See Richard J. Aldrich (Ed.), *British Intelligence, Strategy and the Cold War 1945–51* (Routledge, London 1992), p. 221.

Chapter 5: The Plan – 'Total War'

1. Major S.J. Watson, 'A Comparison of the Russian, American and British Field Armies', *The Army Quarterly & Defence Journal*, April 1950.

2. 'Operation Unthinkable', CAB 120/691, NA, p. 2. Also James Lucas, *War on the Eastern Front* (Greenhill Books, London 1991), pp. 106–7.

3. Dmitri Volkogonov (Trans. Harold Shukman), *The Rise and Fall of the Soviet Empire. Political Leaders from Lenin to Gorbachev* (HarperCollins, London 1998), pp. 114–15. Stalin still had a problem with Ukraine, where nationalists continued to agitate. Much of the local population had nursed a deep hatred of Stalin and his policies since the 1930s, when he had forced through collectivisation, resulting in starvation and the deaths of approximately 8 million people.

4. Mass identity checks were carried out on men between the ages of 16 and 50 and anyone suspected of AK allegiance was arrested. See Antony Polonsky and Bolesław Drukier (Eds.), *The Beginnings of Communist Rule in Poland* (Routledge & Kegan Paul, London 1980), p. 65. Also Anita Prażmowska, *Civil War in Poland 1942–1948* (Palgrave Macmillan, London 2004), p. 124–6. Also Dr Tomasz Łabuszewski to author, 31 October 2012. DSZ took over Nie's army personnel and materials.

5. In the original 'Tempest' plan, the AK called for a nationwide uprising against the Germans, which, if successful, would mean the underground state could meet the incoming Soviet Army as 'equals'. In the event the rising was confined to Warsaw. Hidden weapons and ammunition, protected in oiled cloth, are still being found during redevelopment work in Warsaw. Piotr Śliwowski to author, 31 October 2012.

6. Dr Tomasz Łabuszewski and Dr Jacek Sawicki to author, 31 October 2012. See also R.M. Hankey memorandum, 26 March 1945, FO 371/47709, NA.

7. WiN was slowly eroded as a source of opposition power, particularly during late 1946. The NKVD extracted intelligence via torture. For a study of the extent of this treatment see Marek Jan Chodakiewicz, 'The Dialectics of Pain: The Interrogation Methods of the Communist Secret Police in Poland, 1944–1955', a paper presented at the 61st Annual Meeting of the Polish Institute of Arts and Sciences of America, McGill University, Montreal, Canada, 6–7 June 2003. Also Piotr Śliwowski to author, 31 October 2012.

8. Mark Harrison, *Accounting for War. Soviet Production, Employment, and the Defence Burden 1940–1945* (Cambridge University Press, Cambridge 1996), p. 11.

9. Roy Douglas, *From War to Cold War, 1942–48* (Macmillan, London 1981), pp. 122–3. Whereas the Soviet destruction of German offensive power in 1941–42 was funded by their domestic supply, their pursuit and destruction of the Wehrmacht through to Germany in 1945 was funded by Western resources. See Harrison, *Accounting for War*, p. 130.

10. An example of his tactical weakness was his assault on the heavily defended Zeelöwe Heights around the German capital. He allowed the German 'flexible defence' to fall back, draw his forces in and then subject them to successful counter-attack. Similarly, his use of searchlights to dazzle the enemy merely served to silhouette his own men as easy targets.

11. Dr Sergei Kudryashov, 'D-Day and Russia' in *Everyone's War*, No. 11, Spring 2005.

12. Lieutenant-Colonel David Summerfield RM to author, 16 February 2013.

13. It was not until August 1945 that SIS was officially sanctioned to take over SOE, but the intelligence agency was particularly keen to acquire SOE's sabotage skills. SOE was not formally disbanded until 31 December 1945, though there has been some dispute between two SOE authorities, M.R.D. Foot and David Stafford, over the practical date of dissolution as well as the extent of SIS absorption. See William Mackenzie, *The Secret History of SOE. Special Operations Executive 1940–1945* (St. Ermin's Press, London 2000), p. 715; also M.R.D. Foot, *SOE. The Special Operations Executive 1940–1946* (Pimlico, London 1999), p. 356.

14. SOE memorandum, 22 November 1945, COS (45) 671, CAB 80/98, NA.

15. David Stafford, *Britain and European Resistance 1940–1945. A Survey of the Special Operations Executive with Documents* (Macmillan, London 1980), p. 203.

16. Mackenzie, *The Secret History of SOE*, pp. 675–6. For Turkey see James Schnabel, *The History of the Joint Chiefs of Staff*, p. 57. The claims also included retrocession of the Turkish provinces of Kars and Ardahan in East Turkey.

17. For an assessment of Soviet strength in the East see 'Possible Russian Participation in the War against Japan', 10 July 1945, CAB 84/72, NA. Also 'Operation Unthinkable', p. 4. There was always the possibility that US forces could subsequently attack the Soviet Union via China, using the Nationalist Chinese to help them.

18. 'Operation Unthinkable', p. 3.

19. Dr Jacek Sawacki and Piotr Śliwowski to author, 31 October 2012. In Silesia, for example, one notable resistance band, the 'Warta' Wielkopolska Independent Group only numbered about 100 fighters.

20. Piotr Śliwowski to author, 31 October 2012. It has been estimated that during the Warsaw Rising the local population comprised 25 per cent fighters, 5 per cent who opposed the rising and 70 per cent who just wanted to survive.

21. Dr Tomasz Łabuszewski and Dr Jacek Sawicki to author, 31 October 2012. Also Prażmowska, *Civil War in Poland*, pp. 121–2, 156. Also Krzysztof Persak and Łukasz Kamiński (Eds.), *A Handbook of the Communist Security Apparatus in East Central Europe 1944–1989* (Institute of National Remembrance, Warsaw 2005), pp. 222–3.

22. Lucas, *War on the Eastern Front*, pp. 74–5.

23. Dr Heinrich Haape, Moscow Tram Stop, p. 182.

24. For a detailed assessment of the preparations and operations during Barbarossa see Richard Overy, *Russia's War* (Penguin, London 1999).

25. Haape, *Moscow Tram Stop*, p. 181. Although the bitter winter had defeated the Germans in the Second World War, the Allies would probably have some Finns and Norwegians to help in the winter campaign.

26. Harrison, *Accounting for War*, Table 1.1, p. 10.

27. On 26 December 1941 the *Melbourne Herald* published Curtin's highly controversial message. Churchill was duly appalled at the Australian prime minister's rejection of Britain in favour of the US, but at least the speech highlighted Australia's vulnerability to the Japanese. The author is most grateful for an insight into Australia's political/military situation in 1945 by Dr Ross Bastiaan, 4 December 2012.

28. John Curtin died on 5 July 1945. He would have still been in office at the date of Unthinkable on 1 July. He was succeeded as prime minister by Ben Chifley, another Labor Party stalwart, whose views on foreign policy largely resembled those of Curtin.

29. Only a year after the war a meeting of Commonwealth prime ministers had failed to agree on various dominions taking responsibility for Commonwealth security. See Julian Lewis, *Changing Direction. British Military Planning for Post-war Strategic Defence, 1942–1947* (Routledge, London 2003), pp. 267–71. For Smuts see Roy Jenkins, *Churchill* (Pan Macmillan, London 2002), p. 789.

30. Shelford Bidwell, 'The Use of Small Nuclear Weapons in War on Land', *The Army Quarterly & Defence Journal*, April 1971.

Chapter 6: War Clouds

1. The shift in the US attitude to the Soviet Union in the early months of the Truman presidency is examined by Frank Costigliola in 'After Roosevelt's Death: Dangerous Emotions, Divisive Discourses and the Abandoned Alliance' in *Diplomatic History*, January 2010, Volume 34, #1; also James Schnabel *The History of the Joint Chiefs of Staff*, p. 32.

2. Lord Halifax to WSC, 23 April 1945, FO 954/20 #635, NA. See also Wilson Miscamble, 'Anthony Eden and the Truman-Molotov Conversations, April 1945' in *Diplomatic History*, Volume 2, #2, April 1978.

3. It seems that Molotov was at odds with Stalin over the 'inevitable war'. He was also opposed to Khrushchev's later concept of peaceful coexistence. See Albert Resis (Ed.), *Molotov Remembers. Inside Kremlin Politics* (Ivan Dee, Chicago 1993), p. 7.

4. Martin H. Folly, *Churchill, Whitehall and the Soviet Union, 1940–1945* (Macmillan, London 2000), pp. 80–1.

5. The basics of a United Nations organisation had already been agreed during the Dumbarton Oaks Conference, Washington, held between 21 August and 7 October 1944. This included a Security Council and General Assembly. For Stettinius's career see Thomas Campbell and George Herring (Eds.), *The Diaries of Edward R Stettinius Jr., 1943–1946* (New Viewpoints, New York 1975), Introduction.

6. Venona Transcript no. 1822, 30 March 1945. The release of previously top-secret material in 1995 confirmed Hiss's guilt. He appeared in the early 1970s ITV production *The World at War* when he made a predictable defence of Stalin's tactics at Yalta.

7. Christopher Andrew and Oleg Gordievsky, *KGB. The Inside Story of its Foreign Operations from Lenin to Gorbachev* (Sceptre, London 1991), pp. 344–5. For White's implication see the Venona Transcripts, www.nsa.gov/publicinfo/files/venona/1945.

8. WSC to Stalin, 28 April 1945, telegram No. 450, Char 20/216, CAC.

9. Ibid.

10. The sixteen-man delegation included: Leopold Okulicki, Jan Stanisław Jankowski, Adam Bień, Stanisław Jasiukowicz, Antoni Pajdak, Kazimierz Bagiński, Józef Chaciński, Eugeniusz Czarnowski, Kazimierz Kobylański, Józef Stemler-Dąbski, Stanisław Michałowski, Franciszek Urbański, Zbigniew Stypułkowski, Stanisław Mierzwa, Aleksander Zwierzyński, Kazimierz Pużak. For Churchill's telegram see WSC to Stalin, 28 April 1945, no. 450, Char 20/216, CAC. Also Józef Garliński, *Poland, SOE and the Allies* (George Allen and Unwin, London 1969), pp. 223–33.

11. Quoted in Donald Thomas, *Freedom's Frontier. Censorship in Modern Britain* (John Murray, London 2007), p. 173.

12. WSC to Truman, 30 April 1945, PREM 3/473, NA.

13. Allied Force HQ to War Department, 15 March 1945, CAB 88/56, NA.

14. The name 'Venezia' alludes to the Venetian cultural links of the region. The more recent name of 'Julian March' comes from the nearby Julian Alps and the old word for a border (march).

15. Minutes of British Cabinet Meeting, 13 May 1945, CAB 65/52, NA. For Churchill's later assessment of the crisis see Winston S. Churchill, *The Second World War. Volume VI*, pp. 480–9; also Peter Clarke, *The Last Thousand Days of the British Empire* (Allen Lane, London 2007), pp. 320–1, and Schnabel, *History of Joint Chiefs*, pp. 41–6.

16. FM Alexander to WSC, 1 May 1945, Char 20/217, CAC. See also WSC to Stalin, 15 May 1945, Char 20/225, CAC.

17. WSC to FM Alexander, 6 May 1945, Char 20/218, CAC.

18. FM Alexander to WSC, 17 June 1945, Char 20/224, CAC. The 10th Indian Division, the South African Armoured Division and the New Zealand Division were all to leave Italy and return to their homelands within weeks of the end of the war, while seven US divisions were scheduled to be shipped back to the US for demobilisation.

19. WSC to FM Alexander, 18 June 1945, Char 20/224, CAC. Also FM Alexander to WSC, 19 June 1945, Char 20/224, CAC. For Truman quote see Schnabel, *History of Joint Chiefs*, p. 48.

20. John Colville, *The Fringes of Power. Downing Street Diaries 1939–1955* (Hodder & Stoughton, London 1985), 1 May 1945, p. 595.

21. Quoted in Anthony Montague Browne, *Long Sunset. Memoirs of Winston Churchill's Last Private Secretary* (Cassell, London 1995), p. 116.

22. Lord Alanbrooke diary, 2 May 1945, Alanbrooke Papers, LHCMA.

23. WSC to Anthony Eden, 4 May 1945, FO 954/20 #710, NA.

24. Charles E. Bohlen, *Witness to History 1929–1969* (WW Norton, New York 1973), pp. 214–15.

25. Stalin to WSC, Telegram no. 456, 4 May 1945, FO 954/20, NA.

26. Stalin to WSC, 5 May 1945, FO 954/20 #714; and British Embassy to Foreign Office, #724, both NA. SOE correspondence on the matter of clandestine wireless stations was not sympathetic to the Poles; see MPP to A/DH, 10 May 1945, HS4/145, NA.

27. For Okulicki's appointment and command see Marek Ney-Krwawicz, *The Polish Resistance Home Army 1939–1945* (PUMST, London 2001), pp. 128–33.

28. *Daily Telegraph*, 8 May 1945.

29. Colonel David Smiley to author, 16 September 2003. The Soviets also destroyed the opposition by offering two successive false amnesties, allowing them to capture leading underground figures. Although at the proposed start date of Operation Unthinkable WiN was in its infancy. During 1945 the movement grew to become a formidable force and established ties with Britain's security services. It was destroyed several years later by infiltration by the communist authorities.

30. Jonathan Walker, *Poland Alone. Britain, SOE and the Collapse of the Polish Resistance 1944* (The History Press, Stroud 2010), pp. 217, 238, 262–3. In his task of relaying intelligence to Britain, Sergeant Ward was greatly assisted by resistance members Władek and Sofie Miłkowska, who instructed and sheltered him. For Operation Freston see Jonathan Walker, *Poland Alone*, pp. 272–8; also Dr Jacek Sawicki to author, 31 October 2012.

31. Top secret memorandum, 'Post-war Rehabilitation of SOE Agents', undated but probably April 1945, HS4/291, NA. For developments on the mission see Christopher Warner to Henry Sporborg, 12 March 1945 and 'Foreign Office Polish Mission Report', 21 April 1945, both HS4/262, NA. An earlier military mission to Poland in January 1945 (Operation Freston) was largely a failure. See also cipher, 10 March 1945, report on 'SOE –

NKVD Cooperation', undated, and 'Notes on First Meeting with Colonel Graur', 6 June 1945, all in HS4/335, NA. Intelligence later started coming back from the newly established British Embassy in Warsaw, which was operating out of the Hotel Polonia and using the services of a good number of old 'Polish hands'.

32. Prime minister's memorandum, 30 April 1945, CAB 120/690, NA.
33. WSC to FM Montgomery, 6 May 1945, Char 20/225, CAC; Churchill, *Triumph and Tragedy*, p. 469. Also Admiral Cunningham diary 1945, MS 52578, Cunningham Papers, British Library (hereafter BL). Churchill was subsequently relieved to hear that an Allied airborne company had reached Copenhagen and that the party of Soviet parachutists only amounted to two men.
34. Admiral Cunningham, of the Chiefs of Staff Committee, believed that if after Hitler's death Dönitz had called on all German forces to surrender, he would have been 'the biggest man in Germany'. See Cunningham diary, 2 May 1945, BL.
35. Anna Piekarska (Ed.), *PRL- Tak daleko, tak blisko* (Institute of National Remembrance, Warsaw 2007), p. 10. Also Dr Tomasz Łabuszewski to author, 31 October 2012.
36. Hugh Lunghi, quoted in Martin Gilbert, *The Day the War Ended. VE Day 1945 in Europe and Around the World* (HarperCollins, London 1995), p. 325.
37. John Butler, *The Red Dean of Canterbury. The Public and Private Faces of Hewlett Johnson* (Scala, London 2011), pp. 76–9.
38. Frank Roberts, *Dealing with Dictators*, p. 85.
39. Hewlett Johnson, *Soviet Success* (Hutchinson, London 1947), p. 17.
40. Quoted in Gilbert, *The Day the War Ended*, p. 303.
41. Harry S. Truman to Eleanor Roosevelt, 10 May 1945, Box 13, #394, Truman Library, www.trumanlibrary.org.
42. Roy Jenkins, *Truman* (Papermac, London 1995), p. 68.
43. Orme Sergeant, 'Stocktaking after VE Day', 11 July 1945, Char 23/14, CAC.
44. WSC to Truman, 6 May 1945, Char 20/225, CAC.
45. WSC to Truman, 11 May 1945, PREM 3/473, NA. Churchill sent a similar telegram about the prospect of a Third World War to Anthony Eden, who was attending the San Francisco Conference. See WSC to Eden 11 May 1945, Churchill, *Triumph and Tragedy*, p. 500.
46. WSC to Truman, 12 May 1945, PREM 3/473, NA.
47. Minutes of British War Cabinet, 13 May 1945, CAB 65/52, NA.
48. Henry Stimson diary, 14 May 1945, LoC.
49. Truman to WSC, 12 May 1945, PREM 3/473, NA.

50. Alanbrooke diary, 13 May 1945, LHCMA. Admiral Cunningham also records that 'PM very thrilled at getting Truman's support'. See Cunningham diary, 13 May 1945, BL.

51. Ibid., 14 May 1945.

52. Colville, *The Fringes of Power*, 14 May 1945, p. 599. Also Cunningham diary, 21 May 1945, BL.

53. Quoted in Charles Whiting, *Finale at Flensburg. The Story of Field Marshal Montgomery's Battle for the Baltic* (Leo Cooper, London 1973), p. 158.

54. Robert Rasnus, in Studs Terkel, *'The Good War'. An Oral History of World War Two* (Ballantine Press, New York 1985).

55. FM Montgomery, 'The Truth about the Telegram', in microfiche 'The Woodford Speech of Nov 1954 and the famous telegram!' BLM 162 reel 15, Montgomery Papers, IWM. Lüneburg Heath, near Hamburg, was the scene where Montgomery took the final surrender of German forces in northern Germany, Holland and Denmark.

56. Churchill, *Triumph and Tragedy*, pp. 499–500. Also see *The Times*, 25 November 1954.

57. 'Secret Memorandum', Appendix C, CPS 158/2, CAB 88/56, NA.

58. WSC to General Ismay (COS Committee), 17 May 1945, Churchill, *Triumph and Tragedy*, p. 500.

59. For the difficulties in planning a conflict see Admiral Sir R.P. Ernle-Erle-Drax, 'Some Problems of the Next War', in *The Army Quarterly*, January 1947, Volume LIII, #2. For demobilisation see Schnabel, *History of Joint Chiefs*, pp. 212–26.

60. Quoted in Roy Douglas, *From War to Cold War 1942–48* (Macmillan, London 1981), p. 88.

61. PREM 3 396/12, NA. For Churchill's use of 'iron curtain' see David Reynolds, *From World War to Cold War: Churchill, Roosevelt, and the International History of the 1940s* (Oxford University Press, New York 2006), pp. 248–9.

62. Reynolds, *From World War*, p.478, and also Laurence Rees, *World War Two: Behind Closed Doors. Stalin, the Nazis and the West* (BBC Books, London 2008), p. 369. For Byrnes and Truman see Jenkins, *Truman*, p. 70–1.

63. Truman appointment sheet, 19 May 1945. Quoted in Robert H. Ferrell (Ed.), *Off the Record. The Private Papers of Harry S Truman* (Harper & Row, New York 1980), p. 31.

64. The 'Morgan Line' split the region into a western 'Zone A', to be run by an Allied military administration, and an eastern 'Zone B', to be controlled by the Yugoslav People's Army. This only served as a temporary arrangement, pending confirmation of the exact border at a subsequent

peace conference. Importantly, Trieste and Gorizia remained within Allied control. The Kremlin may well have exerted pressure on Tito to accept this demarcation, for he signed up to it on 10 June, a move that certainly took the heat out of an extremely dangerous dispute. The Morgan Line was succeeded by a proper border in September 1947, when the provisions of the Paris Peace Conference moved the border several miles to the west. Today the old Morgan Line remains in Slovenian territory.

65. Lord Moran diary, 20 May 1945, p. 251.
66. Ibid., 4 June 1945.

Chapter 7: The Plan Delivered

1. The report was dated 22 May 1945, but only reached the chiefs on 24 May.
2. Lord Alanbrooke diary, 24 May 1945, Alanbrooke Papers, LHCMA.
3. Lord Alanbrooke, 'Notes on my Life', Volume 15, ref. 5/2/27 (1955–1956), 4 Feb–3 July 1945, Alanbrooke Papers, LHCMA. Brooke often confused time spans in his descriptions. On 24 May 1945 he refers to a meeting 'a few weeks earlier', yet this took place on 2 October 1944, more than 30 weeks before. Similarly, he refers to 24 May 1945 as 'a few days after VE Day', yet it was sixteen days later.
4. Alanbrooke diary, 7 May 1945, LHCMA.
5. Cunningham diary, 26 May 1945, MS 52578, Cunningham Papers, BL.
6. See Cunningham diary, 25 May 1945. Also Alanbrooke diary, 26 May 1945.
7. Truman to WSC, 2 June 1945, FO 954/20 #780, NA.
8. WSC to Truman, FO 954/20 # 786, NA.
9. Memorandum #24 by Charles E. Bohlen, '1st Conversation at the Kremlin, 8pm, 26 May 1945', Ref 740.00119 (Potsdam) 6-645, Potsdam Briefing Book, US Department of State, US National Archives.
10. Christopher Thorne, *Allies of a Kind. The United States, Britain, and the War Against Japan 1941–1945* (Hamish Hamilton, London 1978), p. 499.
11. Harry S. Truman diary, 13 June 1945, Harry S. Truman Library, www.trumanlibrary.org; also Charles E. Bohlen, *Witness to History 1929–1969* (WW Norton, New York 1973), p. 215. For Hopkins see Christopher Andrew and Oleg Gordievsky, *KGB. The Inside Story of its Foreign Operations from Lenin to Gorbachev* (Sceptre, London 1991), p. 147.
12. Charles Mee, *Meeting at Potsdam* (Andre Deutsch, London 1975), pp. 33–6.
13. Earl of Avon, *The Eden Memoirs. The Reckoning* (Cassell, London 1965), p. 539. See also Winston S. Churchill, *The Second World War. Volume VI. Triumph and Tragedy* (Cassell, London 1954), pp. 501–5, and Roy Douglas, From

War to Cold War, 1942–48 (Macmillan, London 1981), pp. 92–3. See also W. Averell Harriman and Elie Abel, *Special Envoy to Churchill and Stalin 1941–1946* (Hutchinson, London 1976), p. 452.

14. Alanbrooke diary, 31 May 1945.

15. John Colville, *Footprints in Time* (Collins, London 1976), pp. 206–7.

16. WSC to Truman, 2 June 1945, PREM 3/473, NA. See also WSC to FM Alexander, 29 May 1945, Char 20/225, CAC.

17. Churchill, *Triumph and Tragedy*, p. 487.

18. WSC to Truman, 23 June 1945, PREM 3/473, NA.

19. One of the most notorious *foibe* was discovered at Basovizza (in fact it was a mine shaft). Because of the agendas of certain modern political parties, much of the debate over the massacres has been clouded in Left/Right rhetoric. This also applies to much of the literature on the subject. See studies by Glenda Sluga, *The Problem of Trieste and the Italo-Yugoslav Border. Difference, Identity and Sovereignty in Twentieth-century Europe* (State University of New York, New York 2011). Also Joze Pirjevec, *Foibe. Una storia d'Italia* (Giulio Einaudi Editore, Turin 2009).

20. WSC to Truman, 4 June 1945, PREM 3/473, NA.

21. Alanbrooke diary, 8 June 1945.

22. Soviet official sources listed even greater odds when recording the Red Army's final assault on Germany in January 1945. Soviet superiority over German forces was calculated at 7:1 in infantry and 4:1 in tanks. See James Lucas, *War on the Eastern Front* (Greenhill Books, London 1991), p. 50.

23. The chiefs' report included a breakdown of the total allied tactical aircraft of 6,048. It showed the US providing 3,480; Britain and dominions, 2,370 and Poland, 198. Of the 2,750 total strategic aircraft available, the US would provide 1,008; the British and dominions 1,722 and the Polish Air Force 20. See Joint Chiefs report, 8 June 1945, CAB 120/691.

24. 'Report on Operation Unthinkable', chiefs of staff, 8 June 1945, CAB 120/691, NA.

25. Ibid.

26. WSC to General Ismay, 10 June 1945, CAB 120/691, NA.

27. Alanbrooke diary, 11 June 1945.

28. Truman diary, 13 June 1945.

29. Ralph Ingersoll, *Top Secret* (Partridge Publications, London 1946), pp. 271, 273.

30. Truman to WSC, 12 June 1945, Char 20/221, CAC. See also Cunningham diary, 12 June 1945. VCIGS to FM Montgomery, 15 June 1945, ref. 11, Alanbrooke Papers, LHCMA. Also, WSC to FM Alexander, 9 June 1945, Char 23/14, CAC; and WSC to Truman, 14 June 1945, Char 20/224, CAC.

31. Montgomery to Brooke, 14 June 1945, cipher message, BLM 162/2, Montgomery Papers, IWM.

32. Montgomery Memoir, June 1959, 'The Truth about the Telegram' in microfiche 'The Woodford Speech of Nov 1954 and the famous telegram!' BLM 162 reel 15, Montgomery Papers, IWM.

33. Churchill to FM Montgomery, cipher, 23 June 1945, ref. 19; FM Montgomery to FM Brooke, 22 June 1945, ref. 18. Both Alanbrooke Papers, LHCMA.

34. See John Ray Skates, *The Invasion of Japan: Alternative to the Bomb* (The University of South Carolina Press, Columbia 1994).

35. 'Redeployment of US and British Forces after the Defeat of Germany', 1 April 1945, CAB 88/56, NA.

36. WSC to British Embassy, Moscow, 15 June 1945, Char 20/224.

37. WSC to M. Mikołajczyk, 26 June 1945, Char 20/225, CAC.

38. The PPR and their allies held fourteen of the twenty available seats in the cabinet, which was headed by the pro-Soviet socialist Osóbka-Morawski. The two deputies to the prime minister were Mikołajczyk and the communist Władysław Gomułka.

39. For details of the trial and imprisonment of the sixteen see Józef Garliński, *Poland, SOE and the Allies* (George Allen and Unwin, London 1969), pp. 227–33. For *Pravda* account see Zaslavsky memorandum, 20 June 1945, HS4/139, NA.

40. Nigel Cawthorne, *The Iron Cage* (Fourth Estate, London 1993).

41. Stalin to WSC, 23 March 1945, Ministry of Foreign Affairs USSR; J.V. Stalin, *Stalin's Correspondence with Churchill and Attlee 1941–1945* (Capricorn Books, New York 1965).

42. 'MPP' to Victor Cavendish Bentinck, 22 June 1945, HS4/145, NA.

43. War Office to FM Montgomery, 1 July 1945, Alanbrooke Papers, LHCMA.

44. Alanbrooke diary, 2 July 1945, LHCMA.

45. WSC to Truman, 3 July 1945, Char 20/222, CAC.

46. US Department of State. Diplomatic Papers: The Conference of Berlin 1945. Briefing Book Paper # 224.

47. Lord Moran, *Winston Churchill. The Struggle for Survival 1940–1965* (Constable, London 1966), p.253.

48. Andrzej Suchitz and Jan Ciechanowski, 'The History of the Polish Intelligence Archives after 1945' in Tessa Stirling, Daria Nałęcz and Tadeusz Dubicki (Eds.), *Intelligence Co-operation Between Poland and Great Britain during World War II, Volume I. The Report of the Anglo-Polish Historical Committee* (Valentine Mitchell, London 2005), pp. 13–28.

49. The Conservative politician Robert 'Bob' Boothby recalled a miserable lunch with his old friend the Czech foreign minister, Jan Masaryk, who confessed

that he had been ordered to recognise the new Polish administration, but could not bring himself to do it. See Robert Boothby, *Boothby. Recollections of a Rebel* (Hutchinson, London 1978), p. 204.

50. Anita Prażmowska, *Civil War in Poland 1942–1948* (Palgrave Macmillan, London 2004), pp. 145–7.

51. For servicewomen see WSC to Cabinet, 'Manpower', 5 July 1945, Char 23/13, CAC. For general demobilisation see Alan Allport, *Demobbed. Coming Home After the Second World War* (Yale University Press, New Haven 2009), pp. 26–9. For demobilisation in the Red Army see Catherine Merridale, *Ivan's War. The Red Army 1939–45* (Faber & Faber, London 2006), pp. 306–7.

52. Bohlen, *Witness to History*, p. 226.

53. Ibid., 7, 9 July 1945. Also Peter Clarke, *The Last Thousand Days of the British Empire* (Allen Lane, London 2007), p. 321.

Chapter 8: Fortress Britain

1. Jock Colville, *The Fringes of Power. Downing Street Diaries 1939–1955* (Hodder & Stoughton, London 1985), p. 610.

2. For a detailed study of Churchill's life as an artist see David Coombs, with Minnie Churchill, *Sir Winston Churchill's Life Through His Paintings* (Chaucer Press, London 2003).

3. Vladislav Zubok and Constantine Pleshakov, *Inside the Kremlin's Cold War. From Stalin to Khrushchev* (Harvard University Press, Cambridge MA 1996), pp. 48–50.

4. Tom Bower, *The Perfect English Spy. Sir Dick White and the Secret War 1935–90* (Heinemann, London 1995). Sir Dick White became chief of SIS in 1956.

5. Throughout the spring of 1945, large numbers of Ukrainians were forcibly deported to Siberia, to be replaced by ethnic Russians. However, large numbers of anti-Soviet partisans managed to escape into underground bunkers in the Carpathian Mountains, out of the reach of the Red Army. See A.H.S. Candlin, 'Czechoslovakia, Ukrainian Separatism and Soviet Security', *The Army Quarterly & Defence Journal*, January 1972.

6. JPS report on 'Operation Unthinkable', 11 July 1945, p. 1.

7. Ibid., p. 2.

8. Jonathan Walker, *Poland Alone*, pp. 243–4.

9. Irmgard Gröttrup, *Rocket Wife* (André Deutsch, London 1959), p. 179.

10. For details of the immediate post-war years of Soviet rocket development see Frederick Ordway and Mitchell Sharpe, *The Rocket Team* (Heinemann, London 1979), pp. 318–43.

11. WSC to Sir Archibald Sinclair, 28 March 1945, CAB 120/750, NA.

12. JPS report on 'Operation Unthinkable', 11 July 1945, CAB 120/691, NA.

13. Ibid.

14. In the post-war years conjecture has been rife concerning the likely destination of a British government-in-exile. A dominion in the Caribbean has been mooted, as has Kimberley in South Africa. Jasper Humphreys to author, 13 May 2012.

15. The Home Fleet would comprise two battleships, four cruisers, three destroyer flotillas and three submarine flotillas. The east coast would be protected by three destroyer flotillas and six MTB/MGB flotillas. The south coast would be patrolled by two cruisers, three destroyer flotillas and six MTB/MGB flotillas. JPS report, 11 July 1945, CAB 120/691, NA.

16. This combined air force equates to the approximate strength at the end of the Second World War.

17. JPS report, 11 July 1945, CAB 120/691, NA.

18. Lord Moran, *Winston Churchill*, p. 257.

19. Winston S. Churchill, *The Second World War. Volume VI*, p. 553.

20. Although it is commonly believed that Truman only learned about the bomb just after Roosevelt's death, there is some evidence that Roosevelt may have told Truman about the bomb up to eight months before he died.

21. James Leasor, *War at the Top*, p. 289.

22. Lord Moran diary, 16 July 1945.

23. Harry S. Truman diary, 16 July 1945, Harry S. Truman Library, www.trumanlibrary.org.

24. Ibid., 17 July 1945. Inevitably, Truman would later revise his opinion of Stalin.

25. Leasor, *War at the Top*, p. 291.

26. Stephen Walker, *Shockwave. The Countdown to Hiroshima* (John Murray, London 2005), pp. 65–74. Also Dr Peter Pedersen, 'On the Trail of the Bomb' in *Battlefields Review*, Issue 20.

27. Fred Freed (Prod.), NBC White Paper. The Decision to Drop the Bomb, broadcast in 1965.

28. Colville, *Fringes of Power*, p. 610.

29. See Venona transcripts, especially 16 April 1945, where 'Charl'z' [Fuchs] is commended on his information about the magnetic method of separation in the atomic bomb. www.nsa.gov/publicinfo/files/venona/1945.

30. Amy Knight, *Beria. Stalin's First Lieutenant* (Princeton University Press, Princeton 1993), pp. 135–6. Two weeks after Hiroshima Stalin and Beria set up the 'Special Committee on the Atomic Bomb' to boost the existing

'Scientific-Technical Council'. The Soviet spy John Cairncross was private secretary to Lord Hankey, whose office was involved with the early Tube Alloys development. Donald Maclean, as one of the secretaries on the Anglo-American Combined Committee, had access to US atomic secrets, especially the vital knowledge that the US and Britain had access to 90 per cent of uranium deposits outside the Soviet Union; see Robert Cecil, *A Divided Life. A Biography of Donald Maclean* (The Bodley Head, London 1988), p. 71. For Stalin and Khartin quote see Zubok and Pleshakov, *Inside the Kremlin's Cold War*, pp. 39–42.

31. Alanbrooke diary, 23 July 1945, Alanbrooke Papers, LHCMA.

32. Lord Moran, 22 July 1945, op. cit. For atomic bombs see Alanbrooke diary, 23 July 1945. Ironically, Churchill had only recently railed at Air Marshal Portal that the destruction of German civilian targets, such as Dresden, were 'acts of terror'. See 'The Final Act' in Max Hastings, *Finest Years. Churchill as Warlord 1940–45* (Harper Press, London 2009).

33. Lord Alanbrooke, 'Notes on My Life', 23 July 1945, LHCMA.

34. The US and Britain would share information on nuclear programmes until the 1946 Atomic Energy Act, when the co-operation was severed and Britain developed her own programme. The first British atomic bomb was tested in 1952.

35. Stephen Ross, *American War Plans, 1945–1950* (Frank Cass, London 1996), pp. 12–15. The US Joint Chiefs highlighted twenty population centres that also contained industrial targets. These included Moscow, Gorki, Kuibyshev, Sverdeovak and Leningrad.

36. 'Record of Private Talk between the Prime Minister and Generalissimo Stalin', 18 July 1945, Char 23/14, CAC.

37. Mary Soames, *A Daughter's Tale* (Doubleday, London 2011), p. 361. Churchill's departure from Chequers did not prove to be final. He returned as prime minister in October 1951.

38. Colville, *Fringes of Power*, p. 611. Also Zubok and Pleshakov, *Inside the Kremlin's Cold War*, p. 39.

39. The border realignment made Poland dependent on the Soviet Union for support in any future move by Germany to restore her pre-war borders. See Truman diary, 25 July 1945. Also Jerzy Lukowski and Hubert Zawadzki, *A Concise History of Poland* (Cambridge University Press, Cambridge 2006), p. 278.

40. Kenneth Harris, *Attlee* (Weidenfeld & Nicolson, London 1982), p, 266.

41. General Hollis memoir, p. 40, Hollis Papers, 86/47/1, p. 112, IWM.

42. Frank Roberts, *Dealing with Dictators*, pp. 123–4.

43. Quoted in Anne Deighton, *The Impossible Peace: Britain, the Division of Germany and the Origins of the Cold War* (Clarendon Press, Oxford 1993), pp. 15, 232–3.

44. Paul Tibbets was the commander of the *Enola Gay*. Unknown to his crew on take-off, he carried cyanide capsules for them all. If they had delivered the bomb and had been shot down afterwards, they were expected to kill themselves rather than endure capture and inevitable torture. James Cooke, 'VJ Day and the Bomb' in *Everyone's War*, No. 12, Autumn 2005.

45. Roy Jenkins, *Truman*, p. 77.

46. Peter Hennessy, *The Secret State. Whitehall and the Cold War* (Allen Lane, London 2002), pp. 15–17. Also Harold Shukman (Ed.), *Agents for Change. Intelligence Services in the 21st Century* (St. Ermin's Press, London 2000), pp. 22–7.

47. Quoted in Christopher Andrew and Vasili Mitrokhin, *The Mitrokhin Archive. The KGB in Europe and the West* (Allen Lane, London 1999), p. 166.

48. Pavel Fitin, quoted in Christopher Andrew and Oleg Gordievsky, *KGB. The Inside Story of its Foreign Operations from Lenin to Gorbachev* (Sceptre, London 1991), p. 376. For details of documents passed to the Soviet Union see Nigel West and Oleg Tsarev (Eds), *Triplex. Secrets from the Cambridge Spies* (Yale University Press, New Haven 2009).

49. Andrew and Mitrokhin, *Mitrokhin Archive*, p. 167.

50. For details of Maclean's treachery in this area see the Venona transcripts in Nigel West, *Venona. The Greatest Secret of the Cold War* (HarperCollins, London 1999), pp. 121–40. Also Cecil, *Divided Life*, p. 76.

Chapter 9: US Hawks

1. An agreement on a post-war strategic plan between the USJPS and its subsidiary committees was actually dated 4 August 1945. See memorandum, 8 August 1945, JPS PM-44 CCS 381 (5-31-45), US National Archive (hereafter USNA).

2. James Schnabel, *The History of the Joint Chiefs of Staff*, p. 140.

3. Christopher Thorne, *Allies of a Kind. The United States, Britain, and the War Against Japan 1941–1945* (Hamish Hamilton, London 1978), p. 508.

4. For *Los Angeles Enquirer* journalist see 'Notes on Tour of USA', 15 February 1946, File H4/4, Major-General F.H.N. Davidson Papers, LHCMA.

5. JIC 329, 3 November 1945; see Larry Valero, 'The American Joint Intelligence Committee and Estimates of the Soviet Union 1945–1947. An Impressive

Record' in *Studies in Intelligence* (CIA), Summer 2000. Also Stephen Ross, *American War Plans*, pp. 5–8.

6. Nelson MacPherson, *American Intelligence in War-Time London: The Story of OSS* (Frank Cass, London 2003), pp. 232, 237–9.

7. At the end of 1945 the US Joint War Plans Committee (JWPC) and Joint Intelligence Committee (JIC) worked closely with their Joint Planning Staff to produce a plan for the US Joint Chiefs of Staff, in the event of war with the Soviet Union.

8. For a discussion of the 1946 threats to peace see Eduard Mark, 'The War Scare of 1946 and its Consequences' in *Diplomatic History*, Volume 21, Issue 3, Summer 1997. Also Gian P. Gentile, 'Planning for Preventative War 1945–1950', *Joint Force Quarterly*, Spring 2000.

9. Harry S. Truman to James Byrnes, 5 January 1946. Quoted in Robert H. Ferrell, *Off the Record. The Private Papers of Harry S Truman* (Harper & Row, New York 1980), p. 80.

10. Interview with Prof. George Kennan, 'Comrades', *Cold War*, National Security Archive, George Washington University, www.nsarchive.org. Sheer war-weariness, exhaustion and an immediate desire to see their men demobilised all contributed to this gestation period. Prof. Anita Prażmowska to author, 17 January 2013.

11. Anne Deighton, *The Impossible Peace: Britain, the Division of Germany and the Origins of the Cold War* (Clarendon Press, Oxford 1993), p. 224; also Victor Rothwell, *Britain and the Cold War 1941–1947* (Jonathan Cape, London 1982), p. 420. Although France and her European neighbours did not turn communist, elections in France in 1946 saw the communists gain 30 per cent of the vote. It must be remembered that Stalin hated the French, especially since their capitulation to Germany, which allowed Hitler to attack the Soviet Union in 1941. See Anthony Beevor and Artemis Copper, *Paris After the Liberation 1944–1949* (Penguin, London 1944), p. 118.

12. JIC (46) 1 (0), CAB 81/132, NA.

13. Quoted in the *Daily Mail*, 25 November 1954. For a study of the attitudes of the press see Alan Foster, 'The British Press and the Coming of the Cold War' in Anne Deighton (Ed.), *Britain and the First Cold War* (Macmillan, London 1990).

14. Dmitri Volkogonov (Trans. Harold Shukman), *The Rise and Fall of the Soviet Empire. Political Leaders from Lenin to Gorbachev* (HarperCollins, London 1998), p. 150.

15. Schnabel, *History of Joint Chiefs*, p. 93.

16. Ross, *American War Plans*, pp. 10–11. By 1946 US army and air force numbers were expected to have declined from more than 8 million at VE Day to fewer than 2 million in 1946. Within eighteen months the number had declined to fewer than a million.

17. Ross, *American War Plans*, pp. 34–5. Also 'Estimate Based on Assumption of Occurrence of Major Hostilities', 0061 Reel I, JCS 20 April 1946, Records of Joint Chiefs of Staff GB 0099 KCLMA MF 1-70, LHCMA.

18. FM Wilson to General Ismay, 30 August 1946, CAB 120/691, NA.

19. Roy Douglas, *From War to Cold War, 1942–48* (Macmillan, London 1981), p. 144.

20. FM Wilson to General Ismay, 30 August 1946, CAB 120/691, NA.

21. FM Montgomery to Prime Minister Attlee; also Price to General Hollis. Both 16 September 1945; also Price to Hollis, 11 October 1945. All CAB 120/691, NA.

22. Hollis to Price, 16 September 1946, and Attlee to FM Wilson, undated; also Hollis to Attlee, 8 October 1945. All CAB 120/691, NA.

23. Price to Colonel Mallaby, 15 October 1946, and also undated memorandum # 563. Both CAB 120/691, NA. Had a mass of Soviet divisions poured through Turkey, they would have bunched up around the natural obstacles of Istanbul and the Dardanelles when they attempted the next move into the Middle East. Even with their very limited stock of atomic bombs, the US could have decimated these troop concentrations in this restricted area. See Diane Clemens, UC Berkeley, 14 July 1997.

24. By June 1947 the number of serviceman had fallen again to 1.5 million. See Schnabel, *History of Joint Chiefs*, p. 238.

25. Schnabel, *History of Joint Chiefs*, pp. 159–68. Also James F. Byrnes, *Speaking Frankly* (Harper & Bros., New York 1947), p. 256.

26. Harris ended his account of Bomber Command's role in the Second World War with a melancholy view of the future. See Sir Arthur Harris, *Bomber Offensive* (Collins, London 1947), p. 280.

27. Jerzy Lukowski and Hubert Zawadzki, *A Concise History of Poland* (Cambridge University Press, Cambridge 2006), p. 275.

28. George Kennan, in 'Comrades'. For Joint Chiefs see Schnabel, *History of Joint Chiefs*, pp. 107, 123. It was agreed that Britain would supply military aid to Greece and Turkey, and the US bolstered Iran's military capability by $10 million.

29. *Daily Telegraph*, 26 November 1954; *Observer*, 28 November 1954.

30. *Daily Telegraph*, 27 November 1954.

31. Quoted in David Reynolds, *From World War to Cold War: Churchill, Roosevelt, and the International History of the 1940s* (Oxford University Press, New York 2006), p. 251.

Epilogue

1. The scale of famine is discussed in Keith Lowe, *Savage Continent. Europe in the Aftermath of World War II* (Viking, London 2012), pp. 34–40.

2. For Czech war plans see Petr Luňák, 'War Plans from Stalin to Brezhnev: The Czechoslovak Pivot' in Vojtech Mastny (Ed.), with Sven Holtsmark and Andreas Wenger, *War Plans and Alliances in the Cold War. Threat perceptions in the East and West* (Routledge, London 2006), pp. 72–94.

BIBLIOGRAPHY

UNPUBLISHED SOURCES

'Russia. Threat to Western Civilisation'

The first time that Operation Unthinkable came to public notice was when the second volume of Lord Alanbrooke's wartime diaries was published in 1959. The volume, titled *Triumph in the West*, contained only selected extracts from the diaries of Alanbrooke's later war years, but the editor, Sir Arthur Bryant, did include references to a 1945 contingency plan, ordered by Winston Churchill, for an attack on the Soviet Union. It was explosive material, especially as it was published as the Cold War was reaching a climax. But it was still only a reference to the plan. The original plan, if it still existed, remained tantalisingly under wraps. When the records of the Joint Planning Staff (JPS) were subsequently released into the public domain in 1972, they appeared in several bound folders of minutes and reports placed in the National Archives (then known as the Public Record Office, or PRO). One folder, containing the records of the JPS for 1945, had a number of reports and minutes missing for May – marked as 'Withdrawn'. There was no indication of the dramatic content that these weeded documents contained, but it is highly likely that they included the sensitive plans relating to a conflict with the Soviet Union. The Cold War was still very much alive in 1972, and such a disclosure would have been inconceivable. Indeed, when pressed by the defence expert Dr Julian Lewis in 1980, the Cabinet Office confirmed that they had no further papers on Operation Unthinkable. Then, suddenly, in 1998, nearly eight years after the collapse of the Soviet Union, a file titled 'Russia – The Threat to Western Civilisation' was released by the Ministry of Defence and placed in the PRO. It contained the final reports on Unthinkable from the JPS, together with related correspondence between the prime minister and the chiefs of staff, but there was no sign of the maps originally attached to the reports.

Polish Intelligence Papers

The Anglo-Polish Historical Committee, which was formed in 2000, was given the brief of identifying and sourcing surviving documents that illustrated the huge contribution of Polish intelligence to the Allied cause in the Second World War. Despite exhaustive searches in public and private archives, as well as the normally inaccessible archives of the British Secret Intelligence Service (SIS), no record was found of the important Polish II Bureau documentation, deposited at the end of the war with British authorities. The committee concluded that these papers were destroyed at some time during the following decade. Nonetheless, as this diligent group of historians and academics found, there remain large quantities of intelligence-related material spread across archives in Poland, Britain and the US.

Soviet Records

As that great analyst of Anglo-Soviet relations Professor Fraser Harbutt has stressed, Soviet sources available since 1989 have been a disappointment. There is a dearth of wartime archival material available, especially for the period of this study, and most of the records released into the public domain cover the later years of the Cold War rather than its beginnings. Stalin destroyed most of the written evidence of his years in power, years in which he exercised total domination of Soviet domestic and foreign policy.

ARCHIVES AND MUSEUMS

BBC Written Archives Centre, Reading
    Daily Digests of World Broadcasts, March–July 1945.

British Library, London
    Admiral Cunningham Papers (MS 52578)

Central Archives of Modern Records in Warsaw (*Archiwum Akt Nowych*)
    Records of the Polish Underground State during WWII.
    Records of underground movements during Soviet occupation.

Churchill Archives Centre, Churchill College, Cambridge University
    Sir Winston Churchill Papers including:

    Official: War Cabinet: Prime Minister's Directives by Prime Minister
    (Char 23/14)

Official: Prime Minister: Correspondence 1943–5 (Char 20/192)
Prime Minister: Personal Telegrams (Char 20/222, 20/224, 20/225)
Personal Photographs May-July 1945 (Chur 1/97 A-G)
Sir Percy Grigg Papers (GBR/0014/PJGG)

Imperial War Museum, London
  Papers of General Sir Leslie Hollis (86/47/1)
  Papers of FM Lord Montgomery (BLM 162)

Institute of National Remembrance, Warsaw (*Instytutu Pamięci Narodowej*)

Liddell Hart Centre for Military Archives, King's College, London
  (LHCMA)
  Lord Alanbrooke Papers. Original diary 9/5/1945 (Apart from the
  deletion of some exclamation marks, the published version of the
  diaries, edited by Alex Danchev and Daniel Todman, is a verbatim
  transcription of the original).
  'Notes on My Life', Volume XIII, 19/7/44–20/10/44.
  Records of Joint Chiefs of Staff. Part II 1946–1953 (GB 099 KCLMA
  MF 1–70).
  Lord Ismay Papers (GB099 KCLMA Ismay).
  Major-General F.H.N. Davidson Papers (GB099 KCLMA Davidson)

Museum of the Warsaw Rising, Warsaw (*Muzeum Powstamia Warszawskiego*)

National Security Archive, George Washington University, Washington
  George Kennan Papers
  Venona Transcripts

Polish Institute & Sikorski Museum, London (*Instytut Polski i Muzeum im.
  gen. Sikorskiego*)
  Deputy Chief of General Staff (AX11 45/1)

Royal Air Force Museum, London
  Air Marshal Sir Douglas Evill Papers (AC74/8)

The Second World War Experience Centre, Leeds (SWWEC)
  Moser Papers

US National Archives and Records Administration (NARA), Washington DC
US Department of State: The Conference of Berlin (Potsdam) 1945.
Briefing Book Papers, Volume I, 'European Questions/The Hopkins
Mission to Moscow.
Photographic Archives of World War II.

PUBLISHED SOURCES

Journals

The Army Quarterly
Battlefields Review
Diplomatic History
East European Quarterly
Everyone's War
Joint Force Quarterly
Studies in Intelligence

Books

Aldrich, Richard J., *British Intelligence, Strategy and the Cold War 1945–51*
(Routledge, London 1992).
——*The Hidden Hand* (John Murray, London 2001).
Allen, Debra, *The Oder-Neisse Line. The United States, Poland and Germany in
the Cold War* (Praeger, Westport 2003).
Allport, Alan, *Demobbed. Coming Home after the Second World War* (Yale
University Press, New Haven 2009).
Anders, Lietenant-General W., *An Army in Exile. The Story of the Second
Polish Corps* (The Battery Press, Nashville 1981).
Anderson, Terry H., *The United States, Great Britain and the Cold War,
1944–1947* (University of Missouri Press, Columbia 1981).
Andrew, Christopher, and David Dilks, *The Missing Dimension. Governments and
Intelligence Communities in the Twentieth Century* (Macmillan, London 1984).
Andrew, Christopher, and Oleg Gordievsky, *KGB. The Inside Story of its
Foreign Operations from Lenin to Gorbachev* (Sceptre, London 1991).
Andrew, Christopher, and Vasili Mitrokhin, *The Mitrokhin Archive. The KGB
in Europe and the West* (Allen Lane, London 1999).
Applebaum, Anne, *Iron Curtain. The Crushing of Eastern Europe 1944–56*
(Allen Lane, London 2012).

Avon, Earl of, *The Eden Memoirs. The Reckoning* (Cassell, London 1965).

Bader, William, *Austria Between East and West 1945–1955* (Stanford University Press, Stanford 1966).

Barber, J., and M. Harrison, *The Soviet Home Front 1941–1945. A Social and Economic History of the USSR in World War II* (Longman, London 1991).

Barker, Elisabeth, *Churchill and Eden at War* (Macmillan, London 1978).

Beevor, Antony, *Berlin. The Downfall 1945* (Penguin, London 2002).

Beevor, Antony and Artemis Copper, *Paris After the Liberation 1944–1949* (Penguin, London 1944).

Bell, P.M.H., *John Bull & the Bear. British Public Opinion, Foreign Policy and the Soviet Union 1941–1945* (Edward Arnold, London 1990).

Bialer, S. (Ed.), *Stalin and His Generals. Soviet Military Memoirs of World War II* (Cambridge University Press, Cambridge 1982).

Bohlen, Charles E., *Witness to History 1929–1969* (WW Norton, New York 1973).

Boothby, Robert, *Boothby. Recollections of a Rebel* (Hutchinson, London 1978).

Bower, Tom, *The Perfect English Spy. Sir Dick White and the Secret War 1935–90* (Heinemann, London 1995).

Boyd, Alexander, *The Soviet Air Force Since 1918* (Macdonald and Jane's, London 1977).

Broad, Lewis, *Sir Anthony Eden. The Chronicles of a Career* (Hutchinson, London 1955).

Browne, Anthony Montague, *Long Sunset. Memoirs of Winston Churchill's Last Private Secretary* (Cassell, London 1995).

Butler, John, *The Red Dean of Canterbury. The Public and Private Faces of Hewlett Johnson* (Scala, London 2011).

Butler, Rupert, *Stalin's Secret War. The NKVD on the Eastern Front* (Pen & Sword, Barnsley 2010).

Butler, Susan (Ed.), *My Dear Mr. Stalin. The Complete Correspondence Between Franklin D. Roosevelt and Joseph V. Stalin* (Yale University Press, New Haven 2005).

Byrnes, James F., *Speaking Frankly* (Harper & Bros., New York 1947).

Campbell, Thomas, and George Herring (Eds), *The Diaries of Edward R Stettinius Jr., 1943–1946* (New Viewpoints, New York 1975).

Carlton, David, *Anthony Eden. A Biography* (Allen Lane, London 1981).

——*Churchill and the Soviet Union* (Manchester University Press, Manchester 2000).

Cawthorne, Nigel, *The Iron Cage* (Fourth Estate, London 1993).

Cecil, Robert, *A Divided Life. A Biography of Donald Maclean* (The Bodley Head, London 1988).

Charmley, John, *Churchill's Grand Alliance. The Anglo-American Special Relationship 1940–57* (Hodder & Stoughton, London 1995).

Chisholm, Anne, and Michael Davie, *Beaverbrook. A Life* (Hutchinson, London 1992).

Churchill, Winston S., *The Second World War. Volume VI. Triumph and Tragedy* (Cassell, London 1954).

Clarke, Peter, *The Last Thousand Days of the British Empire* (Allen Lane, London 2007).

Colville, John, *Footprints in Time* (Collins, London 1976).

——*The Fringes of Power. Downing Street Diaries 1939–1955* (Hodder & Stoughton, London 1985).

Coombs, David, with Minnie Churchill, *Sir Winston Churchill's Life Through His Paintings* (Chaucer Press, London 2003).

Cox, Geoffrey, *The Road to Trieste* (Heinemann, London 1947).

Cradock, Percy, *Know Your Enemy. How the Joint Intelligence Committee Saw the World* (John Murray, London 2002).

Danchev, Alex, and Daniel Todman (Eds), *War Diaries 1939–1945. Field Marshal Lord Alanbrooke* (Weidenfeld & Nicolson, London 2001).

Davies, Norman, *God's Playground. A History of Poland, Volume II. 1795 to the Present* (Oxford University Press, Oxford 2005).

——*Rising '44. The Battle for Warsaw* (Macmillan, London 2003).

Deane, John R., *The Strange Alliance. The Story of Our Efforts at Wartime Co-operation with Russia* (The Viking Press, New York 1947).

Deighton, Anne (Ed.), *Britain and the First Cold War* (Macmillan, London 1990).

——*The Impossible Peace. Britain, the Division of Germany and the Origins of the Cold War* (Clarendon Press, Oxford 1993).

Dickens, Admiral Sir Gerald, *Bombing and Strategy. The Fallacy of Total War* (Sampson Low, London 1946).

Dorril, Stephen, *MI6. Fifty Years of Special Operations* (Fourth Estate, London 2000).

Douglas, Roy, *From War to Cold War, 1942–48* (Macmillan, London 1981).

Eisenhower, Dwight D., *Crusade in Europe* (William Heinemann, London 1948).

Erickson, John, *The Road to Berlin. Stalin's War with Germany. Volume II* (Cassell, London 2003).

Faringdon, Hugh, *Confrontation. The Strategic Geography of NATO and the Warsaw Pact* (Routledge & Kegan Paul, London 1986).

Ferrell, Robert H. (Ed.), *Dear Bess. The Letters from Harry to Bess Truman 1910–1959* (WW Norton, New York 1983).

——*Off the Record. The Private Papers of Harry S Truman* (Harper & Row, New York 1980).

Folly, Martin H., *Churchill, Whitehall and the Soviet Union, 1940–1945* (Macmillan, London 2000).

Foot, M.R.D., *SOE. The Special Operations Executive 1940–1946* (Pimlico, London 1999).

Fraser, David, *Alanbrooke* (Collins, London 1982).

Gaddis, John Lewis, *We Now Know. Rethinking Cold War History* (Clarendon Press, Oxford 1997).

Garliński, Józef, *Poland, SOE and the Allies* (George Allen and Unwin, London 1969).

Gawenda, Dr J., *The Soviet Domination of Eastern Europe in the Light of International Law* (Foreign Affairs Publishing Co., London 1974).

Gilbert, Martin, *The Day the War Ended. VE Day 1945 in Europe and Around the World* (HarperCollins, London 1995).

——*Winston S Churchill. Volume VIII. 'Never Despair' 1945–1965* (Heinemann, London 1988).

Glanz, David, et al, *Slaughterhouse. The Handbook of the Eastern Front* (Aberjona Press, Bedford PA 2005).

Gorodetsky, G. (Ed.), *Soviet Foreign Policy, 1917–1991* (Frank Cass, London 1994).

Graml, Hermann, *Die Allierten und Die Teilung Deutschlands. Konflikte und Entscheidungen 1941–1948* (Fischer Taschenbücher, Frankfurt 1985).

Greig, Ian, *The Assault on the West* (Foreign Affairs Publishing Co., Petersham 1968).

Gröttrup, Irmgard, *Rocket Wife* (André Deutsch, London 1959).

Haape, Dr Heinrich, *Moscow Tram Stop. A Doctor's Experiences with the German Spearhead in Russia* (Collins, London 1957).

Hansen, Reimer, *Das Ende des Dritten Reiches. Die Deutsche Kapitulation 1945* (Ernst Klett, Stuttgart 1966).

Harbutt, Fraser J., *The Iron Curtain. Churchill, America, and the Origins of the Cold War* (Oxford University Press, New York 1986).

——*Yalta 1945. Europe and America at the Crossroads* (Cambridge University Press, New York 2010).

Harriman, W. Averell, and Elie Abel, *Special Envoy to Churchill and Stalin 1941–1946* (Hutchinson, London 1976).

Harris, Sir Arthur, *Bomber Offensive* (Collins, London 1947).

Harris, Kenneth, *Attlee* (Weidenfeld & Nicolson, London 1982),

Harrison, Mark, *Accounting for War. Soviet Production, Employment, and the Defence Burden 1940–1945* (Cambridge University Press, Cambridge 1996).

Hastings, Max, *Armageddon. The Battle for Germany 1944–45* (Macmillan, London 2004).

——*Finest Years. Churchill as Warlord 1940–45* (Harper Press, London 2009).

Hennessy, Peter, *Never Again. Britain 1945–1951* (Penguin, London 2006).

——*The Secret State. Whitehall and the Cold War* (Allen Lane, London 2002).

Herring, G.C., *Aid to Russia, 1941–1946. Strategy, Diplomacy, and the Origins of the Cold War* (Columbia University Press, New York 1973).

Hilderbrand, Robert C., *Dumbarton Oaks. The Origins of the United Nations and the Search for Postwar Security* (University of North Carolina Press, Chapel Hill 1990).

Hinsley, F.H., *British Intelligence in the Second World War. Its Influence on Strategy and Operations, Volume III, Part 2* (HMSO, London 1988).

Holmes, Richard, *The World at War. The Landmark Oral History* (Ebury Press, London 2007).

Howarth, Patrick, *Undercover. The Men and Women of the SOE* (Phoenix Press, London 2000).

Hull, Cordell, *The Memoirs of Cordell Hull, Volume II* (Hodder & Stoughton, London 1948).

Ingersoll, Ralph, *Top Secret* (Partridge Publications, London 1946).

Instytut Pami Eci Narodowej Komisja Scigania, *Operacja 'Sejm' 1944–1946* (Warsaw & Kiev, 2007).

Ismay, General Lord, *The Memoirs of General Lord Ismay* (Heinemann, London 1960).

Jablonsky, David, *Churchill, the Great Game and Total War* (Frank Cass, London 1991).

Jenkins, Roy, *Churchill* (Pan Macmillan, London 2002).

——*Truman* (Collins, London 1986).

Johnson, Hewlett, *Soviet Success* (Hutchinson, London 1947).

Jurgielewicz, W., *Ludowe Wojsko Polskie 1943–1973* (MON, Warsaw 1974).

Kent, John, *British Imperial Strategy and the Origins of the Cold War, 1944–49* (Leicester University Press, Leicester 1993).

Kersten, Krystyna, *The Establishment of Communist Rule in Poland 1943–1948* (University of California Press, Berkeley 1991).

——*Repatriacia Ludności Polskiej po II Woinie Światowej* (Studium historyczne, Wrocław 1974).

Khrushchev, Nikita S. (Trans. Strobe Talbot), *Khrushchev Remembers* (Little Brown, Boston 1970).

Kitchen, Martin, *British Policy Towards the Soviet Union during the Second World War* (Macmillan, London 1986).

Knight, Amy, *Beria. Stalin's First Lieutenant* (Princeton University Press, Princeton, 1993).

Kochanski, Halik, *The Eagle Unbowed. Poland and the Poles in the Second World War* (Allen Lane, London 2012).

Koehl, Robert Lewis, *The Black Corps. The Structure and Power Struggles of the Nazi SS* (University of Wisconsin Press, Madison WI 1983).

Koehler, John, *Stasi. The Untold Story of the East German Secret Police* (Westview Press, Oxford 1999).

Kolko, Gabriel, *The Politics of War. The World and United States Foreign Policy 1943–1945* (Vintage Books, New York 1970).

Korboński, Stefan, *Fighting Warsaw. The Story of the Polish Underground State 1939–1945* (Hippocrene Books, New York 2004).

Kuniholm, Bruce, *The Origins of the Cold War in the Near East. Great Power Conflict and Diplomacy in Iran, Turkey and Greece* (Princeton University Press, Princeton 1980).

Łabuszewski, Tomasz, *Rzeczpospolita Utracona* (Instytut Pamięci Narodowej, Warszawa 2011).

Leahy, William, *I Was There. The Personal Story of the Chief of Staff to Presidents Roosevelt and Truman Based on his Notes and Diaries at the Time* (Gollancz, London 1950).

Leasor, James, *War at the Top. Based on the Experiences of General Sir Leslie Hollis* (Michael Joseph, London 1959).

Lewis, Julian, *Changing Direction. British Military Planning for Post-war Strategic Defence, 1942–1947* (Routledge, London 2003).

Linge, Heinz, *With Hitler to the End. The Memoirs of Adolf Hitler's Valet* (Frontline Books, London 2009).

Linz, S.J. (Ed.), *The Impact of World War II on the Soviet Union* (Rowman & Littlefield, New York 1985).

Louis, William, *Imperialism at Bay. The United States and the Decolonisation of the British Empire 1941–1945* (Oxford University Press, New York 1978).

Lowe, Keith, *Savage Continent. Europe in the Aftermath of World War II* (Viking, London 2012).

Lucas, James, *War on the Eastern Front* (Greenhill Books, London 1991).

Lüdde-Neurath, Walter, *Regierung Dönitz. Die letzten Tage des Dritten Reiches* (Scientific Publishers, Göttingen 1950).

Lukacs, John, *1945. Year Zero* (Doubleday, Garden City NY 1978).

Lukowski, Jerzy, and Hubert Zawadzki, *A Concise History of Poland* (Cambridge University Press, Cambridge 2006).

Lundestad, Gier, *The American Non-Policy towards Eastern Europe 1943–1947* (Universitetsforlaget, Oslo 1984).

Mackenzie, William, *The Secret History of SOE. Special Operations Executive 1940–1945* (St. Ermin's Press, London 2000).

MacPherson, Nelson, *American Intelligence in War-Time London. The Story of OSS* (Frank Cass, London 2003).

Maisky, Ivan, *Memoirs of a Soviet Ambassador* (Hutchinson, London 1967).

Mastny, Vojtech, *The Cold War and Soviet Insecurity. The Stalin Years* (Oxford University Press, Oxford 1996).

Mastny, Vojtech (Ed.), with Sven Holtsmark and Andreas Wenger, *War Plans and Alliances in the Cold War. Threat Perceptions in the East and West* (Routledge, London 2006).

Meacham, Jon, *Franklin and Winston. A Portrait of a Friendship* (Granta Books, London 2003).

Mee, Charles, *Meeting at Potsdam* (Andre Deutsch, London 1975).

Merridale, Catherine, *Ivan's War. The Red Army 1939–45* (Faber & Faber, London 2006).

Moran, Lord, *Winston Churchill. The Struggle for Survival 1940–1965* (Constable, London 1966).

Nel, Elizabeth, *Mr Churchill's Secretary* (Hodder & Stoughton, London 1958).

Ney-Krwawicz, Marek, *The Polish Resistance. Home Army 1939–1945* (PUMST, London 2001).

Nicolson, Nigel (Ed.), *Harold Nicolson Diaries 1907–1964* (Phoenix, London 2005).

North, John (Ed.), *The Alexander Memoirs* (Cassell, London 1963).

Ordway, Frederick, and Mitchell Sharpe, *The Rocket Team* (Heinemann, London 1979).

Ovendale, Ritchie (Ed.), *The Foreign Policy of the British Labour Governments 1945–1951* (Leicester University Press, Leicester 1984).

Overy, Richard, *Russia's War* (Penguin, London 1999).

Pepłoński, Andrzej, *Wywiad Polskich Sił Zbrojnych na Zachodzie 1939–1945* (Warszawa 1995).

Persak, Krzysztof, and Łukasz Kamiński (Eds), *A Handbook of the Communist Security Apparatus in East Central Europe 1944–1989* (Institute of National Remembrance, Warsaw 2005).

Petrov, Nikita, *The First Chairman of the KGB. Ivan Serov* (Materick, Moscow 2005).

Petrova, Ada, and Peter Watson, *The Death of Hitler* (WW Norton, New York 1995).

Piekarska, Anna, (Ed.), *PRL- Tak daleko, tak blisko* (Instytut Pamięci Narodowej, Warszawa 2007).

Pirjevec, Joze, *Foibe. Una storia d'Italia* (Giulio Einaudi Editore, Turin 2009).

Plokhy, S.M., *Yalta. The Price of Peace* (Penguin, London 2011).

Polonsky, Antony, and Bolesław Drukier (Eds), *The Beginnings of Communist Rule in Poland* (Routledge & Kegan Paul, London 1980).

Prażmowska, Anita, *Civil War in Poland 1942–1948* (Palgrave Macmillan, London 2004).

Pylat, Joanna, Jan Ciechanowski and Andrzej Suchitz (Eds), *General Władysław Anders. Soldier and Leader of the Free Poles in Exile* (Polish University Abroad, London 2007).

Raack, R.C., *Stalin's Drive to the West 1938–1945. The Origins of the Cold War* (Stanford University Press, Stanford 1995).

Rawson, Andrew, *Organizing Victory: The War Conferences 1941–1945* (Spellmount, Stroud 2013).

Rees, Laurence, *World War Two: Behind Closed Doors. Stalin, the Nazis and the West* (BBC Books, London 2008).

Reshetnikov, Vasiliy, *Bomber Pilot on the Eastern Front* (Pen & Sword, Barnsley 2008).

Resis, Albert (Ed.), *Molotov Remembers. Inside Kremlin Politics* (Ivan Dee, Chicago 1993).

Reynolds, David, *From World War to Cold War. Churchill, Roosevelt, and the International History of the 1940s* (Oxford University Press, New York 2006).

——In Command of History. Churchill Fighting and Writing the Second World War* (Penguin, London 2005).

Roberts, Frank, *Dealing with Dictators. The Destruction and Revival of Europe 1930–70* (Weidenfeld & Nicolson, London 1991).

Roberts, Geoffrey, *Stalin's General. The Life of Georgy Zhukov* (Icon Books, London 2012).

Roosevelt, Elliott, *As He Saw It* (Duell, Sloan & Pearce, New York 1946),

Ross, Stephen, *American War Plans, 1945–1950* (Frank Cass, London 1996).

Rothwell, Victor, *Britain and the Cold War 1941–1947* (Jonathan Cape, London 1982).

Saunders, Hilary St George, *Royal Air Force 1939–1945, Volume III. The Fight is Won* (HMSO, London 1954).

Schnabel, James, *The History of the Joint Chiefs of Staff. The Joint Chiefs of Staff and*

National Policy, Volume I. 1945–1947 (Michael Glazier, Wilmington 1979).

Scott, Harriet Fast, and William F. Scott, *The Armed Forces of the USSR* (Westview Press, Boulder 1979).

Seaton, Albert, and Joan Seaton, *The Soviet Army. 1918 to the Present* (The Bodley Head, London 1986).

Sherwin, Martin, *A World Destroyed. The Atomic Bomb and the Grand Alliance* (Alfred Knopf, New York 1975).

Shore, Marci, *Caviar and Ashes. A Warsaw Generation's Life and Death in Marxism 1918–1968* (Yale University Press, New Haven 2009).

Shukman, Harold (Ed.), *Agents for Change. Intelligence Services in the 21st Century* (St Ermin's Press, London 2000).

Skates, John Ray, *The Invasion of Japan. Alternative to the Bomb* (The University of South Carolina Press, Columbia 1994).

Sluga, Glenda, *The Problem of Trieste and the Italian-Yugoslav Border. Difference, Identity and Sovereignty in Twentieth-century Europe* (State University of New York, New York 2011).

Soames, Mary, *A Daughter's Tale* (Doubleday, London 2011),

Stafford, David, *Britain and European Resistance 1940–1945. A Survey of the Special Operations Executive with Documents* (Macmillan, London 1980).

Stalin, J.V., *Stalin's Correspondence with Churchill and Attlee 1941–1945* (Capricorn Books, New York 1965).

Steininger, R., and J. Foschepoth (Eds), *Die Britische Deutschland und Besatzungspolitik 1945–1949* (German Historical Institute, London 1984).

Stimson, Henry L., and McGeorge Bundy, *On Active Service in Peace and War* (Hutchinson, London 1947).

Stirling, Tessa, Daria Nałęcz and Tadeusz Dubicki (Eds), *Intelligence Co-operation Between Poland and Great Britain during World War II, Volume I. The Report of the Anglo-Polish Historical Committee* (Valentine Mitchell, London 2005).

Suvorov, Viktor, *Inside the Soviet Army* (Hamish Hamilton, London 1982).

Suvorov, Viktor (Vladimir Rezun), *Icebreaker. Who Started the Second World War* (PL UK Publishing, Bristol 2009).

Sword, Keith, Norman Davies and Jan Ciechanowski, *The Formation of the Polish Community in Great Britain 1939–50* (School of Slavonic and East European Studies, London 1989).

Szkopiak, Zygmunt (Ed.), *The Yalta Agreements. Documents Prior To, During and After the Crimea Conference 1945* (Polish Government-in-Exile, London 1986).

Terkel, Studs, *'The Good War'. An Oral History of World War Two* (Ballantine Press, New York 1985).

Thomas, Donald, *Freedom's Frontier. Censorship in Modern Britain* (John Murray, London 2007).

Thomas, Hugh, *Armed Truce. The Beginnings of the Cold War 1945–46* (Atheneum, New York 1987).

Thorne, Christopher, *Allies of a Kind. The United States, Britain, and the War Against Japan 1941–1945* (Hamish Hamilton, London 1978).

Thorwald, Jürgen, *Das Ende an der Elbe. Die letzten Monate des Zweiten Weltkriegs im Osten* (Steingrüben, Stuttgart 1954).

Toland, John, *Adolf Hitler* (Doubleday, London 1976).

Tubbs, D.B., *Lancaster Bomber* (Macmillan, London 1972).

van Tuyll, H. P., *Feeding the Russian Bear. American Aid to the Soviet Union, 1941–1945* (Westport 1989).

Ulam, Adam, *Expansion and Coexistence. The History of Soviet Foreign Policy 1917–1967* (Praeger, New York 1968).

Volkogonov, Dmitri (Trans. Harold Shukman), *The Rise and Fall of the Soviet Empire. Political Leaders from Lenin to Gorbachev* (HarperCollins, London 1998).

Walker, Jonathan, *Poland Alone. Britain, SOE and the Collapse of the Polish Resistance 1944* (The History Press, Stroud 2010).

Walker, Stephen, *Shockwave. The Countdown to Hiroshima* (John Murray, London 2005).

West, Nigel, *Venona. The Greatest Secret of the Cold War* (HarperCollins, London 1999).

West, Nigel, and Oleg Tsarev (Eds), *Triplex. Secrets from the Cambridge Spies* (Yale University Press, New Haven 2009).

Wheeler-Bennett, Sir John (Ed.), *Action This Day. Working with Churchill* (Macmillan, London 1968).

Whiting, Charles, *Finale at Flensburg. The Story of Field Marshal Montgomery's Battle for the Baltic* (Leo Cooper, London 1973).

Wilmot, Chester, *The Struggle for Europe* (Collins, London 1952).

Yergin, Daniel, *Shattered Peace. The Origins of the Cold War* (Penguin, London 1990).

Zaloga, Steven, *The Polish Army 1939–45* (Osprey, Oxford 2005).

Zubok, Vladislav, and Constantine Pleshakov, *Inside the Kremlin's Cold War. From Stalin to Khrushchev* (Harvard University Press, Cambridge MA 1996).

INDEX